Contemporary Anthropolc

Series Editors
Don Seeman
Department of Religion
Emory University
Atlanta, GA, USA

Tulasi Srinivas
Department of Liberal Arts and Interdisciplinary Studies
Emerson College
Boston, MA, USA

Contemporary Anthropology of Religion is the official book series of the Society for the Anthropology of Religion, a section of the American Anthropological Association. Books in the series explore a variety of issues relating to current theoretical or comparative issues in the study of religion. These include the relation between religion and the body, social memory, gender, ethnoreligious violence, globalization, modernity, and multiculturalism, among others. Recent historical events have suggested that religion plays a central role in the contemporary world, and Contemporary Anthropology of Religion provides a crucial forum for the expansion of our understanding of religion globally.

More information about this series at
http://www.palgrave.com/gp/series/14916

Mani Rao

Living Mantra

Mantra, Deity, and Visionary Experience Today

palgrave
macmillan

Mani Rao
Bengaluru, Karnataka, India

Contemporary Anthropology of Religion
ISBN 978-3-030-07184-4 ISBN 978-3-319-96391-4 (eBook)
https://doi.org/10.1007/978-3-319-96391-4

Softcover re-print of the Hardcover 1st edition 2019

This Palgrave Macmillan imprint is published by the registered company Springer Nature Switzerland AG
The registered company address is: Gewerbestrasse 11, 6330 Cham, Switzerland

Satyam Sai Jai
Shivam Sai Jai
Sundaram Sai Jai

Acknowledgements

Mantra-practitioners constitute this book. They entrusted me with narratives of their experiences and engaged with me over questions, speculations and findings. There were also practitioners who gave me clues and pointed me in the right direction, even if they declined to be formally interviewed; and there were many people who told me about someone who knew someone with the phone number of someone else whom I really, really ought to meet. I am deeply grateful to every informant on this journey. The research for this book was done for a PhD in Religious Studies at Duke University. I was fortunate to have Leela Prasad as the chair of my dissertation committee—her informed understanding of the subject and responsiveness during critical moments of my fieldwork enabled the realization of this project. My preliminary advisor at Emory and Duke was Laurie L. Patton whose courses in vedic studies stood me in good stead even as my research took a different direction. Dissertation committee members Srinivas Aravamudan (1962–2016), David Morgan, Velcheru Narayana Rao and Hwansoo Kim helped expand my horizons with insights from their own areas of specialization. Hwansoo Kim's response convinced me to include some auto-ethnography in the book version; he also suggested the title "Living Mantra" for this book. Bhavani Adimoolan painstakingly listened to hours of recordings and drafted a number of transcripts. A dissertation-to-book workshop at the Madison South Asia Conference was both timely and useful, and I especially thank faculty and editorial advisor Joyce Fleuckiger at this workshop for engaging with my work and for her feedback. A number of people helped steer this book toward publication at Palgrave Macmillan—in particular, the series co-editor Tulasi Srinivas, who introduced me to her co-editor Don Seeman and the Contemporary Anthropology of Religion series, the Palgrave Macmillan editor Mary Al-Sayed and the editorial assistant team, and the anonymous reviewers whose comments led to clarifications and a more rigorous book.

As I plodded through academic hoops and requirements, it was the presence of other scholars and a shared intellectual life that gave me solace. A number of cohorts and senior colleagues shared their own research and writing with me, especially Antoinette de Napoli, Luke Whitmore, Gil Ben-Herut, Yasmine Singh, Carter Higgins, Alex McKinley, Yael Lazar and Torang Asadi. Many friends inspired, supported and encouraged me over this time. In Iowa, conversations with Frederick M. Smith shaped my interest in a Religious Studies Ph.D., and Jan Myers and Nataša Ďurovičová persuaded me of its value. Subhasree Raghavan, Amit Bararia and Subbarayudu Kameswara kept an eye on me as I traveled on fieldwork. Discussions with Subasree Krishnaswamy, Rahul Soni, Shinie Antony and Madhavi Mahadevan helped me reassess the potential readership for this book. Karuna Sivasailam was my first reader—she read an early draft of my dissertation, and later, the manuscript for the book benefited from her responses. My parents bore my absences and travels bravely these last several years. My brother Madhu's persistent question, "what was it you said you were researching?" was more valuable to me than he may ever realize. My husband, John Nemo Bancroft, *aka* Jaideva, came along for the adventure, moving cities and countries and creating his own thoughtful participation.

Finally, practitioners who shared with me their experience, practice and knowledge of mantra, arranged like in an *aksharamala* (syllabary mantra): Akella Venkatalakshmi; Anuradha Beempavu; Apparao D. V. (Appaji); Arul Murugan P.; Aruna Nandagopal; Arup Kumar; Aspi B. Mistry; Avadhanulu R. V. S. S.; Babu, G. Y. N.; Basavaraj (Prema Chaitanya); Bhagyalata Pataskar; Chirravuri Sreerama Sarma; Donald S. McKenna; Geetha Lakshmi K.; Gopichand Balla; Janice Craig; Karthiyayini Sugumaran; Krovi Parthasarathy; Madhavananda Saraswati; Maheshwari M.; Mani Prasanna Y. N. S. S.; Manikya Somayaji; Mantha Vasudeva Sastry (Swami Vasudevananda); Maunish Vyas; Maureshwar Ghaisas; Monisha Sen; Nachiketananda Puri; Narasimhan M. A.; Narendra Kapre; Neel Kulkarni; Potturi Venkateswara Rao; Prahlada Sastry N. (Amritanandanatha Saraswati); Prayaga Dhanalakshmi;

Prema Reddy; Ramya Yogini; Sandhya Rani; Satpurkar V. V.; Sheela; Siddheswarananda Bharati; Sivananda Puri; Subbarao Kompella (Karunamaya); Tadepalle Balakrishna Sarma; Tadepalle Lakshmidhara Somayajulu; Usha R. Balakrishnan; Usha Rajagopalan; Vadlamudi Venkateswara Rao; Vasundhara Reddy; Vedatmananda Saraswati; Veda Vidyananda Giri; Vidyasagar Sarma G. V. L. N.; Vivek Shastri Godbole; and Yadnyeshwar Ranganath Selukar—thank you, *Namaste*!

Contents

Part I Preparation

1 Introduction 3
1.1 Seeds 3
1.2 Homing In: Andhra-Telangana 5
1.3 Overview 8
References 12

2 A Mountain of Scholarship 13
2.1 Early Indian Concepts 13
2.2 Modern Scholarship 17
References 23

3 Crossing Over 27
3.1 Positioning 27
3.2 Navigating Subjectivity 31
3.3 Practice for Theory 34
3.4 Unbracketing Experience 39
References 46

4 Are There Revelations Today? 51
4.1 "Possible" 51
4.2 Who Is a Rishi? 52

4.3 *Maharshi Daivarata (1892–1975)* 54
4.4 *Chandole Sastry (1886–1990)* 57
References 62

Part II Fieldwork

5 Body-Yantra: Sahasrakshi Meru Temple, Devipuram 67
5.1 *The Thousand-Eyed Goddess* 67
5.2 *Hierophany at Devipuram* 69
5.3 *Invitation to Cosmic Energies* 72
5.4 *Goddess Bala* 76
5.5 *Goddess Chandi* 83
5.6 *Goddess Kali* 88
5.7 *Goddess Lalita* 93
5.8 *Amritanandanatha Saraswati (1934–2015)* 100
References 111

6 Self-Made: Svayam Siddha Kali Pitham, Guntur 113
6.1 *When the Goddess Arrives* 113
6.2 *A Poet Becomes a Guru* 114
6.3 *An Atheist Turns to Mantra* 119
6.4 *Experiments with Mantra* 122
6.5 *Devotion as Investment* 127
6.6 *Persistence Pays* 130
6.7 *After Many Lives* 135
6.8 *Calling Deities* 140
References 148

7 "I Am in Mantra, Mantra Is in Me": Nachiketa Tapovan, Kodgal 149
7.1 *The Ashram at Nachiketa* 149
7.2 *Ocean of Mantra* 152
7.3 *Openness to the Divine* 155
7.4 *Repetition of Mantra* 161
7.5 *Transported by Sound* 163
7.6 *The "No"-Mantra* 166
7.7 *Guru-Disciple Bond* 170

7.8 Diksha 173
7.9 Inner Silence and Anahata 175
References 179

Part III Conclusions

8 Understanding Mantra Again 183
8.1 Anchored Spaces: Mandalas 183
8.2 Primary Sources 185
8.3 Relating to Deities 187
8.4 What Is Vision? 190
8.5 How Mantra Works in Sadhana 196
8.6 Natural Form 200
8.7 OṂ 202
8.8 Summary 205
References 207

Glossary 209

Index 211

Translation, Transliteration and Names

The conversations and narratives of this fieldwork were in Telugu, English and Hindi, and people rarely quoted from Sanskrit doctrinal sources. Translating from Telugu and Hindi, I err on the side of the literal to help communicate the voice of the speaker. When connotations of words or idiomatic expressions would be significantly lost in translation, I include them in parenthesis. Thus, in my conversation with Narendra Kapre, "there are winds of change" is followed by his original Hindi expression "*dhire dhire hava ban rahi hai.*" Kapre's expression in Hindi communicates a gathering momentum and a revolution taking shape, and readers who know Hindi can relish the flavor of the expression. Terms "sadhana," "mantra-sadhana" and "siddhi" are used so frequently in conversations here that I explain them in the introduction, and then use them without translation. Readers may refer to the glossary for all the important, recurring terms.

Many informants spoke in a combination of English and Telugu, and it would neither be comprehensible nor possible to indicate every shift with open and close quotes. Instead, I indicate significant words or phrases in the source language *like this*—this also draws the reader's attention to the speaker's characteristic voice or usage. In a transcript, when I retain the original Sanskrit or Telugu word, that word is in italics and my translation is in parenthesis (like this). If I need to add words to help intelligibility, I add them (like this), but when I have to intervene with a comment for clarification, I use brackets [like this]. When speakers use technical words, I retain them in the transcript and include the translation in parenthesis. In a transcript, I use the Sanskrit forms of words so that the reader does not have to keep track of variants—thus, I change Telugu forms of "mantram" or "mantramu" and "homam" or "homamu" to "mantra" and "homa."

I do not use diacritical marks within the body of the text, as those familiar with the terms will pronounce them correctly anyway; thus, it is "sadhana," rather than "*sādhana.*" Also, names and proper nouns are transliterated without diacritics—I use "ch" and "chh" instead of the diacritical marks "*c*" and "*ch,*" "ri" or "ru" instead of "*ṛ*" and "sh" for both "*ṣ*" and "*ś.*" Thus, the scholar Bhartrihari, "Ishvar" for "God" in Hindi, deity Krishna, the temple of Goddess Sahasrakshi and the Gayatri-mantra. I use "a" for both long and short articulations of the vowel "a," using diacritics only when a short "a" would convey a different meaning—thus *māraṇamu* (killing) vs. *maraṇamu* (death). Names of sources and literary works are also without diacritical marks, whether such popular sources as Ramayana and Mahabharata, or such scholastic sources as Vakyapadiya and Vaksudha. Having said that, several Indian legends tell of disasters that befall an inadvertent mispronunciation, or an accent in the wrong place. Therefore, I do use diacritical marks for and within all mantras, for example: "*Kṛṣṇa,*" "*Sahasrākṣī*" and "*Gāyatrī.*" Additionally, I include the diacritical marks in the index for the reader's reference, and the list at the end of this section should help accurate pronunciation.

So that the reader understands I am talking about a deity and not a person, I use descriptors "goddess" and "god" and "deity" before their names. I translate references to deities in transcripts as "He" and "She" to replicate the equivalent difference established by the respectful nouns and pronouns used for such references in Telugu—"*Ammavaru* (Mother Goddess)" and "*ame.*" I include honorifics of renunciates the first time I mention their name (e.g., Swami Siddheswarananda Bharati); however, subsequent mentions are of their main name (e.g., Siddheswarananda). In practice, I would address people as "Guruji," "Swamiji" or "Mataji" and address most adults with the respectful suffix of "*-garu*" (the Telugu equivalent of the Hindi "*ji*"). However, in the writing of this book, and in transcripts, I use the names by which they are known—that helps identify the speakers to the reader who may be turning to a page at random (after having read it all sequentially at first, of course).

How to Pronounce Diacritical Marks

This guide is not comprehensive, but will help the reader pronounce most names correctly. Basic tips: A dash over a vowel makes it a longer syllable; "*h*" after consonants calls for aspiration, or an out-breath. Curl your tongue back when there is a dot under the letter, except for ṃ, ḥ and ṛ (see below).

Vowels:

a as in cut
ā as in father
i as in pit
ī as in creed
u as in put or foot
ū as in brute or cool
e as in bay or fate
ai as in sigh or aisle
o as in hope
au as in sound or flautist
ṛ (which is a vowel in Sanskrit) similar to brunch, or rig
ṃ nasalize the preceding vowel so that oṃ as in the French bon
ḥ softly echoes the preceding vowel

Consonants: as for English except for:

v as wall
ś as shame (whereas s as in so)
ṣ similar to dish
c as church or chutney
t as pasta
ṅ as sung
ñ as canyon
ṇ has no equivalent in English, but it is a retroflex; the tongue needs to curl backward to touch the palate and then hit the back of the teeth.
d as in the, ḍ as in dart

When pronouncing the aspirated consonants kh, gh, ch, jh, th, dh, ph, bh, the h is pronounced along with an out-breath. This sound has no exact equivalent in English, but the following example will help approximate the sound. Thus, k as in skate but kh similar to Kate; g as in gate but gh as the country Ghana; ch as in much honey; and so on.

List of Figures

Fig. 5.1	Sahasrakshi Meru temple, Devipuram (Photograph by Mani Rao)	68
Fig. 5.2	Syllable positions—Kalavahana workshop handout	74
Fig. 5.3	Mani Prasanna (Photograph by Mani Rao)	77
Fig. 6.1	Goddess Svayam Siddha Kali (Photograph by Mani Rao)	115
Fig. 6.2	Potturi Venkateswara Rao (Photograph by Mani Rao)	121
Fig. 6.3	Swami Siddheswarananda Bharati (Photograph by Mani Rao)	141
Fig. 6.4	Puja to the deity Kala-Bhairava (Photograph by Mani Rao)	143
Fig. 7.1	Nachiketa Tapovan ashram (Photograph by Mani Rao)	150
Fig. 7.2	Swami Nachiketananda Puri (Photograph by Mani Rao)	150
Fig. 7.3	Swami Sivananda Puri, Navaratri 2014 (Photograph by Mani Rao)	153
Fig. 7.4	"Ramakrishna at Studio"	159
Fig. 8.1	Ferdinand Saussure's diagram	199

PART I

Preparation

Preparation is crucial to sadhana.
—Swami Nachiketananda Puri

CHAPTER 1

Introduction

1.1 Seeds

Mantras are codified sounds, clusters of syllables or words, or hymns uttered aloud or silently during religious rituals or contemplative practice. Recitations of mantras invoke deities, consecrate images of deities and mark rites of passage, from birth to marriage and cremation. In a *yajna* or *homa* ritual, mantras are offered to deities, typically via the fire-deity Agni, along with other offerings.[1] *Puja* (worship) in Hindu temples and homes is conducted with mantras, and mantras are also integral components of individual spiritual practice called "*sadhana*."

The seeds of my interest in mantra were planted in 2005. Returning to India after an advertising and television media career, and in response to a dream of Sathya Sai Baba, I began to spend some time at his ashram (spiritual community) in Puttaparthi, in the South Indian state of (what was then) Andhra Pradesh. Although Sai Baba's teachings were pluralistic, one of his missions was to promote the vedas; therefore, students at his schools and universities learned a set of vedic mantras as a part of their syllabus. These mantras were memorized and chanted on their own, detached from rituals. The word "veda" means "to know," and the term "veda" refers to a corpus believed to be the oldest source in Sanskrit and considered a revelation. This corpus is divided into four parts—Rigveda, Yajurveda, Samaveda and Atharvaveda, and at the core of each of these is

M. Rao, *Living Mantra*, Contemporary Anthropology of Religion,
https://doi.org/10.1007/978-3-319-96391-4_1

a collection of mantras (*samhita*). In the daily gatherings at Sai Kulwant Hall in Baba's ashram, the sound of vedic mantras filled the air—many in the crowd chanted along by memory. Whereas across India, mantras are mostly heard at temples or on religious and mythological programs on television, they are ubiquitous in Puttaparthi. The shopping center played mantras on a loop and the shops outside the gates of the ashram sold handbooks of mantras. Twice-daily *bhajans* (devotional songs) began and ended with mantras for peace (*shanti*). Additionally, among the crowds waiting in the Poornachandra auditorium for Sai Baba's public appearance, many would be occupied in *japa*, the repetitive utterance of a mantra, often using a rosary (*japamala*). I had heard about and witnessed several extraordinary phenomena attributed to Sai Baba such as manifestations of *vibhuti* (sacred ash) and materialization of objects, but did not have any understanding about spiritual practice. Living in Puttaparthi those few months, I became familiar with the idea of *sadhana*. Derived from the verbal root "*siddh*" (to achieve), *sadhana* carries the idea of earnest, hard work and of aspiring toward achievement. The culmination of sadhana is "*siddhi*" which means power, mastery or achievement. One imagines an athlete in training—no matter how many trainers she has, it is she who has to train; every sprint calls for single-minded attention and helps improve ability. A person who does sadhana is called a "*sadhaka*." When sadhana is centered around mantras, the siddhi involves gaining siddhi over a mantra, or having the ability to harness its power.

At the time, my own responses to mantras were aesthetic. Outside my day job, I was a poet and placed particular emphasis on sound structures. Admiring the rigor of mantra-sounds, I wondered, what prosodic elements made the chant of Srisuktam different in mood and effect from the chant of Rudram? What were the differences between mantras and Sanskrit classical poetry? If I accentuated the "Ṃ" in the utterance of "OṂ" (or "AUṂ") which prefaced so many mantras, I could feel the vibration on the top of my head; did the "A" and "U" also resonate in my body, and where? I was intrigued by such popular mantras as the Gayatri.[2] In vedic recitations, it was chanted in a jagged tone (*svara*) but commercial establishments in Puttaparthi played dulcet versions of it sung by the popular singer, Lata Mangeshkar.[3] During my stay on that visit, I developed a rudimentary sadhana; attracted to the Gayatri mantra—I thought, for its lofty meaning and jagged rhythms—I would often chant it silently.

It was in late 2005 when I was on a writing fellowship in Iowa City, USA, that I had what I would later call my first "mantra-experience." It was Fall, the leaves had turned red, rust and orange, and I would take a walk in the evening after a day of writing and meditation. On a walk one day, I heard a continuous tone in my right ear. I could tell it did not originate from *outside* me, and I could still hear it. The tone stayed with me, and while it was not unpleasant, it made me anxious, for I remembered reading about such a symptom in relation to some kind of motor imbalance. Searching for this symptom on the internet, I found information that suggested it could be related to meditation—an effect of certain *chakras* (energy centers) during meditation. Chakras are funnel-like structures at different points along the spinal path of the *kundalini* "energy" that may rise during spiritual practice, and the process is described as an awakening of the coiled-serpent-like *kundalini* from the *muladhara chakra* at the base of the spine to the *sahasrara chakra* at the crown. I phoned a Puttaparthi friend who engaged in full-time sadhana. She asked me a few questions—was it in my right ear, or the left? Was it continuous, and did I hear it all the time? It was in my right ear, it was quite loud, and if I forgot it, the slightest attention would bring it back to my hearing. She told me it was the *Pranava* (OṂ) and just a sign of a step forward in spiritual practice, I should pay no attention to this. I knew—from my general reading of early Indian ideas—that the sound of OṂ was said to be present in the *akasha* (etheric space), but I had never read about *hearing* it, and did not know quite what to make of it. Why me? Was there something I was supposed to do? What could I do with it? What next? Over the next few weeks, I lost this sound. Sometimes, I would hear a smallish wind-like *swoosh-swoosh* sound in the ear, but never a full-fledged and continuous sound like that first time. A decade later, when I began to study early Indian sources formally, mantra became my first scholarly project. Reviewing the scholarship, I found little or no study of the practice and experience of mantra. My methodology became ethnography; it was when I was deep into fieldwork that I realized the gaps in scholarship were also my own, eager to be bridged.

1.2 Homing In: Andhra-Telangana

Andhra-Telangana is one of the five Southern states of India. Previously a single state called "Andhra Pradesh," it was divided into two states of "Andhra Pradesh" and "Telangana" on 2nd June 2014, when I had just begun fieldwork there. Historically, vedic communities settled along the banks of the river Godavari which flows all the way from western India's Nasik in Maharashtra for over 900 miles into Telugu-speaking regions of southeast India. Compared to other regions of India, the population of vedic ritualists is more dense in the Godavari delta (Knipe 1997, 2015). At the same time, this region is home to tantric Hinduism including the Shakta Srividya tradition in which the Goddess, Shakti, is the absolute divine power. A number of places in Andhra are *Shakti pithas*, or "seats" of Shakti (Sircar 1950), and associated with legends about Shakti.

The primary language spoken across this region is Telugu, and one of the popular explanations for the derivation of the word "Telugu" is that it may come from "*Tri-linga*," denoting three *Shivalingas* (aniconic forms of Shiva) manifested at Kaleshwaram in Telangana, Srisailam in Rayalaseema and Draksharamam in Andhra—these three locations are also *Shakti pithas* (seats of Goddess Shakti). Telugu is replete with words from Sanskrit and has retained the same alphabet (unlike Hindi which has dropped some of the letters). Sanskrit texts circulate in the Andhra region in the Telugu script; therefore, many Telugu people are familiar with Sanskrit religious texts and mantras even though they may not be able to read the Nagari script. This results in a population of Sanskrit pundits as well as Telugu-speaking laity with access to religious literature. Those who have trained in veda schools become professional priests and are called upon to conduct rituals for the laity, especially rites of passage such as weddings and after-death ceremonies. The laity may also have their own mantra-sadhana including extracts from vedic mantras and tantric mantras, often not overtly understood as such.

One may categorize ideas and/or practices at the three locations of this fieldwork as tantric Hindu, or even as folk tantra,[4] and the central role of Goddess Tripurasundari and Goddess Kali marks them as "Shakta." Typically, "sadhana" refers to Hindu tantric practices; however, many foundational ideas about mantra (e.g., Vak, or divine Speech) in tantric sources are to be found in vedic sources. Unless one is speaking to orthodox vedic practitioners, both veda and tantra are considered *shruti* (revelations). On-ground, veda and tantra are neighbors, and neighbors do speak to each other. There are several instances in the narratives of this book where vedic pundits have a private mantra-sadhana.

Therefore, staying close to ground realities in this fieldwork, while I focused on three Hindu tantric locations, I did not exclude cases of visionary experience or insights from vedic ritualists. Finally, discussions with practitioners suggested that revelations and visions occur beyond and may even confound categories. Just as Hindu religious sources may be classified as vedic (from vedas), tantric (from tantras) or pauranic (from puranas), mantras done by sadhakas in this research range wide, from *Gayatri* (vedic) to *Shodashi* (tantric) and *Panchakshari* (pauranic).[5]

My preliminary fieldwork had been in Pune and surrounds where I interviewed a number of professional vedic ritualists. Conversations were full of quotations from established religious sources. Was there no tradition of discourse about experience among vedic practitioners here, or had language been a barrier? Whatever the reason, it was when I turned to Andhra-Telangana that I met people who spoke from their own experience. A chance conversation helped provide a focus—*visionary* experience of mantra. One clue led to another, and I found myself refocusing on mantra-sadhakas with visionary experience. An advantage of working with Telugu people was that I—a native Telugu speaker—did not have to translate concepts mentally as I conversed. Not that I felt conceptual distance in the location of my preliminary fieldwork, Pune, but not as many jokes and subtleties had whizzed about in Hindi, which was neither their, nor my, language. In Andhra-Telangana, my communication challenges were after the fieldwork when I was preparing transcripts and writing; that was when I would consider how to translate Telugu expressions as closely and accurately as possible into English. One or two conceptual points become important to note at this juncture. The specific verbs attached to mantra in Telugu indicate how people think about mantras and they are also indicative of how people speak and think about mantras in many Indian languages. In English, it is more common to say "chant mantras," and this indicates singing; in Telugu, we "do" (*chesenu*) or "put" (*vesenu*) mantras. When one person instructs another in a mantra, we do not say she "said" the mantra (*chepperu*), we say she gave the mantra (*iccheru*). Already, this indicates how a mantra is an entity, a thing, as well as an action, rather than a language to be spoken. Even when the verb "to read" is used (*chadavadamu* in Telugu, and in Hindi, *padana*), it does not necessarily mean that the mantra has been read from a book or written source, for it may have been accessed from memory. In order to specify that a mantra was said aloud, we specify, "*uccarinchenu*," or "I articulated it." "*Mantramu vinipincheru*" means "s/he had me hear it" and this shows how the source of the mantra is not a composer or speaker, but an enabler.

1.3 Overview

This chapter began with a disclosure about the experience from which the questions of this research germinated, and provided some information about Andhra-Telangana, the location of this research, and the popularity of mantra here.

Chapter 2, "A Mountain of Scholarship," surveys the literature about mantra. Such Indian sources as vedas and tantras considered authoritative contain and explain mantras as cosmic emanations, divine revelations or a priori forms that can be perceived by a *rishi*—a Sanskrit word often translated as "sage," and which means one who can *see*, thus, "seer." In many mantras and all vedic mantras, the rishi/seer is named along with the deity and the meter for that mantra. Indian legends have many anecdotes of how mantras solve problems and confer extraordinary powers upon those who utter them. Speculations about the origin of mantras, debates about their meaningfulness or meaninglessness, and commentaries and discussions including dialogs about applications and interpretations have been ongoing for over two millennia. Modern scholarship focused on mantra has mostly been of two kinds: those that categorize, translate and recapitulate early Indian sources, and those that attempt to understand mantra via music and myth and via language-based concepts including metaphors and cognitive theory, semiotics, speech act theory, prosody and structuralism including performance theory and ideological analysis. Immersing myself in this vast library of mantra, I found few insights into mantra-experience, and began to turn to fieldwork as a source of information.

Chapter 3, "Crossing Over," is about the methodological challenges and strategies in this research. From Émile Durkheim to Lévi Strauss, I thought, it was fieldwork that led to theory, and could one not also consider Sigmund Freud's interviews, fieldwork? Could I theorize mantra based on fieldwork? Determining that fieldwork would be my recourse also posed methodological issues. Can a scholar gain access to experience, or only to narratives of experience? Reading the views of anthropologist Clifford Geertz (1974) about experience-near and experience-distant locations, I wondered if I could be experience-*open*—and that still left the question whether experience was culturally constructed. What was my culture, and how would I position myself, or find myself positioned *vis-à-vis* the people I would interview? How to navigate subjectivity? In this chapter, I discuss methodological challenges and how mantra-sadhana and mantra-experience had to become a part of my life. I became sensitized to the subject, was welcomed into the in-circles of practitioners and discovered the questions that were of consequence to them.

Practitioners also live in the modern context and apply empirical parameters to many areas of their life; how do they deal with questions of verifiability for themselves? What kind of experience leads a rational person to embrace a lifelong mantra-practice? Do practitioners consider mantras, language, and do they care for meaning, or appreciate the aesthetics of mantras? How are mantras for different deities different in practice? What inspires steadfast practice? Is efficacy an expectation, and what do these expectations, or the lack of, do to mantra-practice? Are there useless mantras? Do practitioners think they can stop the effects of a mantra? Are some mantras more speedy or effective than others? Is there room for uncertainty and doubt? On what does the relationship between a practitioner and a deity depend? Is it as simple as Aladdin rubs the lamp and genie appears, or is the genie freer than that? How does a practitioner know it is a deity (i.e., visitation) and not imagination (i.e., hallucination)? Does the practitioner have the freedom to reject one deity and find another? Why is a deity appearance gratifying? Once a deity has been accessed with mantra, who is the audience for the continued practice of a mantra? When mistakes are made in mantras, a *kshama*-mantra seeking forgiveness for errors is often uttered … do deities not know what is really meant? If a mantra does what it is expected to do, where is the need for gratitude, or even devotion? How do contemporary understandings compare with traditional Indian ideas? Do mantras go out of date? Can and does a guru take back a mantra? Are there revelations today?

In Chapter 4, "Are There Revelations Today?," I probe the link between mantra and *rishi*/seer with two narratives to help illustrate two kinds of vision: revelation of mantra, and of deity. I use the term "seer" instead of "guru" (spiritual master/teacher) to stay close to the concept of visionary experience. My main fieldwork sites were identified based on informants for whom mantra was part of an intense religious or spiritual practice, many of whom had ideas about mantra and the visionary process based on their own visionary experience. These practitioners had been engaged with mantra-sadhana for years, if not decades, and many of them were gurus to other sadhakas.

Chapters 5, 6, and 7 are ethnographic and explore mantra-experience at three different communities. Chapter 5 takes place in Devipuram, Anakapalle, where a temple in the shape of a three-dimensional Sriyantra (aniconic Goddess form) was established by the guru-seer Amritanandanatha Saraswati. Chapter 6 connects with the community surrounding Swami Siddheswarananda Bharati whose primary location is the Svayam Siddha Kali Pitham in Guntur, where the *murti* (image) of the deity manifested in front of a group of people. Chapter 7 is about the experience of mantras at Nachiketa Tapovan ashram near Kodgal with Paramahamsa Swami Sivananda Puri and her guru, Swami Nachiketananda Puri. In the last chapter, I propose that such communities are akin to *mandalas* (circles of influence, chapters).

Practitioners describe their experiences including visions of deities and mantras, and how mantras transformed them and brought desired and unexpected results. They speak about deities they have seen and deities they witnessed taking shape *from* the mantras, discuss distinct characteristics of different deities, and explain how it is that deities can reside both outside and inside us. But the discussions go well beyond amazing experiential stories to engage in clarifications about processes involved in the reception and use of mantras. Practitioners share their processes, doubts, interpretations and insights into the nature of mantras and deities. While they care to discriminate between what is imagined and what actually occurred, they also consider imagination crucial to success and explain how imagination coupled with feeling or generative intention connects with deities and generates results. We learn about mantras received from deities, seen and heard mantras, hidden mantras, lost mantras, dormant mantras, mantras given silently, mantras done unconsciously and even a "no"-mantra. The experience of mantra unravels around phenomena, deities and results. As practitioners immerse themselves in mantra-sadhana, they find themselves mediating new mantras and practices, reshaping tradition. Chapter 8, "Understanding Mantra Again" (with grateful acknowledgment of Harvey P. Alper's [1989] important anthology titled "Understanding Mantra") arrives at a fresh understanding about mantra based on fieldwork.

Notes

1. Yajña or Homa: A ritual worship and exchange, typically involving such offerings as mantras, clarified butter (*ghee*) and other substances, to gods via Agni, the Fire god and messenger to gods. In return, the cosmic order is upheld and/or those who perform the ritual get benefits which can range from health, longevity and prosperity to enjoying heavenly realms in the afterlife. "*Yajña*" is often mistranslated as "sacrifice."
2. When people refer to the Gayatri mantra, they typically mean: *OṂ bhur bhuvaḥ svaḥ tat savitur vareṇyaṃ bhargo devasya dhīmahi dhiyo yonaḥ pracodayāt.* It is also called the Savitri mantra and is in numerous sources. Rigveda 3.62.10, dedicated to deity Savitar and revealed to the seer Vishvamitra in Gayatri meter, does not include *OṂ bhur bhuvaḥ svaḥ* (*Rigveda Samhita* [1890] 1966, 337). Many other mantras which are in the Gayatri meter dedicated to other deities are also called Gayatri. Tracing the history of the Gayatri mantra, Krishna Lal (1971) shows that it was not predominant in the early vedic period, and its popularity increased over the centuries.
3. Many professional vedic priests say that if vedic mantras are uttered without vedic tones (svaras), they are no longer mantras—from this perspective, non-svara versions of Gayatri mantra would not be considered mantras.
4. André Padoux (1987, 274) defines tantrism as "a practical way to attain supernatural powers and liberation in this life through the use of specific and complex techniques based on a particular ideology, that of a cosmic reintegration by means of which the adept is established in a position of power, freed from worldly fetters, while remaining in this world and dominating it by a union with (or proximity to) a godhead who is the supreme power itself." Teun Goudriaan (1979, 7–9) points out a number of features that mark tantrism including mantra, yantra, diksha (initiation) and hybrid goals (both mundane and spiritual). June McDaniel (2016) distinguishes classical tantra from folk tantra—the former more scholastic, and the latter based on pragmatic concerns and the charismatic leadership of those with visionary experience.
5. The Puranas include stories about the gods, and Pauranic mantras tend to be structured around the name of the deity. A typical Pauranic mantra begins with OṂ, followed by the name of the deity in the dative case (e.g., *Hanumaté, Śivāya*) and "*namaḥ*" (hail). Many mantras are also in multiple sources and categories—for example, the Panchakshari is a part of Yajurveda's Rudram-mantra which has Kashyapa for its rishi, but it is widely regarded as a pauranic mantra. The Gayatri/Savitri mantra (considered vedic) is used in combination (called "samputikarana") to yield a range of mantras.

References

Alper, Harvey P., ed. 1989. *Understanding Mantras.* Albany: State University of New York Press.

Geertz, Clifford. 1974. "From the Native's Point of View": On the Nature of Anthropological Understanding. *Bulletin of the American Academy of Arts and Sciences* 28 (1): 26–45.

Goudriaan, Teun. 1979. "Introduction: History and Philosophy." In *Hindu Tantrism*, edited by Sanjukta Gupta, Dirk Jan Hoens, and Teun Goudriaan, 1–67. Leiden: E. J. Brill.

Knipe, David M. 1997. "Becoming a Veda in the Godavari Delta." In *India and Beyond: Aspects of Literature, Meaning, Ritual and Thought: Essays in Honour of Frits Staal*, edited by Dick van der Meij, 306–332. Leiden: International Institute for Asian Studies.

———. 2015. *Vedic Voices : Intimate Narratives of a Living Andhra Tradition.* New York, NY: Oxford University Press.

Lal, Krishna. 1971. "Sāvitrī—From Saṁhitās to Gṛhyasūtrās." *Annals of the Bhandarkar Oriental Research Institute* 52 (1/4): 225–229.

McDaniel, June. 2016. "Tantric Mysticism and Some Issues of Religious Authority." *Prabuddha Bharata* 121 (1): 96–108.

Padoux, André. 1987. "Hindu Tantrism." In *The Encyclopedia of Religion*, edited by Mircea Eliade, 14 of 16, 274–280. New York: Macmillan.

Rigveda Samhita, Together with the Commentary of Sayanacarya. [1890] 1966. Edited by Max F. Müller, 2nd ed., 4 vols. Varanasi: Chowkhamba Krishnadas Sanskrit Series.

Sircar, Dineschandra. 1950. *Sakta Pithas.* Delhi: Motilal Banarsidass.

CHAPTER 2

A Mountain of Scholarship

Scholarship and practice are not necessarily disparate, nor opposed, and it would be difficult to divide the history of ideas on mantra into mutually exclusive and opposing factions of theoretical vs. practical, or academics vs. practitioners. Early Indian thought about mantra may be the result of practice as well as scholarship and is a resource for both practitioners and scholars. The thoroughness in the books of Frits Staal could only come from a familiarity with practical aspects and his intervention has not only influenced but helped finance the performance of large-scale vedic rituals.[1] On the other hand, Swami Pragyatmananda Saraswati (1971) is theoretical, even though his insights seem derived from observation during practice.

2.1 Early Indian Concepts

Across a range of early sources including veda, tantra, yoga and philosophy of grammar, mantras are regarded as natural, preexisting forms revealed to seers (*rishis*). However, there are a range of proposals about the relationship of mantras to the material world, and debates, commentaries and discussions about applications and interpretations. The following criteria are accepted as evidence (*pramana*) in Indian philosophies (*darshanas*): perception (*pratyaksha*), inference (*anumana*), comparison (*upamana*), non-apprehension (*anupalabdha*), postulation (*arthapatti*) *and shabda*. "*Shabda*" typically refers to veda, but is also used to refer to authoritative revelations called *tantra*. Vedas and tantras are both

M. Rao, *Living Mantra*, Contemporary Anthropology of Religion,
https://doi.org/10.1007/978-3-319-96391-4_2

considered *shruti*—15th CE Kulluka Bhatta wrote that revelation is two-fold, vedic and tantric (Padoux 1990, 34).[2]

Shabda/veda is uncreated (*autpattika*) and not created by any person (*apaurusheya*) and this also excludes *Brahman*—the formless and name-less absolute (and thus a) non-object, translatable for convenience as "God." Veda is called Brahman's exhalations[3] and as the core of vedas, vedic mantras are considered authorless, uncreated and self-evident. If we had to reconcile this idea with that of veda without a beginning, we must also conclude that veda—as the breath of Brahman—was not created by Brahman. Every vedic mantra has three identifiers—*rishi* (seer), *chandas* (meter) and *devata* (deity). A mantra's seer is understood literally—s/he is not regarded as the author of that mantra, but as the person who has come to know it through extraordinary perception. Students learn the vedic meter along with the mantra they are chanting. The presiding deity of a vedic mantra may or may not be named within a mantra, and a mantra may also refer to a number of deities. Formal aspects of vedic mantra recitation are so important that phonetics (*shiksha*) is considered auxiliary to the veda. Taittiriya Upanishad 1.2 lists six elements of chanting: phoneme (*varna*), accent (*svara*), quantity (*matra*), strength (*balam*), articulation (*sama*) and connection (*santana*) (Olivelle 1998, 291). The emphasis is on invariability, and a system of tones (*svaras*) helps with exact replication.[4] It is possible that vedic mantras were first used in yajnas and later in private recitation called "*svadhyaya*" (Killingley 2014). Fourth-century BCE Mimamsa-Sutras of Jaimini state in sutra 2.1.31 that mantras express assertions connected to ritual (Sandal 1923, 50). But, in the preface to his commentary (*bhashya*) on Rigveda samhita, fourteenth-century CE Sayana describes two applications for mantras: ritual and private recitation ([1870] 2006). Discussing which veda is more important, Sayana gives primacy to Yajurveda for its ritual instructions, but concedes first place to Rigveda for study (*adhyayana*), reading (*parayana*) and repetitive utterance (*japa*) (1).

Debates about the meaningfulness and meaninglessness of mantra have been ongoing for over two millennia. In *Nirukta* 1.15–1.16, first-century CE etymologist Yaska refutes Kautsa who claimed mantras meaningless or purposeless (*anarthaka*), and asserts that veda has meaning because it uses the same words as ordinary language. Next, mantras are a part of veda; therefore, they too are meaningful (Sarup 1920–1927, 16). Second-century CE *Shabarabhashya*, a commentary on Jaimini's

Mimamsa-sutras, gives us glimpses of debates among philosophers (Jha 1933).[5] The starting point for this is that Jaimini's Mimamsa-sutras set up veda as *dharma* (obligation, right action) and dharma as known from vedic injunctions. Such a circular reasoning places mantra in an unjustifiable position. The opponents in the debate protest that mantras are unintelligible, and the reason they tend to be in an invariant order is because they are not expressive; no wonder then, that meaning is not taught to students who train in vedic chanting. If mantras have no meaning, they cannot help understand dharma. The defense then explains that mantras can be directives for they help follow the sequence of rituals, and attach to ritual procedures. Meanings of mantras can be deduced from etymology with the help of commentaries, lexicon and grammar. If mantras are not understood, the fault is that of the person who is idle or careless. Any mantra that seems meaningless ought to be taken figuratively. A "four-horned deer" is explained as the four priests who stand like the four horns of the sacrifice. Meanings of mantras are not learned because it has no bearing on the actual performance. Besides, understanding and remembering meaning is easy, it is learning and remembering the mantras that is difficult (74–86). Across the centuries, even if mantra's meaningfulness has been defended, it has not superseded a conviction in the power of its form. Mantras are thought to produce results regardless of the intentions of the speaker—this is called having "*shabda-bhavana*" not just "*artha-bhavana*" (Taber 1989, 158).[6]

Shabda means "sound" as well as "word," and absolute or divine "Word" as well as word within language. Shabda is also described as "Vak" (Speech), and Rigveda samhita includes many mantras about Vak ([1870] 2006). In Rigveda mantra 10.125, Vak is a female rishi who is the source of the universe. Rigveda mantra 1.164.45 mentions that there are four parts to absolute Speech that wise Brahmins know about, and of which three are kept in secret; human beings speak only the fourth part.[7] While this mantra does not elaborate on the three mysterious parts, there are interpretations in other sources. Sayana acknowledges a number of interpretations including that of the levels of *Para*, *Pashyanti*, *Madhyama and Vaikhari*, stating that this is known to wise people who are masters of their mind, those who do yoga and those adept in mantra ([1870] 2006, 818). *Vaikhari* is the audible level with differentiated sounds upon which human speech takes place; *Madhyama* occurs at the level of thought; *Pashyanti* is the level where there is no distinction between word and meaning and there is no temporal sequence; and *Para* is the unmanifest level of language, equivalent to shabdabrahman. (Practitioners today refer to Pashyanti as the state of mind where revelations occur.)

In fifth-century CE Bhartrihari's *Vakyapadiya*, a treatise on the philosophy of grammar, the origins of language are attributed to shabdabrahman (1.1–1.4). It is the eternal shabda in the mind (*buddhi*) that causes discrete speech sounds (1.46), as well as the world (1.120). All knowledge is possible only because of shabdabrahman, and consciousness (*chaitanya*) is preceded by Vak (1.126). Word and meaning are intrinsically linked and meaning is conveyed by the bursting of "*sphota*"—like a spore—which is held in shabdabrahman, and perceived by a supersensuous entity called "*pratibha*" (Subrahmanyam 1992).

Mantras are depicted as magical forces in the vast oral literature of the Puranas where humans, *suras* (gods) and *asuras* use mantras to achieve extraordinary feats.[8] Pauranic mantras tend to be simpler—e.g., *OṂ Namaḥ Śivāya* begins with OṂ and includes the name of a deity in dative case. Vedic and Pauranic mantras were also used extensively in daily activities and life-cycle rites (from birth to marriage and death), and there are prescriptions for mantras in the Dharmashastras, early first millennium treatises about rights and obligations. Puranas and Dharmashastras are also consulted today across India for applications of mantras.

In the numerous treatises of tantra, mantras are linked to the dyad of Shiva and Shakti, where Shiva is absolute consciousness and Shakti animates this consciousness into the material world. Tenth-century CE Abhinavagupta's Tantraloka, a source of Kashmir Shaiva thought, proposes a detailed process by which all of cosmic creation is contained in and emanated by Shiva, reflecting and condensing on lower levels. Passing through resonance, Shiva's creative energy of *nada* (cosmic sound) becomes a *bindu* (dot) of phonic energy and gives rise to *matrikas* (matrix of phonemes), which in turn results in the world of objects and meanings. Mantra has a vital role in tantric worship. Deities are ritually constructed with mantras, and specific mantras invoke and install deities into their iconic and aniconic images. The emphasis is on identification, so the worshiper's body is imaginatively dessicated, burned and annihilated and then reconstituted with mantras before commencing the worship of, and identification with, the deity. The reconstitution happens with *nyasa*, where mantric syllables are placed on specific areas of the body. Individual syllables are prominent in tantric mantras, and adding the nasal *ṃ* sound (*anusvara*) to each letter/syllable turns the entire alphabet into a mantra called *Aksharamala* (Padoux 1990).

Yoga and tantra share conceptions about mantra, and mantra has a strong presence even in the compilation of yoga principles, the Patanjali Yogasutras. In *sutra* (aphorism) 1.27–1.29, OṂ is the very designator or expression of *Ishvara* (God); its constant repetition and meditation helps consciousness turn inward and removes obstacles to the practitioner's progress. Sutra 2.44 notes that the desired deity becomes visible through the svadhyaya of mantra, and sutra 4.1 lists mantra as one of five methods to gain powers (Dwivedi 1980). Over the centuries, yoga treatises including sixteenth-century CE Purnananda Giri's *Shadchakranirupana* describe how "seed syllables" (*bija-mantras*) are present at different energy centers (*chakras*) of the human body; as the yoga-practitioner advances, these chakras are energized, enabling better faculties. Thus, mantras impact and transform the mantra-practitioner because they are constituents of an intricate network that links the cosmological and physiological (Woodroffe [1918] 2012).

Mantras include sounds and words; therefore, it is feasible to discuss the prosody of mantras as well as aesthetics, but this approach would have been considered entirely out of line by early Indian thinkers. A non-worldly origin means mantras do not attract the same modes of evaluation as does literature. Besides, an uncreated and infallible object cannot be critiqued—vedic interpreters argue that human authors are fallible, mantra is authorless, and therefore, mantra is infallible. Mantra is not poetry (*kavya*); poetry comes from the world of human craft. Indian theorists circumscribed aesthetic dimensions to kavya. Mantras have authority, and kavya has authors.

2.2 Modern Scholarship

Academics tend to study mantras in categories, especially vedic and tantric. This is pragmatic, for mantras are a part of rituals and ritual traditions; moreover, the vast repertoire of ritual and related philosophical literatures makes it difficult for any one scholar to straddle diverse traditions. Thus, Jan Gonda (1905–1991) focused on vedic, and André Padoux (1920–2017) focused on tantric, sources. If mantras were to be understood from a range of perspectives within Indology, *Understanding Mantras* (1989b) edited by Harvey P. Alper includes a specialist for each of them.[9] Alper's "Working Bibliography" of over a hundred pages in the same volume is exhaustive and needs neither imitation nor annotation. My purpose in this section is to discuss frameworks, categories and methodologies under which mantra has been studied by modern scholars—this becomes useful both for what it illuminates about mantra-sadhana, and what it does not.

Along with an appreciation of the evident patterns in the structures of mantras, the discussion about meaning comes to the fore in scholarship. Beginning with an essay in 1979 and subsequently in several essays and books (1985, 1989a, b, 1993), especially *Rules without Meaning* (1989b), Staal decodes the rules or structures of rituals (e.g., embedding, omitting, transforming and modifying) to conclude that rituals carry no intrinsic meaning and that mantras are prelinguistic, even regressive, utterances.[10] Scholarship after Staal necessarily includes troubled comments disputing his pronouncement and defending mantra's meaningfulness. Meanwhile, scholarship on vedic hermeneutics and commentaries also highlights the significance and meaningfulness of mantras within the tradition (Francis Clooney 1990; Cesary Galewicz 2009).[11] There are also studies focusing on the history of specific mantras; recently, F. M. Moore Gerety (2015) takes a philological approach focusing on the Pranava (OṂ), tracing how mantras, music and discourse play a role in its spread across a range of religious milieus and centuries.

As ideas about language developed, they also helped reinterpret mantra through the lens of language-based frameworks. J. L. Austin and John Searle's speech act theory has been highly influential in this area (Wade Wheelock 1985, 1989; John Taber 1989; Ellison Banks Findly 1989).[12] The cognitive theory of Turner, Lakoff and Johnson has also proved useful for scholars attempting to make sense of the apparent disconnectedness between what is stated in the mantras and their applications. Laurie L. Patton (2005) works with cognitive theory to theorize how vedic mantra-practitioners may work with mental associations for new applications across changing contexts. Sthaneshwar Timalsina (2015) uses cognitive theory as well as Indian aesthetics to appraise tantric language. Arguing against the convention and that 10th-century CE Abhinavagupta authored a treatise on tantra (Tantraloka) and commentaries on aesthetics (Bharata's Natyashastra and Anandavardhana's Dhvanyaloka), but never blended the two platforms, Timalsina reads tantric images (i.e., deities) via *rasa* theory (in Indian aesthetics). Patton's book does not feature in Timalsina's discussions and bibliography, illustrating the deep divide and lack of exchange of ideas between vedic and tantric scholars. A third theme from language philosophy that has proved a rich resource for scholars is that of Charles Sanders Peirce (1839–1914). A detailed application of Peircean semiotics is undertaken by Robert A. Yelle (2003) in *Explaining Mantras—Ritual, Rhetoric and the Dream of a Natural Language in Hindu Tantra*. Yelle points out the limitations of J. L. Austin's theory in the context of mantras and is concerned with how mantras explicitly aim to influence reality—discussing them as an intensified language that use such poetic devices as palindromes, alliteration, repetition, etc.[13]

Such a use of language-related analytical frameworks helps move the subject away from incomprehension to reconceptualization, and avoids the use of the derogatory term "magic," perhaps also revealing the effort to correct colonial de-authorizations of ritual practices in colonized cultures.[14] In "The 'Magical' Language of Mantras," Patton E. Burchett (2008) takes the next step. Burchett surveys magic as a derogatory category and how it perpetrates enlightenment values of rationalism; disapproving of the term, Burchett even pins it firmly within scare quotes. He proposes calling mantras "natural language" in line with ancient Indian theory, noting in passing Robert Yelle's implicit rejection of the idea of a natural language by calling it a "dream" in his title. At this stage, scholarship is still far from discussing mantras as "natural" phenomena.

Scholars have also turned to categories of myth and music. Patton (1996) studies an Indian indexical source on deities to show how mantras are placed in a prominent and even an autonomous position in myths that function as arguments as well as commentary, tidying up and reformulating canon. In two books, Guy Beck (1993, 2012) discusses the role of sound in religious traditions and in the Indian tradition. Revisiting Indian theories from Shaiva, Shakta and Vaishnava[15] sources as well as Bhartrihari, Beck shows how contemporary devotional singing is linked to classical Indian music that uses melodic scales (*ragas*) as well as vedic tones (*svaras*). Among literature that describes the contemporary practice of mantras, Gudruun Bühnemann (1988) writes on mantras in daily Hindu rituals of Maharashtra, and Madhu Khanna (1986) on the *Concept and Liturgy of the Srichakra* based on 13th-century CE Sivananda's works.

The need for fieldwork in mantras was indicated by André Padoux decades ago, in 1978.

> All the researches hereto enumerated, important as they are, still do not suffice for a complete understanding of the problem of mantra, if only because they remain on the surface: they limit themselves to reporting what different texts, schools, authors, say on the subject. They report a discourse, they contribute to clarify it, they unveil its relations to other discourses, or its historical origins and developments, but they do not explain it: what really are mantras? How do they <function>? What can one say about the mantric phenomenon as a peculiar type of human praxis and discourse? Those, indeed, are the most important problems. (238–239)

Padoux runs through all the possible but unexplored directions in the research of mantras. He begins with indological and scientific types of research, and within the indological, suggests inventories and indexes, historical and comparative studies, traditional theories, linguistic and even psychological studies. Finally, he recommends that mantras are social facts and therefore must be approached from the anthropological side (239). Many of his suggestions (whether following his cue, or not) have been fulfilled in the last three decades, but not yet adequately, anthropology.

In the field of vedic studies, the ethnographic method has been used by David Knipe, Frederick M. Smith, Timothy Lubin, Laurie Patton and Borayin Larios. Drawing from interviews spanning over two decades, Knipe (1997, 2015) presents biographies of generations of vedic families from settlements in coastal Andhra, and describes vedic ritual life, careers and attitudes. Smith's (2001) ethnographic work is about changes or adaptations in vedic rituals, especially in contemporary Maharashtra.[16] An ideological focus comes from Lubin (2001), who looks at vedic ritual in the context of Hindu revivalism. Lubin draws attention to how vedism and devotion (*bhakti*) blend and how the rhetorical aspects of the packaging and promotion link the ritual to patriotic concerns, Hindu identity and even ecological and scientific goals. Larios (2017) does an in-depth ethnographic study of veda schools in Maharashtra, documents pedagogical systems and points to how contemporary veda schools accommodate Hindu devotion. All these ethnographies are focused on vedic rituals rather than mantras per se and interested in social context and/or ideology. An exception is Patton whose essay "Cat in the Courtyard" (2007) considers ethnographic material via Charles Briggs to propose how verbal texts have a performative context with an emotional impact. Across the modern period, scholars have not sought the insights of authoritative practitioners who are influencing present and future understandings of mantra.[17]

Speeding toward the galaxy of scholarship, a growing body of literature from mantra-practitioners and sympathizers aims to prove the efficacy of mantras. Not all of them are indigenous, and some are driven by nationalist ideology as critiqued by Agehandanda Bharati (1970) and Meera Nanda (2003).[18] Such universities and institutes as Maharishi Institute of Vedic Science (Fairfield, USA), S-VYASA (Bangalore, India) and Vaidika Samshodhana Mandala (Pune, India) have been the base for several research publications. When research is conducted to test or prove the efficacy of mantras (e.g., yajna brings rain; mantra causes healing), it is a *fait accompli* and implies or assumes that practitioners do mantras for results; moreover, we still do not learn anything about practice and experience. Among the ambitious works in this group, Tony Nader's (2000) *Human Physiology* aims to prove or translate equivalences between vedic material and modern science. Ideology and apologetics notwithstanding, this literature demonstrates an effort by practitioners to be accepted by modern norms of verifiability and perhaps also to communicate with scholars.

In "Rite out of Place," Ronald L. Grimes (2006) writes about a play titled after a polar bear, and a Byzantine screen through which it is observed. Grimes leverages this anecdote to think about the position of the religious studies scholar observing the enactment of religious life. The Byzantine frame becomes a means of working out alternative interpretive frameworks—aesthetic, religious, ritual and practical. A scholar too works with a screen, observing an activity at some remove from what s/he studies; the screen is theory, which is also the metaphoric move. Meanwhile, an improvisation artist observes the audience from behind the stage curtains, gaining a peculiar perspective, and later leaps into the role of a polar bear, triggering revelations for the audience and the playwright. The improvisation artist/fool of the opening anecdote illustrates how traditional or predictable scripts may be overturned for new insights by a scholar. Both, says Grimes, are necessary.

Notes

1. In 1975, Frits Staal (1930–2012) helped fund, organize and document a 12-day Agnicayana (vedic ritual) in Panjal, Kerala.
2. "*Śrutiś ca dvividhā vaidikī tāntrikī ca*"—Kulluka Bhatta in his commentary on the Mānavadharmaśastra, as qtd. by André Padoux (1990, 34).
3. "*Yasya Niḥśvasitaṃ Vedā*" in the benedictory verse of 14th-century CE Sayana's commentary on the Rigveda ([1870] 2006, 1). If we had to reconcile this idea with that of a veda without a beginning, we must also conclude that veda—as the breath of Brahman—was not created by Brahman.
4. Vedic mantras are taught along with specifications of the three tones—rising (*udātta*), falling (*anudātta*) and mixed (*svarita*).
5. Francis X. Clooney (1990) thinks that these debates may have been a defensive response to the rise of Buddhist critique of Vedic practices.
6. John Taber draws from the Artha Sangraha of 17th CE Laugakshi Bhaskara, a treatise on Mimamsa.
7. RV1.164.45: In the mantra beginning "asya vāmasya." [...] *catvāri vāk parimitā padāni / tāni vidur brāhmaṇā yé manīṣíṇaḥ guhā trīṇi nihitā néṅgayanti / turīyaṃ vāco manuṣyā vadanti.*
8. In Indian mythology, suras or devas (gods) and asuras are the sons of Aditi and Diti, respectively (co-wives of Kashyapa), and tend to compete with each other. "Asura" is sometimes mistranslated as "demons," but there are good and bad asuras.
9. In Harvey Alper's (1989b) anthology, Frits Staal writes on vedic mantras, Ellison Banks Findly on Rigvedic mantras and Kenneth G. Zysk (1989) on Ayurvedic mantras; Harold Coward explains mantras via philosophy of grammar of Bhartrihari, and Alper via Kashmir Shaivism; Gerhard Oberhammer (1989) discusses the use of mantra in yogic meditation; Ludo Rocher (1989) covers the puranic period of the first millennium as exemplified in the Shivapurana; and Sanjukta Gupta explains how Pancharatra tradition differs from Shaiva tradition.
10. In addition to Frits Staal's work on the structures of vedic mantras, there are other studies. Wade Wheelock (1985) looks at how mantras are used in definite patterns in vedic rituals as exemplified by a new-moon full-moon sacrifice. Jayant Burde (2004) adopts Staal's methods and includes mantras across non-vedic traditions to show how they share patterns with other forms of music, dance and even gymnastics.
11. Francis X. Clooney (1990) extracts the Jaimini Mimamsa-Sutras from the interpretive layer of Shabara's commentary, underlining a long tradition of intelligent debate about vedic mantras. Cesary Galewicz (2009) studies how 14th-century CE Sayana's exegetical commentary on the entirety

of the samhita (the mantras of the veda) was a core political project of the southern Vijayanagara kingdom—indicating how important it was to understand the meanings of vedic mantras.

12. Wade Wheelock (1985, 1989) discusses mantras via J. L. Austin and John Searle's speech-act theory. In Alper's (1989b) anthology, John Taber reconsiders and proposes some modifications to Wheelock's analysis, and Ellison Banks Findly discusses mantras as performative utterances.
13. An essay that draws from semiotics to analyze a specific liturgy is "Pedagogy and Practice" by John R. Freeman (2010). Freeman works with Peircean semiotics and Michael Silverstein's linguistic anthropology to show how words point to larger worlds.
14. Ariel Glucklich (1997) traces the history of anthropologists' reflections about magic and notes how with the demise of J. G. Frazer, "the literalist-occultist path has been sealed off; except to researchers in the area of para-normal phenomena," and "sociology and symbolism of magic have come to dominate academic interest" (83).
15. Vaishnava traditions honor Vishnu, Shaiva traditions honor Shiva, and Shakta traditions honor Shakti, as their main deity.
16. Frederick M. Smith finds that historically, vedic sacrificers lived in relative obscurity, dedicating their lives to their practice. The need for patronage generated a new breed of ritualists whom Smith calls "vedic activists"—ritualists promoting revivalism, seeking public patronage, and often with new interpretations and understandings—this contrasts with my informants in Andhra-Telangana.
17. The relevance of such a method became more evident as I went deeper into mantra fieldwork. Studying ritual treatments in Tamil Nadu for nagadosham (snake-blemish), A. L. Allocco (2009) comes across conflicting reports as well as what she calls "off-stage-left" references to nonexistent textual material for authentication (9). Researching mantra in Andhra Pradesh, I did come across a number of handbooks, but the mantra-practitioner's authoritative reference was always a guru, and/or visionary experience.
18. Agehananda Bharati (1970) discusses the apologetic use of science, and the relationship between Hinduization and westernization in post-independence India; Meera Nanda (2003) describes a full-fledged industry in scientistic discourse and argues how it becomes a guise for Hindu supremacist ideology.

References

Allocco, Amy. L. 2009. "Cacophony or Coherence: Ethnographic Writing and Competing Claims to Ritual and Textual Authority." In *Method and Theory in the Study of Religion* 21: 3–14.

Alper, Harvey P. 1989a. "The Cosmos as Śiva's Language-Game: "Mantra" according to Kṣemarāja's Śivasūtravimarśinī." In *Understanding Mantras*, 249–294. Albany: State University of New York Press.
———, ed. 1989b. *Understanding Mantras*. Albany: State University of New York Press.
Banks Findly, Ellison. 1989. "Mantra Kaviśastá. Speech as Performative in the Ṛgveda." In *Understanding Mantras*, 15–47. Albany: State University of New York Press.
Beck, Guy L. 1993. *Sonic Theology: Hinduism and Sacred Sound*. Columbia: University of South Carolina Press.
———. 2012. *Sonic Liturgy: Ritual and Music in Hindu Tradition*. Columbia: University of South Carolina Press.
Bharati, Agehananda. 1970. "The Hindu Renaissance and Its Apologetic Patterns." *The Journal of Asian Studies* 29 (2): 267–287.
Bühnemann, Gudrun. 1988. *Puja : A Study in Smarta Ritual*. Vienna: Sammlung De Nobili.
Burchett, Patton E. 2008. "The 'Magical' Language of Mantra." *Journal of the American Academy of Religion* 76 (4): 807–843.
Burde, Jayant. 2004. *Rituals, Mantras, and Science: An Integral Perspective*. Delhi: Motilal Banarsidass.
Clooney, Francis X. 1990. *Thinking Ritually: Rediscovering the Pūrva Mīmāṃsā of Jaimini*. Vienna: De Nobili Press.
Coward, Harold. 1989. "The Meaning and Power of Mantras in Bhartṛhari's Vākyapadīya." In *Understanding Mantras*, edited by Harvey P. Alper, 165–176. Albany: State University of New York Press.
Dwivedi, M.N., ed., and trans. 1980. *Yoga-Sutras of Patanjali: Sanskrit Text and English Translation Together with an Introduction and Notes*. Delhi: Sri Satguru Publications.
Freeman, John R. 2010. "Pedagogy and Practice: The Meta-Pragmatics of Tantric Rites in Kerala." In *Ritual Dynamics and the Science of Ritual*, vol. 1, edited by A. Michaels and A. Mishra, 275–305. Wiesbaden: Harrassowitz.
Galewicz, Cezary. 2009. *A Commentator in Service of the Empire: Sāyaṇa and the Royal Project of Commenting on the Whole of the Veda*. Wien: Sammlung de Nobili.
Glucklich, Ariel. 1997. *The End of Magic*. New York: Oxford University Press.
Grimes, Ronald L. 2006. *Rite Out of Place: Ritual, Media, and the Arts*. Oxford and New York: Oxford University Press.
Gupta, Sanjukta. 1989. "The Pancaratra Attitude to Mantra." In *Understanding Mantras*, 224–248. Albany: State University of New York Press.
Jha, Ganganatha, trans. 1933. *Shabarabhashya*, vol. 1. Baroda: Oriental Institute.
Khanna, Madhu. 1986. "The Concept and Liturgy of the Srīcakra Based on Śivānanda's Trilogy." PhD dissertation, University of Oxford.

Killingley, Dermot. 2014. "Svadhyaya: An Ancient Way of Using the Veda." *Religions of South Asia* 8 (1): 109–130.
Knipe, David M. 1997. "Becoming a Veda in the Godavari Delta." In *India and Beyond: Aspects of Literature, Meaning, Ritual and Thought: Essays in Honour of Frits Staal*, edited by Dick van der Meij, 306–332. Leiden: International Institute for Asian Studies.
———. 2015. *Vedic Voices: Intimate Narratives of a Living Andhra Tradition.* New York: Oxford University Press.
Larios, Borayin. 2017. *Embodying the Vedas: Traditional Vedic Schools of Contemporary Maharashtra.* Berlin: Walter de Gruyter GmbH.
Lubin, Timothy. 2001. "Veda on Parade: Revivalist Ritual as Civic Spectacle." *Journal of the American Academy of Religion* 69 (2): 377–408.
Moore Gerety, Finnian McKean. 2015. *This Whole World Is OM: Song, Soteriology, and the Emergence of the Sacred Syllable.* Doctoral dissertation, Harvard University, Graduate School of Arts & Sciences.
Nader, Tony. 2000. *Human Physiology: Expression of Veda and the Vedic Literature: Modern Science and Ancient Vedic Science Discover the Fabrics of Immortality in Human Physiology.* Vlodrop: Maharishi Vedic University.
Nanda, Meera. 2003. *Prophets Facing Backward : Postmodern Critiques of Science and Hindu Nationalism in India.* New Brunswick, NJ: Rutgers University Press.
Oberhammer, Gerhard. 1989. "The Use of Mantra in Yogic Meditation: The Testimony of the Pasupata." In *Understanding Mantras*, 204–223. Albany: State University of New York Press.
Olivelle, Patrick. 1998. *Early Upaniṣads—Annotated Text and Translation.* New York: Oxford University Press.
Padoux, André. 1978. "Some Suggestions on Research into Mantra." *Indologica Taurinensia* 6: 235–239.
———. 1990. *Vāc: The Concept of the Word in Selected Hindu Tantras.* Translated by Jacques Gontier. Albany: State University of New York Press.
Patton, Laurie L. 1996. *Myth as Argument : The Bṛhaddevatā as Canonical Commentary.* Berlin: Walter de Gruyter.
———. 2005. *Bringing the Gods to Mind : Mantra and Ritual in Early Indian Sacrifice.* Berkeley: University of California Press.
———. 2007. "The Cat in the Courtyard: The Performance of Sanskrit and the Religious Experience of Women." In *Women's Lives, Women's Rituals in the Hindu Tradition*, 19–34. Oxford: Oxford University Press.
Pragyatmananda Saraswati, Swami. 1971. *Japasutram, the Science of Creative Sound.* Madras: Ganesh.
Rigveda Samhita, Together with the Commentary of Sayanacarya. [1870] 2006. 2nd ed., 4 vols, edited by Max F. Müller. Varanasi: Chowkhamba Krishnadas Sanskrit Series.

Rocher, Ludo. 1989. "Mantras in the Sivapurana." In *Understanding Mantras*, 177–203. Albany: State University of New York Press.

Sandal, Mohan Lal, trans. 1923. *Mimamsa Sutras of Jaimini, Chapters I–III.* Sacred Books of the Hindus, vol. 27. Allahabad: Panini Office.

Sarup, Lakshman, ed., and trans. 1920–1927. *Nighantu and the Nirukta, the Oldest Indian Treatise on Etymology, Philology and Semantics.* London: Oxford University Press.

Smith, M. Frederick. 2001. "The Recent History of Vedic Ritual in Maharashtra." In *Vidyarnavavamdamam: Essays in Honour of Asko Parpola*, edited by Klaus Karttunen and Petteri Koskikallio, 443–463. Helsinki: Finnish Oriental Society.

Staal, Frits. 1979. "The Meaninglessness of Ritual." *Numen* 26 (1): 2–22.

———. 1985. "Mantras and Bird Songs." *Journal of American Oriental Society* 105: 549–558.

———. 1989a. "Vedic Mantras." In *Understanding Mantras*, 48–95. Albany: State University of New York Press.

———. 1989b. *Rules Without Meaning: Ritual, Mantras, and the Human Sciences.* New York: P. Lbang.

———. 1993. "From Meanings to Trees." *Journal of Ritual Studies* 7 (2):11–32.

Subrahmanyam, K., trans. 1992. *Vakyapadiyam of Bhartrhari—Brahmakanda.* Delhi: Sri Satguru Publications.

Taber, John. 1989. "Are Mantras Speech Acts? The Mimamsa Point of View." In *Understanding Mantras*, 144–164. Albany: State University of New York Press.

Timalsina, Sthaneshwar. 2015. *Tantric Visual Culture a Cognitive Approach.* New York: Rutledge.

Wheelock, Wade T. 1985. "Patterns of Mantra Use in a Vedic Ritual." *Numen* 32 (2): 169–193.

———. 1989. "The Mantra in Vedic and Tantric Ritual." In *Understanding Mantras*, 96–122. Albany: State University of New York Press.

Woodroffe, John. [1918] 2012. *The Serpent Power: Shat-chakra-Nirupana and Paduka-panchaka—Two works on Laya Yoga, Translated from the Sanskrit, with Introduction and Commentary.* Delhi: New Age Books.

Yelle, Robert A. 2003. *Explaining Mantras: Ritual, Rhetoric, and the Dream of a Natural Language in Hindu Tantra.* New York: Routledge.

Zysk, Kenneth. 1989. "Mantra in Ayurveda: A Study of the Use of Magico-Religious Speech in Ancient Indian Medicine." In *Understanding Mantras*, 123–143. Albany: State University of New York Press.

CHAPTER 3

Crossing Over

3.1 Positioning

Anthropology emphasizes participation; there is no substitute to being *inside* the community being studied. One begins with Bronislaw Malinowski's (1922) pioneering thinking in *Argonauts of the Western Pacific*—the idea of participatory observation—and his example of venturing out and living with the Trobriand. But, eventually, the exotic veneer of Malinowski's empathetic off-the-verandah anthropology was tarnished by his private diaries, published posthumously in 1967, which suggest that he was either a prejudiced racist or just a frightened outsider. E. E. Evans-Pritchard (1962) cautioned against anthropology that did not succeed in entering the *minds* of the people it studied and of scholars who come up with interpretations more akin to their own cultures. Ironic, then, that Stanley Tambiah (1985) critiqued Evans-Pritchard for not living up to these very ideals in his lifelong work especially with Azande communities. Tambiah explains that Azande analogical thinking is different from western methods of induction and verification. Evans-Pritchard and many western anthropologists drew from the pattern of how early Greek thought led to the development of scientific thought, i.e., how their "magic" developed into "science." As a result, Tambiah writes, Evans-Pritchard "misunderstood the semantic basis of magical acts" (61) and tried to determine if it was empirical or mystical. If Malinowski was inside, but never an insider, Evans-Pritchard may never have entered the Azande mind.

M. Rao, *Living Mantra*, Contemporary Anthropology of Religion,
https://doi.org/10.1007/978-3-319-96391-4_3

Tambiah's contemporary Clifford Geertz, however, seems to be over the romance of immersive anthropology. Discussing experience-near and experience-distant approaches, Geertz (1974) compares the goal to catching a joke, rather than achieving communion. He concludes: "Accounts of other people's subjectivities can be built up without recourse to pretensions for more-than-normal capacities for ego-effacement and fellow-feeling" (44). The distance that Geertz pitches as unproblematic comes across as a problem for other scholars. Ann G. Gold (1988) studies pilgrimages and their significance to a Rajasthani Ghatiyali village community in *Fruitful Journeys.* Gold explains her determination to get away from imperialist malaises of anthropology's past. She aims to "record, explore and work within indigenous categories," and "understand text and context as mobilely interlaced" (xiii). An informant tells Ann Gold that her fieldwork narratives are like "*gur* (cane sugar)" to the deaf and dumb—inexpressible by her. Gold then recalls Clifford Geertz: "I knew that I could never share nor replicate native visions" (301). Gold crosses this distance by relying on indigenous categories for her interpretation. Isabelle Nabokov (2000) expresses similar concerns in *Religion Against the Self* about possession and sorcery in Tamil Nadu. Nabokov finds western theory unhelpful—Tamil rituals do not fit into the three-stage model proposed by Arnold Van Gennup or Victor Turner, nor are sacred places distinct from the profane as proposed by Émile Durkheim. It is finally in ancient Tamil concepts of *puram* (outside) and *akam* (inside) that Nabokov finds resonance.[1] However, Nabokov finds her position as an outsider appropriate: "But I could never internalize that reality, and in my case, felt it would be false, presumptuous, even transgressive to try" (180). By contrast, a shared community is evident in the voices of Kirin Narayan and Urmila Sood (1997) who retrieve folk tales from the foothills of the Himalayas for *Mondays on the Dark Night of the Moon.* Naryan and Sood call informants "collaborators," letting them tell as well as actively interpret their stories: "Where actual people exist who are using such stories, I believe that we owe it to them to find out what they – as people of artistry and intelligence – might think" (219). Similarly, Leela Prasad shows no insider–outsider struggle in *Poetics of Conduct* (2007), a book about how the people of Sringeri construct normative values against a tradition of prescribed norms. Prasad also displays shared values—upon losing a ring, she offers *puja* (worship) to the deity of lost objects (5).

However, these examples cannot fall into two simplistic categories of exogenous and indigenous scholars with genealogies suggested by their names. Lila Abu-Lughod (1993) discusses the complexity of her position as a "cultural halfie" and Kirin Narayan (1993) recommends a reorientation in how anthropologists are perceived as inside or outside a community. Today, there is no guessing how an Azande scholar trained at a university in Paris might interpret Azande rituals; neither is identity so rigid, nor is anthropology a western method. It is anthropological traditions that seem more diverse now, and informants, more hybrid.[2] Further, we must think about how ethnographers *choose* to locate themselves, the roles they are *able* to play in the communities they study, and the *results* of their methods. Sometimes, the anthropologist's distance is driven by practical considerations. Antoinette E. DeNapoli (2014) describes her interaction with women ascetics in Rajasthan in *Real Sadhus Sing to God*. Even as she developed personal relationships with her informants, DeNapoli, affectionately called "*pardesi-cheli*" (foreign disciple) by her informants, chose not to become anyone's disciple as she was certain it would change her relationship with other ascetics (37–38). However, smarting under criticism in the early stages of her fieldwork, she began to learn to sing bhajans with and for them—this not only changed her status, but also gave her a better understanding of devotion and asceticism. Geertz's outsider position leads to cultural anthropology, and he deciphers symbols and patterns of meaning. From Nabokov's thesis about how possession rituals result in a rupture of personality, we may consider her position a prudent choice, safe distancing. DeNapoli made a choice, but resourcefully circumvented its disadvantages. Finally, although ethnographers may imagine that they are deliberating and calibrating distances, numerous field narratives illustrate that it is the host community that decides if the visitor is an outsider, and when and why, an insider.

What was my cultural identity? More adept in English than in any Indian language, influenced by French rather than Indian literature, not home-schooled in Hindu religious customs but familiar with the multi-religious values of a guru, and then a non-resident Indian for over two decades, I am a "heritage-learner." But from the informants' point of view, my face immediately identified me Indian, and my ability to pronounce *gha, kṣa, jña* and other sounds from the Indic syllabary suggested I was no foreigner. I remembered the protagonist of Cheuk Kwan's (2003) documentary film that traces the history of Chinese restaurant owners in South Africa, Israel and Turkey. The restaurateur confesses that when he arrived in Israel, he didn't know how to cook Chinese cuisine. His Israeli friends say, "never mind it's easy, we'll show you how – but you cook, you've got the right face." Conversing about my interest in learning vedic chanting, a Pune scholar asked if I was a Brahmin (*varna*, "caste"). The orthodox view is that only male Brahmins are entitled to chant vedic mantras, and I wondered if he cared about traditional rules, or if he asked so that he could respond to similar queries about me from others. "Brahmin," I said, and he seemed relieved; if my desire to learn to chant vedic mantras clashed with my gender, it was at least in line with my varna. The combination of Indian, Hindu and Brahmin set up a framework—freedoms and constraints, rights and responsibilities. Speaking from within a tradition would give me access, as well as scope to take some liberties when necessary, it would also carry restrictions and expectations.

My concerns seemed unnecessary anxieties after I went deeper into sadhana—perhaps neither experience-distant nor experience-near, but just experience-open. An anecdote will help illustrate the considerable difference that it made to interactions with informants. A couple of years before my fieldwork, when I was at Duke University in Durham, USA, I had met Subbarao Kompella *aka* Guru Karunamaya (of Chapter 5). He was on a USA tour and had been invited to conduct a puja at the Duke University chaplain Usha Rajagopalan's home. Karunamaya was known for his devotion to Goddess Lalita and said to enjoy the Goddess's palpable presence. An anecdote describes how, when he was in dire straits during his early years as a sadhaka, the Goddess demonstrated her presence by exuding honey from her iconic image that he worshiped daily.[3] At dinner after *satsang* (spiritual gathering) that evening, I sat beside Karunamaya and his wife Usha Ratna Kompella and tried to thaw ice. I told him I was researching mantra, gave him one of my books, and the next morning, emailed him with some questions. He did not respond to my email then, nor later. In 2015, after a year of fieldwork and by when I had an earnest mantra-sadhana, I met Karunamaya again. This time, to my surprise, we struck a warm rapport. When I commented on this change, he laughed, confessing that back in 2011, he had thought me "just a researcher."

3.2 Navigating Subjectivity

An anthropology of experience goes along with questions about how to maintain objectivity. In "Traditions of Disbelief," David Hufford (1982) writes that scholarship often begins with the presumption that a belief in the supernatural is an error of judgment, and objectively incorrect. It is assumed that informants—who are not acting on the basis of significant experiences—are under unconscious pressures from repressed needs, or have social needs, or creative urges that lead to hoaxes and fabrications, or simply reproduce folk etiologies. Where there is a claim of experience, scholars attribute it to hallucination, misperceptions or illusions and misinterpretations (49). (Hufford's own research suggests that many supernatural traditions are cross-culturally consistent and that it is experience that shapes culture, not vice versa.) Hufford suggests that if the scholar disbelieves the information presented, it is because scholarship too is a "tradition of belief" (54); such a reversal has also been proposed by other thinkers. Bruno Latour (2004) writes that scholars misconstrue themselves as scientists. If a scholar plays jury by adopting objective, critical thinking, he says, "the Zeus of Critique rules absolutely, to be sure, but over a desert" (239). Set in the present, an informant's narrative that pushes the limits of empirical parameters becomes susceptible to skepticism and may be recast as a claim, but rejecting it does not contribute to scholarship either. Studying religious experience within the community of his family for *Between Heaven and Earth* (2005), Robert Orsi reflects on the religious studies scholar who struggles with the space in-between the subjective and the objective, with some suggestions for how a balanced position may be adopted. While informants challenge an anthropologist's distance, scholars suspect entanglement for its biases. Empirical work can seem to endorse the religious worlds it studies, and the scholar has to walk a tightrope, suspending judgment. How can s/he negotiate between the subjective and objective? Orsi says it is not solved by adding autobiographical prefaces or epilogues, and suggests methodological experiments. The scholar may want to be "more clear," and even "disruptive" about the voices s/he includes; and "invite them to challenge our interpretations of them" (158). To illustrate this openness, Orsi provides an example of a scholar he thinks has gone wrong, and a scholar he appreciates. Dennis Covington is of the first type, a journalist who comes close to becoming an insider when conducting research among snake-handlers in Georgia. At a particular point in his research, he faces the misogynist mindset of his subjects and rejects the entire experience he has so far been studying. By contrast, David Haberman, who writes about Krishna worship in Western India, reserves his judgment when he finds himself skeptical about the emotional response of devotees to relics of Krishna's footprints. Orsi quotes Haberman's reflection that "multiple realities or worlds of meaning are available to us" (201). Orsi's conclusion is that a scholar is bound to have a response, but this response needs to become "a pivot for reflection" rather than a moment for judgment. While Orsi advocates empathetic objectivity, he emphasizes that he is agnostic. Similarly, T. M. Luhrmann plays mediator in *When God Talks Back* (2012), explaining to non-believers how evangelical Christians can believe in God. Both these scholars discuss practitioners from a non-committal distance and adopt a position that helps connect with informants as well as the academic community. A scholar who does make a commitment is Karen McCarthy Brown (2001). It is by enrolling as an initiate of the vodou priestess Mama Lola that Brown gains entry to the psychological world of vodou practitioners. McCarthy Brown does not include her own experience, and such silence suggests the problems of so immersive a fieldwork.

By the time I began fieldwork, I was convinced that the constructions and imperatives of scholarly considerations are already available to the scholar, with no risk of losing them; it is the practitioner's world that can expand scholarship. It was crucial to enter fieldwork bracketing skepticism instead of informants' experience. It was irrelevant to argue about the existential reality of deities, and more pertinent to understand the relationship between deity and mantra for practitioners. My goal was to look past belief and disbelief, to listen and to think. Unlike McCarthy Brown, I had multiple locations. It was visionary experience I was researching rather than the life of practice, and a single location or informant-subject would not suffice. I decided not to hire fieldwork assistants and mediators (and I did not need a translator). I chose not to focus on Puttaparthi, as that would be too close to home, and to my guru, Sathya Sai Baba. I discovered a range of perspectives and distances; my interaction with gurus and practitioners was different at different locations. Whereas all fieldwork locations would be referenced in a fieldwork bibliography as "participant observation," it was of many kinds on-ground. At Devipuram (Chapter 5), I intentionally subjected myself to rituals and courses of study; it gave me a taste of their mantra-process and supplemented what I learned from interviews. Siddheswarananda (Chapter 6) seemed to have a larger following compared to gurus at the other two locations and my research here took shape around interviews rather than relationships. Nachiketa ashram (Chapter 7) was where I did mantra-sadhana and where I was persuaded to put aside my recorder and forget about research for specific durations. The three fieldwork chapters reflect such a range of positions. Writing about the approaches to mantra at Nachiketa ashram for Chapter 7, I focus on the nitty-gritty of practice, and include some autoethnography when it contributes to the analysis. Informants are not only resources or screens, they are actors and agents too, and—as Donna Haraway recommends in *Situated Knowledges* (1988)—they too act upon the researcher (592). They did.

At the outset, I had concerns about instrumentality and loyalty. My informants were co-practitioners and did not mind that I would produce a book from the fieldwork, and my questions were actually of interest to them. As for loyalty, every anthropologist—to use a pejorative word—is a double-agent. If anthropology is subjective, it is redeemed by self-awareness for epistemic reasons, and if anthropology exposes, it is redeemed by transparence for ethical reasons. I did not downplay my scholarly motivations to co-practitioner informants. Some of them appreciated such transparence and were comfortable sharing their experience; others extended the hand of friendship upon condition that I would not write about them. More importantly, I saw how my own work with mantra was similar to that of many practitioners.

I did not anticipate that I would go so far as to take mantra-initiation (*mantra-diksha*) at Nachiketa ashram. Becoming a genuine mantra-practitioner opened as if an inner door within myself, as well as within communities of practitioners; I thought this could have been due to my own heightened appreciation of the poetics and experience of mantra-practice. What emerged in my fieldwork and writing was what Kirin Narayan (1993) calls "hybridities." Questioning old definitions of a native anthropologist, she calls for a "melt down" of the divide between narrative and analytical, subjective and objective:

> One wall stands between ourselves as interested readers of stories and as theory-driven professionals; another wall stands between narrative (associated with subjective knowledge) and analysis (associated with objective truths). By situating ourselves as subjects simultaneously touched by life-experience and swayed by professional concerns, we can acknowledge

> the hybrid and positioned nature of our identities. Writing texts that mix lively narrative and rigorous analysis involves enacting hybridity, regardless of our origins. (682)

Scholars from Catherine Bell to Pierre Bourdieu tell us that it is their theory or method which will remove the subjective vs. objective predicament. I found no external theoretical apparatus necessary to achieve this meltdown. If anything, doing sadhana cultivated what Nachiketananda (of Chapter 7) called the "witnessing-I." An old Indian story in several sources including the Mundaka Upanishad tells of two birds perched on a tree.[4] One eats the fruit of the tree, while the other merely looks on. This is considered figurative—the bird that experiences the fruit is the person who participates in the world; and the first bird that looks on is the *atman* ("self," or "soul")—the two birds are one and the same person. Commenting on this parable today, I would name the two birds "Objective" and "Subjective." They are both present at the same time on the branch, and at any given moment, one can morph into the other. It is by slipping in and out of both these positions that analytical fieldwork becomes possible.

The focus on mantra-practice and experience led to a break from ethnographic conventions in this writing. Often, discussions focused on mantras to the extent that there was no chit-chat about personal particulars. This also *matched* the focus on mantras that practitioners had themselves. I rarely provide—and often, do not know—biographical details such as education, family and social backgrounds. I did not attempt to frame the findings via gender and orientation, lineage and caste, socioeconomic particulars, affiliations to tantric and vedic traditions—had these been factors for analysis, it would have been a different project and a different kind of book.

3.3 Practice for Theory

When I began to do mantra-sadhana to research the experience of mantra, little did I know that it was exactly how some of my informants viewed their own sadhana. In their daily lives, mantra-practitioners were teachers, architects, marketers, businessmen and women, medical doctors and nuclear scientists—mantra was their private passion, a vocation. Biographical particulars, if at all volunteered by them, would be relevant to our discussion about mantra. Practitioners who had come to mantras for help with personal problems continued with mantras after these problems had been resolved—and in their narratives, positioned these problems as opportunities that led them to a mantra, or a guru. Subsequently, the unfolding of a mantra in their life was a part of their adventure in actively shaping their lives, writing their lives with mantras.

In conversations, the three main figures of this fieldwork rarely quoted from authoritative sources. Amritananda (2014) writes in *Understanding Sri Chakra Puja:* "Much of the matter presented here is being spoken from a direct personal revelational stand point, and so carries no references" (1). Such assertions are not ignorant of previous commentaries and sources; on the contrary, they displace them using authority. In the same book, Amritananda credits the Parasurama Kalpa Sutra as his source, but observes that the layers of commentaries are complicating.

> But if you see the Kalpa Sutras you will see it in an encoded form. They never write the mantras in a direct form. Every mantra has to be deciphered before you can understand it. That has been done here. In this deciphering process there is an Umanandanatha who has given a commentary on this. But he has added so many other things as well. And then every other upasaka who has written a commentary has also added on to it. They keep on complicating it. (93)

When a disciple reads such an introduction, s/he is not concerned about inconsistencies with previous sources—the revision has already become authoritative. When criticized for not following "shastras," Amritananda is said to have responded—"I don't follow shastras, I make shastras."[5] In my first meeting with Sivananda, she told me that she too was researching mantras. Another time, she said—"I didn't read shastras." Siddheswarananda experimented with rigorous disciplinary practices as a young seeker, and rather than guiding his followers with what to expect in practice, pushed them toward their own conclusions. All three saw *themselves* as primary sources.

This may come across as a transgression in a religious tradition that defines itself with reference to an authoritative canon of revelatory material. However, tradition is not as intransigent as it would seem. A quick review of discussions about the relationship between practice and theory, oral and written, and folk and the classical in Indian intellectual history will prove useful. Scholarship on Indian oral traditions of the *itihasa-puranas* (epic histories, legends) has long debunked the idea of an *ur*-text.[6]

A range of scholars from Paula Richman (1991, 2001), A. K. Ramanujan (1991), and Velcheru Narayana Rao (1991) to Romila Thapar (1999) and Linda Hess (2001) have shown how shifting contexts and participating publics build a dynamic tradition that is open to change, and have challenged hierarchies of written as authoritative and oral as folk, derivative or inferior. However, this has mostly been in the category of itihasa-purana.

Scholars have also given thought to how authoritative sources flourish in India. It was not theism but adherence to vedas that defined orthodoxy and heterodoxy in Indian thought. A person who accepted the *pramana* (evidence) of the veda was called an *astika* (believer) and one who did not, was called a *nastika* (non-believer). Thus, among the *darshanas* (schools of thought), Buddhists, Jains and Charvakas (materialists from ca. sixth-century BCE) were nastikas. The idea of vedic authority is legendary—undaunted, Louis Renou (1965) takes a bird's eye view of centuries of multiple Indian traditions in *Destiny of the Veda* to illustrate how the idea of the veda is more prevalent than adherence to its content. Brian K. Smith's (1988) *Reflections on Resemblance, Ritual and Religion* takes a different angle, and turns this into a positive outcome, repositioning veda as the "vedism" within later Hinduism, locating underlying epistemological principles and continuities. An anthology edited by Laurie L. Patton (1994) *Authority, Anxiety and Canon* focuses on specific texts and traditions to point out rhetorical strategies which allow variations from vedic authority to thrive, while purporting to carry on the tradition. Leela Prasad (2006) has shown how people interact with shastras intelligently, concluding that there is a dialectical relationship between theory and practice. Jonardan Ganeri ([2001] 2011) has shown in *The Lost Age of Reason* how deference has had the unfortunate result of downplaying innovation within the Indian tradition. But the idea of revisions in shruti is an entirely different matter altogether.

In "Theory of Practice, Practice of Theory," Sheldon Pollock (1985) lays out a broad review of the concept of tradition and change in Indian thought. In the ancient period, he writes, veda was called shastra and the vedangas (ancillary vedic sciences) such as *nirukta* (etymology), and *chandas* (prosody) were descriptive, with a taxonomical and non-legislative character. In the next phase, theory began to govern *prayoga* (practice). Pollock explains that the idea of a transcendent source of knowledge created a rule-driven approach. If all shastra or authoritative texts are no more than textualizations of transcendent knowledge, which is incontrovertible, then practice has no room to revise tradition.

In the Patanjali Mahabhasya, a ca. fourth-century BCE commentary on Paninian grammar, there is an exception to this rule—instances that are not provided for in shastra are acceptable in practice if the *shishta* (learned people) employ them. Pollock then examines the meaning of "shishta" and turns to later commentators in the 17th-century CE:

> Where, however, a linguistic science posits as its primary axiom that for usage to be "successful" it must derive wholly from grammatical theory, the presence of "ungrammatical" but acceptable usage can only be accounted for by recourse to the existence of a new member of the speech community who in a way distinct from that of the other members— by transcendent yogic insight as of a ṛṣi [rishi/seer], for example— has mastered the grammatical rules and so can lead us to infer that he has access to a more complete grammar than others possess. This, assert the later commentators on the Mahābhāṣya, is Patañjali's true position here. (505)

What is remarkable about this example is how later commentators reinterpret "a learned person" as a seer. It is also illuminating when we consider how this concept of a rishi comes from the 17th-century CE, which we now classify as early modern.

The example contains an important clue to how change is possible within the Indian tradition. The Indian philosophical tradition does not consider knowledge as being of human origin, but it also considers the actual source as vast, and accessible. Even though there is the idea of absolute, transcendent knowledge, there is also the idea that it is inexhaustible. Even if revelatory material is a priori and authorless, there are happy gaps—the source is inexhaustible, and a seer may have direct access to areas in these sources that have been untapped by his or her predecessors. Therefore, the commentators reason that rishis would have access to a more complete grammar than their predecessors. This very example also dislodges Pollock's thesis—while he is not wrong about theory preceding practice, he is not entirely right either. Practice is the source for past *and* future theories.

John R. Freeman (2010) looks into the liturgical details of a tantric puja where novices learn and rehearse rituals directly from their teachers rather than from manuals. Ritual practice and a textualized source coexist and intersect with each other—Freeman concludes that it is a "partial correlation." When the practitioner performs the ritual, they may abbreviate a group of rituals in a gesture. Performative utterances themselves are referred to by meta-linguistic descriptions. Ritual units are subject to "fusion, fission and ellipsis" (298). Freeman destabilizes understandings of the relationship between text and ritual practice. If novitiates transform texts or create new texts during practice, how much more so would a visionary with the authority to determine what others follow? In actual practice, a revision that claims to proceed with direct access to an original source is sure to proceed with *more* liberty for re-envisioning tradition. My classmate from a Srividya course at Devipuram, Arul Murugan, a welder by profession and a seasoned mantra-practitioner, told me he had come there for a course in order to learn from the person (i.e., from Amritananda) who had learned it directly from Goddess Lalita. At Ma Yoga Shakti Peetham temple in Nachiketa, the artist of the murals on the wall was Sivananda herself. Nachiketaites understand that the mantras in the homas are directed by her based on her visions, and when she dresses up the goddesses for Navaratri, it is understood she is simply replicating how the Goddess appeared to her in person. The point is not whether or not such views are legitimate, but that this is how it works on-ground, in practice. Given such ability, if those with visionary experience do not then go on to reject past material and produce entirely new material, it bolsters the argument for the ontological theory of mantra. Such a conception may also explain why information found in ancient Indian written materials is fragmentary and often incomprehensible without commentary. The dense, epigrammatic style of many early Indian sources makes more sense once we begin to re-envision them as notes, or outtakes of practice rather than as a second-order discourse or a reflection on custom.

In "Meaning in Tantric Ritual," Alexis Sanderson (2006) draws from Sanskrit works of Kashmir Saivism between 9th and 13th centuries CE to explain the tantric system. Kashmir Shaivism exerted a strong influence across the Indian region including South India; therefore, Sanderson calls this an excellent starting point. Sanderson also notes the shortcomings of staying within their ambit. Scholars have been focused on the metaphysical and mystical elements of tantrism, and ignored much else:

> When the prescription and theory of ritual have been neglected in the study of the learned works of the medieval period, it cannot be surprising that these humble manuals should have escaped attention altogether. (15)

Sanderson's point about what awaits scholarly study is valuable for the concerns of this research. The ideas of Sivananda Puri, the books of Siddheswarananda Bharati and Vadlamudi Venkateswara Rao and the manuals of Amritanandanatha Saraswati circulate today and are used as guides by their followers—unless scholarship gets out of the libraries of canonical sources from several centuries ago and into the field, how will it address present concerns? How can categories and modes of worship from centuries ago continue to be the basis and template of scholarly understanding, when in the absence of contact with current practice? And how can there be meaningful contact with current practice without understanding the realities and concerns of practitioners?

When practitioners have moved on to more updated material, it becomes incumbent upon scholars to keep pace. While I had my own list of secondary sources, an academic conversation that I was a part of, I became sensitive to another conversation I was witness to—between practitioners and their textual references. Mantra-sadhakas referred to other books by noted practitioners and thinkers because they regarded them as their practical notes by predecessors. Their approach to these written sources was not that of homage, but of consultation. When reading a book, just as one pauses to look at the bibliography, I browsed the bookshelves of my co-practitioner informants and noted what books they were reading. In the bookshelves at the Nachiketa ashram office, I found books by Chandrasekhara Sarasvati and Aurobindo, and often saw Nachiketananda referring to them. In the office of the manager of Siddheswarananda's ashram in Courtallam, there were several books about Ramana Maharishi and his disciples. A book on Daivarata was given to me by vedic ritualist Narendra Kapre. Vadlamudi cited the Shaiva Panchakshari Kalpa. Amritananda spoke about the Tripuratapini Upanishad and Parashurama Kalpasutra, and the manual that he created at Devipuram was his *revised* version of the Parashurama Kalpasutra. Such sources became a part of my bibliography in addition to early Indian sources and modern scholarship.

3.4 Unbracketing Experience

Gerardus van der Leeuw (1967) distinguishes phenomenology from history of religion, poetics of religion, psychology of religion and the philosophy of religion and theology, and there has already been a history of phenomenology of religion in the western academy—it has seen both a rise and a fall. Derived from the Greek term "*phainomenon*," which means "that which shows itself" or "that which appears," this approach admits a description and discussion of religious experience that may not be admissible in a strictly empirical framework. After William James (1842–1910) underlined the ineffable character of mystical experience (1902), such other thinkers as Rudolf Otto (1869–1937), Gerardus van der Leeuw (1890–1950) and Mircea Eliade (1907–1986) focused on description and insisted that religious experience was *sui generis*, i.e., in a class of its own. Eliade (1961) wrote about how the sacred manifests in hierophanies, Otto (1917) about numinous moments, and van der Leeuw (1967) about divine Power and Will.

Such an essentialist approach has been updated by particularity and reduction to such explanatory modes as social, cultural, psychological, cognitive, narrative, etc. A number of scholars including Wayne Proudfoot (1987) and Gavin Flood (1999) think that experience is only accessible through narratives, which actually also constructs the experience. Ann Taves (1999, 2009) draws attention to the context in which experience occurs, and turns to cognitive science to help reframe supernatural religious experience, helping realize the influence of the contextual frame upon the interpretation of the experience. Finally, some scholars including Russell McCutcheon (1997) find that phenomenology thrives alongside a trend of pluralism and cultural relativism, and suspect it of political motivations. Discussing "experience" as a critical term in religious studies, Robert Sharf (1998) is humorously skeptical—"[I]f only I had a taste of the real thing, I would quickly and humbly forgo my rueful attempt to explain away such phenomena" (94–116). Sharf also proposes that it is a historical anomaly, a "relatively late and distinctively western invention." Relying mainly on Wilhelm Halbfass (1988), Sharf concludes there is no rhetoric of experience in Asian religions before the colonial period. Halbfass had pointed out that in classical philosophy, ***darshana*** meant belief system rather than vision; thus, even the materialistic Charvaka system was called a darshana. Next, he argued that neo-Hindus Sarvepalli Radhakrishnan and Debendranath Tagore were driven by apologetics when they claimed Indian philosophy was based on intuition, vision and perception. However, Halbfass's view has been contested. Reviewing his book, John Taber (1991) challenges the thesis—"how far wrong really were the neo-Hindus about Indian philosophy being rooted in vision?" He points out that in the Upanishads, teachings are attributed to sages with unique capacities of wisdom and insight. Taber presents a range of key thinkers in Indian intellectual history including 8th-century CE Shankara—"Since he emphasizes that scripture should yield a direct experience of the truth, it seems reasonable to assume he was drawing on his own experience." In "Religious Experience in Hindu tradition," June McDaniel (2009) lays out excerpt after excerpt from early Indian sources to establish that the idea of religious experience has been stable through the centuries. I agree with Taber and McDaniel, and not only because of early sources… phenomena are ubiquitous in mantra-practice, and so is an *-ology*.

Conversations with practitioners invariably included reports of appearances by deities or their manifestations through signs and other phenomena. It is rare to find a hagiography of any guru without reports of his or her siddhis. Miracles are also the raw material of Indian legends, and they are understood as signs of the support and favor of deities or other non-human entities. Overall, siddhis are about the contravention of nature, and it has categories and conventions. In Patanjali Yogasutras, phenomena are described systematically—the Vibhuti Pada section from Verse 16 onwards enumerates how a yogi can gain siddhis including knowledge of the past and future, the ability to become invisible and to read the minds of others (Dwivedi 1980). Siddhis (*ashta-siddhis*) in pauranic narratives include the power to become diminutive (*aṇimā*); the power to become huge (*mahimā*); the power to become heavy (*garimā*); the power to become light (*laghimā*); (the power to obtain anything (*prāpti*); the power to achieve any desire (*prākāmya*); supremacy (*īśitva*) and control over anything (*vaśitva*). Other siddhis mentioned in Indian thought and literature include entering the bodies of others (*parakāya praveśam),* being undisturbed by hunger, thirst and other bodily needs (*aṇūrmimatva*) and many such suprahuman powers. Honorifics of gurus are often the markers of capabilities. For instance, a *Paramahamsa* (supreme-swan) is believed to be a person who has attained *Nirvikalpa samadhi* (complete liberation) and is discriminating. In a drink of milk mixed with water, a swan is said to be able to drink the milk and leave the water—such is its ability to discriminate and separate the real from the unreal, the worthy from the unworthy, and the title "paramahamsa" refers to such a quality (*tattva*). Accounts of phenomena in Indian sources are usually within a framework of soteriology or self-improvement. If vedic sources prescribe yajnas for a range of results from conception to rain, if tantric sources divulge the mantra to summon a particular deity, today too, popular manuals describe what siddhis accrue on how many counts of mantra-japa. Sources like these are numerous; if modern scholars of Indian religious studies were to "squirm" (Sharf 1998, 114) about experience and phenomena, the result would be large gaps in our understanding.

There is a crucial difference between "experience" and "experience*s*"—the former suggests wisdom arising from reflection after experiences, and the latter refers to phenomena which may or may not add up to experience. A Sanskrit and Telugu equivalent of experience is "*anubhava*," which is strongly associated with existence, for the term comes from the verb "*bhū*" or "to be;" great people are called "*mahanubhavuru*," i.e., a person with depth of experience. A popular narrative about the 8th-century CE philosopher-guru Shankara illustrates the weight of experience (Tapasyananda 1996). When Shankara and mimamsa scholar Mandana Mishra engage in a debate, Mishra loses and as agreed, he has to become a *sanyasi* (celibate renunciate) and a disciple of Shankara. Peeved, Mishra's wife Ubhaya Bharati tells Shankara that he has to defeat her too, as she is Mishra's other half. In this second debate, she interrogates Shankara on the science and art of love. As a sanyasi, Shankara has no knowledge of this subject and stands to lose the debate; Ubhaya Bharati gives him some time to respond to her questions. Shankara then uses his siddhis to leave his body and inhabit the dead body of a King. After reviving the King's corpse, he gains the necessary experience and returns to win the debate (113). The narrative illustrates a siddhi (*parakāyapraveśa*), but also shows how experience is valued in the Indian imagination—Shankara had to go and get the experience before he could discuss the subject. On the other hand, experience*s* get a negative assessment on the whole. In Dilip Kumar Roy's (1964) *Flute Calls Still*, when Indira Devi finds she has acquired precognition as a result of meditation, she ignores these effects. In Robert Svoboda's (1986) book on the occult practices of *aghoras*, when he describes the mantra-materialization of a demon (*pishaca*), he also shares his guru Vimalananda's warning that *shaktis* (goddesses, powers) can misfire for novices. Novices may gain control over shaktis in this life, but in their next lives they serve these same shaktis. Even though legends about the charisma of gurus tend to be about miracles, we are also told that they themselves would be disdainful of these occurrences. I recall what Subhadra-ma (*aka* Tapovani-ma in Uttarkashi), told me some years ago, when I asked about the miracles that I had heard she was performing—"It happens of its own accord, *it's not important*." This stance about the unimportance of phenomena was mainly among seasoned practitioners, and is also a normative expectation. In Hyderabad, when wrapping up after an hour's conversation, I asked Vadlamudi Venkateswara Rao, tongue-in-cheek—"And you haven't seen any deities, have you?" "OOhnono," he replied, poker-faced, "thankfully, I've seen no deities, I am relaxed as can be." In Telugu, he had been expressive—"*nenu hai ga unnanu*," the onomatopoeic "*h a a i*" imitating a relieved sigh. Everyone in the room laughed. Meaningful grins flew across the room at this adept's humorous but firm refusal to be drawn into mundane interests in deities and visions. The hierarchy is clear—the master or experienced practitioner has discrimination and is uncaring about phenomena, while the novice-practitioner is excited and encouraged by it. Experiences and such minor siddhis as precognition are credentials for the legitimation and evaluation of a practitioner's status; phenomena are every practitioner's instantaneous evidence that *something* is happening. My exchange with Vadlamudi was a joke; conversations with mantra-practitioners were not only about experiences but about aspects of mantra-practice—motivations and processes, concerns and values.

Even as they disagree, Sharf and Taber both seem to regard religious experience as a lofty state or a climactic moment where some ultimate insight or knowledge occurs. The idea that liberation is like a grand finale is widely prevalent, especially in relation to seers. Richard Cohen (2006) has pointed out that "enlightenment" is Max Müller's mistranslation of *nirvana* (3–8). Müller was portraying Buddha as a man appropriate for the modern age and expressing his convictions rooted in the European Enlightenment. My observations in Andhra-Telangana suggested that religious experience occurs on a graded scale. Repeatedly, in India, I listened to descriptions of phenomena that had nothing to do with ultimate knowledge. In Puttaparthi, I asked Ahlad Roy, a kriya yogi, "are you enlightened?" He was reputed to receive visitations from ascended masters and I had heard he had experienced *atma-sakshatkaram*, which means a direct experience of the ultimate-self. He replied: "a little." One wonders if Sharf's discomfort with phenomena is more at home within a theological framework of a formless and nameless God. In India, even God is on a graded scale—"*Brahman*" refers to a formless and nameless god, "*Ishvara*" and "*Bhagavan*" have a form and name, and deities are said to number 33,000.[7] In such an environment, Rudolf Otto's "numinous" and Gerardus Van der Leeuw's "power," "will," and "form" are too general—one wonders if Indian sources could furnish deities for each of Van der Leeuw's abstractions. McKim Marriot's (1990) anthology *India through Hindu Categories* is not new to scholarship in Indian studies, but the importance of this work necessitates a recapitulation. The preface explains why there are no equivalent western categories for many Indian conceptions and realities. Indian thinking does not distinguish between the material and ideological, or between nature and culture. One does not find mutually exclusive, oppositional binaries as material vs. spiritual, body vs. soul, true vs. false, fact vs. fiction, reality vs. imagination, action vs. thought, sacred vs. profane. Thus, a person is thought to be made of *koshas* (sheaths) which interpenetrate—*annamaya* (food-filled), *manomaya* (mind-filled), *pranamaya* (breath/life filled), *vijnanamaya* (wisdom/science-filled) and *anandamaya* (bliss-filled). Where a person's *body* is more than physical, the presence of non-physical entities is not extraordinary. When Robert Orsi (2008) writes about Marian apparitions to illustrate how an "abundance" of phenomena (echoing Otto's "overplus of meaning") awaits in a blind spot of the academic community, his voice is that of protest. Writing about mantra-phenomena in contemporary India is in line with a discourse already present on-ground. In *More than Real* (2012), David Shulman discusses Indian understandings of reality and how imagination, thought or desire *creates* reality. Shulman explains how *bhavana* (ideation) which derives from the verb *bhū* (to be) and *sankalpa* (intentional will) and *kalpana* (imagination) from *klp* (to create) are projections that generate external outcomes. Shulman takes us through a range of examples across two millennia of Indian narratives and focuses on the renaissance of ideas in 16th-century CE India. The same ideas and terms—kalpana, bhavana, sankalpa—came up in my research among mantra-practitioners.

Experience per se is valorized by the group of anthropologists including Michael Jackson and Albert Piette who explain their method in "What Is Existential Anthropology?" (2015).[8] Although Jackson and Piette's fundamentals are comparable with the approach in *Anthropology of Experience* edited by Victor W. Turner and Edward M. Bruner (1986), there are specific concerns that mark their method differently. Discussing their method that necessitated a new terminology, Jackson and Piette identify "a refusal to reduce lived reality to culturally or socially constructed representations" (3–4). Even though they do not deny that processes govern lives, they insist that individual experience is continually shifting, and unique. Dubbing this kind of attention "existence" comes from an allegiance to and acknowledgment of their intellectual traditions and conversation partners. They hope the concept of existence will help overcome the "antinomies" between psychology and anthropology, the singular and shared, biological and cultural. Jackson emphasizes the inter-subjective method, and Piette emphasizes the singularity and subjectivity of experience (10). Jackson and Piette's term works in the space between anthropos and ethnos, between ethnography and phenomenography and between ontology and epistemology (16). In *Existential Anthropology: Events, Exigencies and Effects*, Jackson (2005) sees an interplay between given life-situations and the human capacity to transform it. This puts the focus on practice: "the world is thus something we do not simply live and reproduce in passivity, but actually produce and transform through praxis" (xxii). Jackson seeks out "moments of being" that give him glimpses of what is at stake for the practitioner, this leads to what he calls an anthropology of events (13). I took a lead from such a focus on experience to expose the very grain of experience of mantra-sadhana. While locations impose some commonalities, every practitioner experiences and interprets his or her experience uniquely, and the narratives in this research are about moments of discovery. To emphasize individual voices of practitioners, I adopt a transcript-heavy approach. Stepping away from fieldwork (but not on to a mountain) for the last chapter "Understanding Mantra Again," I notice patterns and differences to theorize mantra via practitioners.

Notes

1. A. K. Ramanujan (1989) observes that Indian thinking is particularly context-bound and contrasts it with western thinking which he calls context free. In context-free cultures, he writes, counter-movements tend to be context sensitive; one of the examples Ramanujan notes is the search for native categories in anthropology.
2. Michael Jackson and Albert Piette (2015) explain how American, British and Continental traditions of anthropological thought are distinct depending on the distinct ways in which anthropologists engage with philosophy (1).
3. Official website of Guru Karunamaya, durvasula.com, "About Guruji," http://www.durvasula.com/gurukaruna/?page_id=2, accessed 11 September 2016.
4. Mundaka Upanishad 3.1.1–2 (Olivelle 1998, 449); Svetasvatara Upanisad 4.6–7 (Olivelle 1998, 425).
5. Vira Chandra. "Guruji Katha," *Amritananda-Natha-Saraswati* (blog), retrieved 27 May 2018.

6. In *Sakuntala: Texts, Readings, Histories*, Romila Thapar (1999) considers multiple versions of a single text to demonstrate how legends are reinterpreted in different historical contexts. Two anthologies edited by Paula Richman (1991, 2001) include essays that discuss the dynamic Ramayana tradition on-ground—*Many Ramayaṇas: The Diversity of a Narrative Tradition in South Asia* and *Questioning Ramayanas: A South Asian Tradition*. Among the essays included in *Many Ramayanas*, two that have become well known are A. K. Ramanujan's "Three Hundred Ramayanas: Five Examples and Three Thoughts on Translation" (22–50) and Velcheru Narayana Rao's "A Ramayana of their Own: Women's Oral Tradition in Telugu" (114–136); and among the essays in *Questioning Ramayanas*, Linda Hess's essay "Lovers' Doubts: Questioning the Tulsi Ramayana" by Linda Hess (25–48) describes how people conduct their questioning of authoritative tradition.
7. In the Brhadranyaka Upanishad 3.9, Vidagdha Shakalya asks Yajnavalkya how many gods there are. Yajnavalkya answers, "three hundred and three, and three thousand and three." Not being satisfied with the answer, Shakalya repeats the question, and this time the answer is "thirty-three." The interrogation continues, yielding a range of answers: six, three, two, one and a half, and finally, one, followed by an explanation that they are all manifestations, that there are thirty-three main manifestations, and the others are only their glories (Olivelle 1998, 93).
8. An ironic instance of scholars being shepherded into schools of thought is Michael Lambek (2015) who notes how he never thought of his work as existential anthropology until invited to redescribe and contribute to this anthology (59).

References

Abu-Lughod, Lila. 1993. *Writing Women's Worlds: Bedouin Stories*. Berkeley: University of California Press.

Amritanandanatha Saraswati. 2014. *Understanding Sri Chakra Puja*. Devipuram, Anakapalle: Sri Vidya Trust.

Cohen, Richard S. 2006. *Beyond Enlightenment: Buddhism, Religion, Modernity*. London and New York: Routledge.

DeNapoli, Antoinette E. 2014. *Real Sadhus Sing to God—Gender, Asceticism and Vernacular Religion in Rajasthan*. Oxford and New York: Oxford University Press.

Dwivedi, M.N., ed., and trans. 1980. *Yoga-Sutras of Patanjali: Sanskrit Text and English Translation Together with an Introduction and Notes*. Delhi: Sri Satguru Publications.

Eliade, Mircea. 1961. *The Sacred and the Profane: The Nature of Religion*. Translated by Willard R. Trask. New York: Harper Torchbooks.

Evans-Pritchard, E. E. [1962] 1967. *Theories of Primitive Religion - 1962 Lectures*. Oxford: Clarendon Press.

Flood, Gavin. 1999. *Beyond Phenomenology: Rethinking the Study of Religion*. London and New York: Cassell.

Freeman, John R. 2010. "Pedagogy and Practice: The Meta-Pragmatics of Tantric Rites in Kerala." In *Ritual Dynamics and the Science of Ritual*, vol. 1, edited by A. Michaels and A. Mishra, 275–305. Wiesbaden: Harrassowitz.

Ganeri, Jonardon. [2001] 2011. *The Lost Age of Reason: Philosophy in Early Modern India 1450–1700*. Oxford and New York : Oxford University Press.

Geertz, Clifford. 1974. "From the Native's Point of View": On the Nature of Anthropological Understanding. *Bulletin of the American Academy of Arts and Sciences* 28 (1): 26–45.

Gold, Ann G. 1988. *Fruitful Journeys: The Ways of Rajasthani Pilgrims*. Berkeley: University of California Press.

Halbfass, Wilhelm. 1988. *India and Europe: An Essay in Understanding*. Albany, NY: State University of New York Press.

Haraway, Donna. 1988. "Situated Knowledges: The Science Question in Feminism and the Privilege of Partial Perspective." *Feminist Studies* 14 (3): 575–599.

Hufford, David. 1982. "Traditions of Disbelief." *New York Folklore* 8 (3–4): 47–56.

Hess, Linda. 2001. "Lover's Doubts: Questioning the Tulsi Ramayan." In *Questioning Ramayanas: A South Asian Tradition*, edited by Paula Richman, 25–48. Berkeley: University of California Press.

Jackson, Michael. 2005. *Existential Anthropology: Events, Exigencies and Effects*. New York: Berghahn.

Jackson, Michael, and Albert Piette, eds. 2015. *What Is Existential Anthropology*. New York: Berghahn.

James, William. [1902] 2012. *Varieties of Religious Experience: A Study in Human Nature*. Edited by Matthew Bradley. Oxford: Oxford University Press.

Kwan, Cheuk. 2003. *Chinese Restaurants: Song of the Exile*. Documentary. Toronto: Tissa Films.

Lambek, Michael. 2015. "Both/And." In *What Is Existential Anthropology*, edited by Michael Jackson and Albert Piette, 58–83. New York: Berghahn.

Latour, Bruno. 2004. "Why Has Critique Run Out of Steam? From Matters of Fact to Matters of Concern." *Critical Inquiry* 30 (2): 225–248.

Luhrmann, T. M. 2012. *When God Talks Back—Understanding the American Evangelical Relationship with God*. New York: Knopf.

Malinowski, Bronislaw. [1922] 1984. *Argonauts of the Western Pacific: An Account of Native Enterprise and Adventure in the Archipelagoes of Melanesian New Guinea*. Prospect Heights, IL: Waveland Press.

———. 1967. *A Diary in the Strict Sense of the Term*. Translated by Norbert Guterman. New York: Harcourt, Brace & World.

Marriott, McKim, ed. 1990. *India Through Hindu Categories*. New Delhi: Sage.

McCarthy Brown, Karen. 2001. *Mama Lola: A Vodou Priestess in Brooklyn*. Berkeley: University of California Press.

McCutcheon, Russell. 1997. *Manufacturing Religion: The Discourse on Sui Generis Religion and the Politics of Nostalgia*. New York: Oxford University Press.

McDaniel, June. 2009. "Religious Experience in Hindu Tradition." *Religion Compass* 3 (1): 99–115.

Nabokov, Isabelle. 2000. *Religion Against the Self: An Ethnography of Tamil Rituals*. New York: Oxford University Press.

Narayan, Kirin. 1993. "How Native is a Native Anthropologist?" *American Anthropologist* 95 (3): 671–686.

Narayan, Kirin, and Urmila Sood. 1997. *Mondays on the Dark Night of the Moon: Himalayan Foothill Folktales*. New York: Oxford University Press.

Olivelle, Patrick. 1998. *Early Upaniṣads—Annotated Text and Translation*. New York: Oxford University Press.

Orsi, Robert A. 2005. *Between Heaven and Earth: The Religious Worlds People Make and the Scholars Who Study Them*. Princeton, NJ: Princeton University Press.

———. 2008. "Abundant History: Marian Apparitions as Alternative Modernity." *Historically Speaking* 9 (7): 12–16.

Otto, Rudolf. [1917] 1970. *The Idea of the Holy: An Inquiry into the Non-Rational Factor in the Idea of the Divine and Its Relation to the Rational*. Translated by John W. Harvey. London and New York: Oxford University Press.

Patton, Laurie L., ed. 1994. *Authority, Anxiety, and Canon: Essays in Vedic Interpretation*. Albany: State University of New York Press.

Pollock, Sheldon. 1985. "The Theory of Practice and the Practice of Theory in Indian Intellectual History." *Journal of the American Oriental Society* 105 (3): 499–519.

Prasad, Leela. 2006. *Poetics of Conduct: Oral Narrative and Moral Being in a South Indian Town*. New York: Columbia University Press.

Proudfoot, Wayne. 1987. *Religious Experience*. Berkeley: University of California Press.

Ramanujan, A.K. 1989. "Is There an Indian Way of Thinking." *Contributions to Indian Sociology* 23 (1): 41–58.

———. 1991. "Three Hundred Ramayanas: Five Examples and Three Thoughts on Translation." In *Many Ramayanas: The Diversity of a Narrative Tradition in South Asia*, edited by Paula Richman, 22–49. Berkeley: University of California Press.

Renou, Louis. 1965. *Destiny of the Veda in India*. Edited by Dev Raj Chanana. Delhi: Motilal Bonarsidass.
Richman, Paula, ed. 1991. *Many Ramayanas: The Diversity of a Narrative Tradition in South Asia*. Berkeley: University of California Press.
———, ed. 2001. *Questioning Ramayaṇas: A South Asian Tradition*. Berkeley: University of California Press.
Roy, Dilip Kumar. 1964. *The Flute Calls Still: Letters on Yoga*. Poona: I. Niloy.
Sanderson, Alexis. 2006. *Meaning in Tantric Ritual*. New Delhi: Tantra Foundation.
Sharf, Robert. 1998. "Experience." In *Critical Terms for Religious Studies*, edited by Mark Taylor, 94–116. Chicago and London: University of Chicago Press.
Shulman, David D. 2012. *More Than Real: A History of the Imagination in South India*. Cambridge, MA: Harvard University Press.
Smith, Brian. 1988. *Reflections on Resemblance, Ritual and Religion*. New York: Oxford University Press.
Svoboda, Robert. 1986. *Aghora: At the Left Hand of God*. Albuquerque, NM: Brotherhood of Life, Inc.
Taber, John. 1991. "India and Europe: An Essay in Understanding by Wilhelm Halbfass." *Philosophy East and West* 41 (2): 229–240.
Tambiah, Stanley J. 1985. "Form and Meaning of Magical Acts" In *Culture, Thought, and Social Action: An Anthropological Perspective*, 60–86. Cambridge, MA: Harvard University Press.
Tapasyananda, Swami. 1996. *Sankara-Dig-Vijaya: The Traditional Life of Sri Sankaracharya*. Madras: Sri Ramakrishna Math.
Taves, Ann. 1999. *Fits, Trances, & Visions: Experiencing Religion and Explaining Experience from Wesley to James*. Princeton, NJ: Princeton University Press.
———. 2009. *Religious Experience Reconsidered: A Building Block Approach to the Study of Religion and Other Special Things*. Princeton, NJ: Princeton University Press.
Thapar, Romila. 1999. *Sakuntala: Texts, Readings, Histories*. New Delhi: Kali for Women.
Turner, Victor, and Edward M. Bruner, eds. 1986. *Anthropology of Experience*. Urbana: University of Illinois Press.
Van der Leeuw, G. 1967. *Religion in Essence and Manifestation*. Gloucester, MA: P. Smith.
Velcheru, Narayana Rao. 1991. "A Ramayana of Their Own: Women's Oral Tradition in Telugu." In *Many Ramayanas: The Diversity of a Narrative Tradition in South Asia*, edited by Paula Richman, 114–136. Berkeley: University of California Press.

CHAPTER 4

Are There Revelations Today?

4.1 "Possible"

Several months into researching the practice of mantras in Andhra-Telangana, among those with whom I became acquainted was veda-pundit Narendra Kapre. Visits to Kapre's house in Hyderabad's Padmarao Nagar brought on wide-ranging discussions about topics past and present, from the legendary sage Dirghatamas to the Indian Prime Minister Narendra Modi. One such day, I argued with him: "If vedas are *anadi-ananta* (without beginning and end), surely it ought to be possible to access them directly, even today?" Kapre stared back. I went on—"We say we now only have fragments of vedas, the rest is *lupta* (eroded) or *supta* (dormant), but if that is so, it ought to be possible to discover? Can it happen even today?" *Aaj bhi ho sakta hai*? I added in Hindi, the language we had been conversing in along with English. I had asked the same question previously to a young vedic priest at Hyderabad's Vedabhavan. He had replied, immediately and with certainty, "impossible" *(asambhav)*, attributing it to the decadence of the times. So I was surprised when Kapre responded in an authoritative tone—"possible." He then told me the story of Daivarata who had a vision of vedic mantras in 1917. He called Daivarata "*maharshi*," which means a great seer (*Maharishi*). Even though oral transmission has preserved veda across the centuries, the extant veda may be a miniscule portion of what was once known. Each of the vedas has branches or recensions called "*shakhas*" and different shakhas are transmitted by different schools or

M. Rao, *Living Mantra*, Contemporary Anthropology of Religion,
https://doi.org/10.1007/978-3-319-96391-4_4

families. There are thirteen branches known today; across the centuries, different literatures refer to many more branches.[1] This was the allusion in my question to Kapre. If a portion of the veda is lost, might it not be possible to find? Are there rishis today?

4.2 Who Is a Rishi?

In Basara, Telangana, nervous that I would not be able to extricate myself, I crawled cautiously into the *guha* (cave) of Vyasa after my young classmates from the veda school. In the far, dim corner, there was a statuette of a sage sitting cross-legged in meditation—"Vyasa-maharshi," announced one of my friends. Basara was once called "Vyasar" after rishi Vyasa who compiled the vedas. Locals speak about how Vyasa left the sacred location of Kashi (i.e., Varanasi) and came south to do penance in this cave by the banks of the river Godavari. Several hundred miles downstream, by the tank at the Draksharamam temple, a stone panel features the legendary *sapta-rishis* (seven sages)—Atri, Bhrigu, Kautsa, Vasishta, Gautama, Kashyapa and Angirasa. It is why the location is called *sapta*-Godavari. At the entrance to the Ma Yoga Shakti Pitham temple at Nachiketa ashram in Kodgal, the deity Lord Dakshinamurthy instructs four "Kumaras," the rishis Sanaka, Sanatana, Sanandana and Sanatkumara. In Andhra-Telangana, the past is rich with rishis; as I was soon to discover, so is the present.

The word "rishi" has a specific meaning related to vision. According to early Sanskrit grammar and etymology, objects take their names from a particular *action* which is the most important and most special to them (Sarup 1920–1927, 69). Thus, nouns can be derived from verbs, and "rishi" can be derived from "*ṛṣ*," an obsolete form of the verb "*dṛṣ*," or "to see." In Yaska's Nirukta (2.11), "*ṛṣir.darśanāt*"—"a seer is (so called) from him having vision" (29). In Indian intellectual history, "darshana" also means a viewpoint or a school of thought and Indian philosophies are classified into six darshanas. In daily life, "darshana" simply means vision, or seeing, and in the context of temples and deities, refers to the mutual seeing between a devotee and deity. In the context of meditation or sadhana, "darshana" refers to a revelation of information—objects, events, and beings—beyond the range of ordinary human perception. A rishi's extraordinary vision is related to the idea of *shruti*, which literally means "what is heard," connoting a revelation which can only be seen/heard (rather than composed); vedas and tantras are both considered shruti. If it is only seen/heard, who says or *shows* it? Veda is called "*apaurusheya*," which means it is not by any *purusha* (person), whether human, or other being. Such an idea of authorlessness enables shruti to remain invariant, not open to revision.

Some scholars have regarded the proposal of shruti's uncreated eternality as a legend, or even a misconception. Frits Staal (2008) writes about shruti: "It nowhere says that the Veda is revealed or *śruti*, literally, "what is heard." It is heard only in the sense that it is transmitted from father to son or from teacher to pupil" (xvi). Many scholars from Louis Renou (1965) and T. G. Mainkar (1977) to more recently Robert Yelle (2003), Laurie L. Patton (1994, 2005) and Stephanie Jamison and Joel Brereton (2014) refer to vedic mantras as "poems," and to their speakers/rishis, as "poets," words that are understood *today* in terms of aesthetics rather than visionary experience. The reason to translate "rishi" as "poet" can be traced back to the vedic mantras themselves, which use "*rishi* (seer)" and "*kavi* (poet)" interchangeably. However, the idea of a poet in the vedic era is a person open to and seeking divine inspiration. Jan Gonda ([1963] 2011) writes in *Vision of the Vedic Poets* that scholars often misunderstand terms "probably as a rule unconsciously—founded on preconceived notions or suppositions anachronistically derived from modern conditions of life, our own Western traditions or agelong habits of thought" (9). He conducts an extensive philological survey of "*dhī*" to establish that it connotes vision in the vedic samhitas, and that to see was to know.

> [T]here was in those ancient times no hard and fast line between "religion" and "poetics", between a "prophet", a poet, a divine man, and a "philosopher." [...] the man fulfilling it was to a considerable extent a tool of Power, emptied of himself and "filled with the god." (14)

Perhaps another reason to translate "rishi" as "poet" is that Rigvedic mantras do not portray rishis as sagacious people with superhuman abilities; instead, they portray them as hard-working people eager for inspiration. In many mantras, the rishi asks for inspiration, addressing deities Vak, Agni, Indra, Soma, Varuna, Mitra, and others. Even the Gayatri mantra of Rigveda 3.62.10 comes across as the individual rishi's voice speaking on behalf of a collective, asking solar deity Savitar for *dhi* (intelligence). In Rigveda 10.71 attributed to rishi Brihaspati and dedicated to Vak, who is sacred language or Speech, rishis have to work for Vak's favor, sifting it as grain is sifted through a sieve, and by performing sacrifices. Kapre's narrative also emphasized Daivarata's hard work.

4.3 Maharshi Daivarata (1892–1975)

Twenty-five-year-old Daivarata was the disciple of Vasishtha Ganapatimuni (1878–1936) who was the disciple of Ramana Maharshi (1879–1950) of Thiruvannamalai in Tamil Nadu, the state neighboring Andhra-Telangana. Ganapatimuni and Daivarata would sit down to meditate on a daily basis, and Daivarata would go into *samadhi* (absorbed meditation) for hours. One day in 1917, Ganapatimuni heard Daivarata muttering when in samadhi. He observed Daivarata the next day too, and when he realized that the utterances were in vedic meters, he began to transcribe them. The process took three hours daily over sixteen days, and fifty *suktas* (hymns) with 448 stanzas were documented in their entirety (xvi–xviii). These are the details of the event as narrated in *Chandodarśana* by Daivarata (1968), a publication given to me as a pdf file by Kapre. The book includes Daivarata's verses and an introduction and commentary by Ganapatimuni. The verses were in four different vedic meters of Gayatri, Anushtubh, Trishtubh and Jagati, invoked forty-two vedic deities of which Sarasvati, identified with Vak, the Goddess of Speech, was predominant—none of the mantras were traceable to any known vedic source. Ganapatimuni describes how he transcribed the mantras:

> Some of the mantras which came out of Daivarata's lips could not be taken down on account of the speed with which they came; some were not distinct enough; some of the Mantras were only half or quarter. All such Mantras have been discarded. Only those Mantras which were complete, clearly audible, and which could be taken down in full have been compiled and commentary has been written by me for their elucidation. Similarly, the Suktas and Mantras and Anuvakas [sections] have been arranged in logical order according to Deities involved. And commentary written accordingly. (vii)

Researching this, I found that Daivarata's fame had spread to the Sanskrit academy across India, inspiring a 1996 doctoral thesis by G. N. Bhat followed by a seminar in Sirsi, North Karnataka in 1997. The papers at this seminar later anthologized by Bhat (2001) include critical appraisals of the *Chandodarśana* mantras vis-à-vis its conceptual and linguistic fit with the Rigveda. In another anthology, G. U. Thite (2000) studies vedisms in *Chandodarśana*. Thite examines accents, refrains, consonants, nominal declensions, particles and indeclinables and concludes that *Chandodarśana* has all the appearance of a Rigvedic chapter (43). He also notes negative points including the absence of such typical vedic figures as Vritra, Varuna or Ashvins and even Soma, with the conclusion that "Chandodarśana is Vedic but not sufficiently archaic" (43). Thite then hopes for its inclusion in the veda:

> I only hope that future history will not only accept Chandodarśana as Veda but will also associate it with some new ritual. The future generations are likely to learn this text by heart in its Samhitā-pāṭha and even with the other Vikṛtis [variations] like Krama, Jaṭā and Ghana etc. The future Mimāṁsakas [veda interpreters], too, will try to establish the apauruṣyatva [authorlessness] of this text and its authoritativeness. (43)

Kapre had given me extra-textual information including an account of how India's first President, Dr Rajendra Prasad, had accidentally run into Daivarata's notes in New Delhi, and was so impressed by the scholarship evident in the fragments that he visited Gokarna and gradually became Daivarata's supporter and follower. Kapre had heard about this from a pundit in Gokarna. The same pundit had also told him about a campaign in progress to include the Daivarata mantras in the vedic corpus. His view was that it should be added in the Atharvaveda mantras. Kapre said (in Hindi):

> There's a debate about that. But to what shakha [branch] can these mantras be added? Everyone wants to keep their own shakha. Like the Muslims say, it is *final,* not a sentence can be added or subtracted. Until now, it is not accepted by the scholar community. *Magar dhire dhire hava ban rahi hai* [But there are winds of change].

An unusual aspect of this phenomenon is that the rishi here is the young disciple Daivarata and it is his guru, Ganapatimuni, who takes on the role of transcriber, commentator and promoter. Three aspects were emphasized in Ganapatimuni's introduction and commentary (in English and Sanskrit) as well as in Kapre's narrative—a special talent, the credibility of those who endorsed the seer, and earnest effort. The commentary by Ganapatimuni includes a chart of Daivarata's horoscope, following a convention of displaying astrological predictions of greatness (xvii). As a respected scholar and sadhaka well known for having promoted Ramana Maharshi, Ganapatimuni's endorsement of Daivarata already carries credibility; Rajendra Prasad's is an additional and weighty testimonial. Daivarata went on to become a scholar of some repute, and his scholarship followed the theme of his visionary experience—*Vedarthakalpalata* (in Sanskrit) is an exposition of the Gayatri-mantra, and *Vaksudha* (in Sanskrit) is about the process of emanation of speech. Another book in Sanskrit, *Yogasudha*, is based on his experience in the practice of yoga. A combination of scholarship and practice shaped his reputation.

When Kapre emphasized Daivarata's hard work, he had quoted from the Mahabharata—"*Yugānte antarhitān vedān setihāsān maharṣayah tapasā lebhire…*," and then repeated, "*lebhire tapasā*."[2] He was quoting a verse from the Mahabharata which means that at the end of the *yuga* (era), the rishis rediscover vedas and epics through their penance (*Mahabharata* 2009, 330–331). The phrase Kapre repeated ("*lebhire tapasā*") is significant—i.e., it was by doing penance that the rishis had attained mantras. The Sanskrit word "*lebhire*" comes from the root "*labh*," which means to obtain, to get, arrive at, or achieve. Mantras received in vision are the goal posts achieved after an arduous journey, and they are also like a key that must be obtained to open yet another secret door. Kapre's quote helps place the new event within the convention of sadhana which is all about hard work, and achievement. What was even more pertinent to my research, though, was the methodology, or know-how of this event. Nowhere in Ganapatimuni's report is there any information about Daivarata's process of darshana or vision. The book is called "Chandodarshana," i.e., the darshana of chandas or the vision of vedic mantras—did Daivarata literally see the mantras, as visuals, images, as a script, and if so, which script? Or, did he hear them, or *also* hear them? Ganapatimuni coins such words as "supersight" and "supersensual" when describing how Daivarata had the mantra-darshana, implying extraordinary perception. Internal evidence in Daivarata's mantras gives us a clue to an elaborate sensory engagement in the vision. In *Chandodarśana* II-11.1–9, Vak (Speech) pairs with "*śrotra* (hearing)," "*tvak* (touch)," "*cakśus* (sight)," "*rasanā* (taste)" via "*jihvā* (tongue)," "*nāsa* (smell)" and "*prāṇa* (life force)." The verse describes the *mithunam* (pairing) between Daivarata and Goddess Vak—suggesting a union between Daivarata and Vak that produces the self-referring mantra (138–147). Daivarata died in 1975; his life, writings and methodology a potential treasure for future study.

4.4 Chandole Sastry (1886–1990)

The next seer I heard about is well known in Andhra-Telangana for his friendship with the Goddess—the story goes that the Goddess frequented his home in her girl child form called "Bala." In his day, Tadepalle Raghava Narayana Sastry was called "Chandole Sastry" after his village Chandole—today, the village is famous because of him. Chandole (or Chanduvole) is a one main-street village south of Guntur, an hour by road toward Repella, and it was easy to find the Chandole Sastry family home. The layout was traditional—a dirt yard in the front with two large Peepal and Neem trees nearly a hundred years old, a pump by the pathway so that visitors may wash their feet before they entered the house, a covered portico with an easy chair for the elder in the family and a built-in concrete bench beside it for visitors. Chandole Sastry's father Tadepalle Venkatappaiah Sastry had started a veda school on the premises and which continues to this day. I was accompanied on this visit by Rani Siva Sankar Sarma, son of late vedic ritualist Rani Appaji Sastry and author of *The Last Brahmin* (2007). Rani was interested in this visit for his own research on Hinduism as *sanatana-dharma* (perennial dharma). As we waited for Chandole Sastry's octogenarian son, Tadepalle Lakshmidhara Somayajulu, we spoke with his grandson Tadepalle Balakrishna Sarma.

The Tadepalles spoke in the same dialect of Telugu as I did. The moment I introduced myself, I was asked my last name and soon, there were no formalities. They knew some of my relatives (whom I did not know) and they knew Rani's father. We could have been new to the village, paying our respects, somewhat helpless as the man with the story held us captive. Over the next hour, Sarma regaled us with stories about his seer grandfather. Chandole Sastry was initiated in the Bala-mantra at the age of five (in 1891) when he had his *aksharabhyasam* (initiation in writing). He did japa steadily, and when he was sixteen years of age, Goddess Bala Tripurasundari began to respond to him. Once, during the Dussehra festival, they paid a bangle seller for outfitting seven girls. The salesman protested, insisting that there had been eight girls.

A lucky man! the bangle seller, he got to see (Goddess) Bala! There was a spot in the nearby forest where Sastry went for meditation. One day, when he came out of samadhi, it was late and dark. Suddenly, he saw Goddess Bala and asked her, "what are you doing in this darkness?" She replied, "aren't you sitting in the dark too?" He returned home with the little Goddess Bala holding his little finger. Someone came to him once for help about a sick child; he wrote a recommendation letter on a palm leaf with a stylus (*ghantam*) and told them to deliver it to Tenali Ganganamma (at her temple) and to say it was sent by him. He was beyond the mundane world (*lokatitam*) and strict about his ritual routines (*anushthanas*). If he had fever, he would tell the fever-deity (*jvara-devata*) to go over to the stick, then the stick would tremble. After he finished his rituals, he would tell the fever-deity, okay come'on come back, and she/it (the fever) would return to him. He never took medicines. The religious pontiff Kanchi Shankaracharya visited to see him and called him "yogi," and said he was really a *sanyasi* (renunciant) at heart, despite being a householder. Chandole Sastry died on December 10, 1990. He was aware of this approaching date, informed people about it in advance and did seven days of *prayopavesham* (resolving to die through fasting). When the cremation happened, the fire took the shape of Goddess in *virasana* (a seated yoga posture) and went up, the rest of the remains were instantly ashen, without a single residual ember. This phenomenon had been photographed and published in the journal *Andhraprabha*, and Sarma made a point about the date of the issue: September 8, 1991.

Chandole Sastry's son, Lakshmidhara Somayajulu, joined us. He had conducted a *somayaga* (a yajna) in 1990 and did not hide his orthodoxy. He railed against Brahmin pundits who went overseas, lay Brahmins who did not do their *sandhyavandanam* (a ritual with Gayatri mantra) and spoke about his father who had studied veda and vedangas from *his* father, logic (*tarka*) and grammar (*vyakarana*) from other scholars, and the sciences of mantra and tantra (*mantra-tantra-shastra*) from a Seetharama Sastry of Podili. He was also a staunch Brahmin and thought invitations to go overseas were a test from the Mother Goddess:

> They offered two crore [twenty million] dollars, asked you [him] to come to America. Father said, "No, my brahmin-ness (*brahmanatvam*) will go away, what is the use of two crore dollars, to burn! You're trying to tempt

me. Why two crores, you don't need to give me even two paise." So what Mother Goddess (*Ammavaru*) does meanwhile? Will he be greedy or not?

Chandole Sastry's grandson, Sarma, was also a mantra-practitioner; he had received mantra from his grandfather and did daily japa of the "Shodashi," the 16-syllable mantra of the Srividya tradition. He spoke about his grandfather's practice:

> Nobody knows about this *pitha* [seat/temple of the Goddess]. It has been a secret (*gudam*). One hundred and fifty years ago Mother Goddess (*Ammavaru*) asked and then came, she said "I will come to your house." Grandfather said "no-no-no." He did Ajapa-Gayatri (mantra). All deities come to that, and then the mental worship (*manasika puja*) happens and it's done. He said to her, "don't come, if you do, how will I do worship of all the deities (*sakala-upasana*)?

Manasika puja is done internally, in the mind, and *sakala* puja meant he was doing the puja to all the deities. Doing *ajapa*-mantra meant that it was being done involuntarily from within, rather than articulated by the sadhaka. Sarma explained that veda is studied so that one gets to know the deities within oneself—"There are Shaktis [deities/powers], *adhishthana devatas* [established deities], it is to know them that there is veda. When this is not known, they say in the veda, that there is no use studying the vedas that are in the books, the *baita-veda* [external veda]."

> SARMA: You know that when they do the brahma-yajna and pitra-yajna [rituals honoring ancestors] they say "*ṛco akśare.*" One man, a vedic pundit, asked grandfather to say the meaning of "*ṛco akśare parame vyoman.*" [….] What it means is this: every person has vedas. They are in the heart, in the heart's etheric space (*daharakasham*). The subtle akasham is there. There are deities, they are following this veda. To know those deities we study the veda.

"*Akasha*," or "ether," is an element or substance that pervades the universe and is the vehicle or medium for life and sound. It is one of the five elements (*panchabhutas*) which are earth, air, fire, water and ether. "Daharakasha" is the tiniest space in which akasha is present, and it refers to the space within the heart (not the anatomical heart). Rani and I both spoke simultaneously:

RANI: They are in the *daharakasham*? Heart?

MANI: When there is no gain by just studying…?

SARMA: There is *daharakasham, akasham*, the deities follow the veda which is there. The person who studies the veda and knows the devatas, *samāsate* … he becomes full of Brahma (*brahmamayam avutadu*).

RANI: What is the mantra you were quoting?

SARMA: "*Satam samāsate*," that's how it ends. Veda itself tells us. The person who comes to know the deities, he becomes full of Brahma. Others who read it externally there is really no use of that. No one knows this meaning. If he (grandfather) knows, it is because he is Shankara. Incarnation (*avatara*) of Ammavaru [Mother Goddess]. *Ardhanarishvara* [Shiva]. Shivalinga [Shiva's iconic form].

MANI: Who gave him initiation?

SARMA: Ammavaru.

Later, I found the mantra Sarma had quoted, in Rigveda 1.164.39 as well as Shvetashvatara Upanishad 4.8.[3] This mantra notes that for the person who does not know *akshara* (syllable) in the highest *vyoman* (heart-space) in whom all the deities are supported/established, the veda is of no use (Olivelle 1998, 425). Interpretations of the terms "akshara" and "vyoman" are wide-ranging—Olivelle translates "akshara" as syllable, while Vinoba Bave (1895–1992) translates it as the OṂ-mantra. This mantra emphasizes experience, and it is not surprising that it is more often quoted in Indian discussion forums than in academic anthologies. A commentary by Bave (2003) presents a response to this mantra. Bave writes:

> Do not carry the burden of any Book – so say the Vedas themselves. The Brahman (the Absolute) alone is the original source of all the Vedas. The Vedic riks (mantrams of Rig-veda) are not meant to be parroted. The Vedas exhort us to give up sectarianism and realize the Brahman. All the riks in the Veda, i.e., the Vedic mantras, are inherent in the sacred syllable or one Word— Akshara (a + kshara =not perishable), that is, the Imperishable, is the name of the Supreme Being who is hiding in the innermost recesses of the heart "What can one do with the Rig-Veda if one does not know that great Akshara on which the whole edifice of the Vedic riks stands?"— this is what the mantra means. That Akshara is AUṂ. […] On its realisation, the need for the Vedas naturally ceases. (30)

Bave sets up an opposition between "Book" and Brahman—the mantras of the veda come from the cosmic OṂ and thus become futile if one does not "know" OṂ and realize Brahman. In early Indian theory (see 2.1), OṂ is the origin of the world including the veda. In the rest of the commentary, Bave discusses the importance of realizing the OṂ-mantra. Quoting the same mantra/lines as Bave, Sarma explained his grandfather's perspective as experiential against a context of vedic priests who simply did external chanting. Sarma's response to my question about initiation referred to Sastry's direct communication with the Goddess which made him an authority for unprecedented rituals. I regarded his epithets as part of a convention where hyperboles represent high regard, but understood his import—it was because Chandole Sastry had experienced, actualized and internalized the veda that he achieved the presence of Goddess Bala. Sarma's comment also informed another line of questioning that had begun to develop in my fieldwork, whether mantra-sadhakas thought deities and mantras were inside or outside us. Sarma also spoke of a new *kalpa* (mantras and ritual procedures) authorized by his seer grandfather around the Sanskrit syllabary.

> Even in daily worship liturgies (*nitya-puja-vidhanas*), he created some new ones. No one in the outside world knows about it. We know about it.

When asked, Sarma said there was no manuscript for this kalpa. But the seer had taught it orally and it became a tradition at their annual Dussehra puja.

Sadhakas I met in my fieldwork were familiar with both the narratives of this chapter through word of mouth, and also through publications—Daivarata's writings are published by the Ramana ashram, and Chandole Sastry's son has written books about his father. After these two recent cases, finding people with visionary experience among *contemporary* mantra-practitioners did not feel like an anachronism.

Notes

1. There are nine branches of the veda today—two of Rigveda, three of Samaveda, six of Yajurveda and two of Atharvaveda. Based on a mention in 10th-century CE Bhagavata Purana 12.3, RVSS Avadhanulu (2007) writes that there are 1131 branches (41). Jan Gonda (1975) notes that we lack precise information on the branches (31).

2. Kapre was quoting a verse from the third chapter of Mahabharata's *Shantiparvan*. Alexander Wynne translates: "At the end of a world age, when the vedas and legends have vanished from the world, the great seers discover them once again through their asceticism, with the prior assent of the self-existent one" (*Mahabharata* 2009, 330–331).
3. *Ṛco akṣare parame vyoman yasmin devā adhi viśve niṣeduḥ/Yas tanna veda kim ṛcā kariṣyati ya it tad vidus te ime samāsate*. Rigveda samhita [1870] 2006, and Shvetasvatara Upanishad (tr. Olivelle 1998).

References

Avadhanulu, R.V.S.S. 2007. *Science and Technology in Vedas and Sastras*. Hyderabad: Shri Veda Bharati.

Bave, Vinoba. 2003. *Vedamrut—Reflections on Selected Hymns from Rigveda*. Varanasi: Sarva Seva Sangh Prakashan.

Bhat, G.N., ed. 2001. *Brahmarshi Daivarata's Chando-Darshana: A Critical Study: A Collection of Research Papers*. Mangalore: Jayashree Prakashana.

Daivarata, Brahmarshi. 1968. *Chhando-Darśana* [Vision of Veda/Meter]. Translated by Vāsiṣṭha Gaṇapatimuni with a Preface. Bombay: Bharatiya Vidya Bhavan.

Gonda, Jan. [1963] 2011. *The Vision of Vedic Poets*. Berlin and New York : De Gruyter Mouton.

———. 1975. *Vedic Literature: Saṃhitās and Brāhmaṇas*. Wiesbaden: Harrassowitz.

Mahabharata Book Twelve, Peace—Volume III "The Book of Liberation." 2009. Translated by Alexander Wynne. Clay Sanskrit Library. New York: New York University Press and JJC Foundation.

Mainkar, T.G. 1977. *Ṛvedic Foundations of Classical Poetics*. Delhi: Ajanta Publications.

Olivelle, Patrick, ed. and trans. 1998. *Early Upanishads*. New York: Oxford University Press.

Patton, Laurie L. 1994. "Poets and Fishes: Modern Indian Interpretation of the Vedic Rishi." In *Authority, Anxiety, and Canon: Essays in Vedic Interpretation*, 281–307. Albany: State University of New York Press.

———. 2005. *Bringing the Gods to Mind: Mantra and Ritual in Early Indian Sacrifice*. Berkeley: University of California Press.

Renou, Louis. 1965. *Destiny of the Veda in India*. Edited by Dev Raj Chanana. Delhi, Motilal Bonarsidass.

Rigveda: The Earliest Religious Poetry of India. 2014. Translated by Stephanie W. Jamison and Joel P. Brereton. New York: Oxford University Press.

Rigveda Samhita, Together with the Commentary of Sayanacarya. [1870] 2006. 2nd ed., 4 vols., edited by Max F. Müller. Varanasi: Chowkhamba Krishnadas Sanskrit Series.

Sarup, Lakshman, ed. and trans. 1920–1927. *Nighantu and the Nirukta, the Oldest Indian Treatise on Etymology, Philology and Semantics*. London: Oxford University Press.

Siva Sankara Sarma, Rani. 2007. *The Last Brahmin*. Translated by Venkat Rao. 2002. Bangalore: Permanent Black.

Staal, Frits. 2008. *Discovering the Vedas*. London: Penguin Books.

Thite, G.U. 2000. "Vedisms in Daivarata's Chandodarshana." In *Makaranda: Madhukar Anant Mehendale Festschrift*, 37–43. Ahmedabad: Sharadaben Chimanbhai Educational Research Centre.

Yelle, Robert A. 2003. *Explaining Mantras: Ritual, Rhetoric, and the Dream of a Natural Language in Hindu Tantra*. New York: Routledge.

PART II

Fieldwork

"For those who are ready to receive it, it's happening right now."
—Amritanandanatha Saraswati

CHAPTER 5

Body-Yantra: Sahasrakshi Meru Temple, Devipuram

5.1 The Thousand-Eyed Goddess

Looking down from one of the surrounding mountains, the Sahasrakshi Meru temple in Devipuram looks like a Sriyantra—interlocking triangles encircled by pink petals and an outer square with four openings (Fig. 5.1).[1] The Sriyantra or Srichakra is an aniconic (*amurti*) form of the primordial Goddess in the Srividya tradition; it is considered the form of the Goddess (and not a symbol). The temple architecture imitates the three-dimensional pyramidal Srichakra called "*meru*," which means "mountain" in Sanskrit. Approaching the Sahasrakshi Meru temple, I climb three levels to the inner sanctum of Goddess Lalita. Different flights of stairs for entry and exit ensure that I have also circumambulated the temple when I leave the space. The ground level of this temple is dedicated to Shiva and features a Shivalinga (Shiva's aniconic form). In this arrangement, as a sadhaka at Devipuram commented, it seems as if Shakti is standing upon Shiva.[2]

"Sahasrakshi," which is a descriptive name of Goddess Lalita, means "thousand-eyed." After I visit the temple, I feel that Her eyes are on me for the rest of the time that I stay at Devipuram—whether I am at the Kamakhya temple, the Shiva temple, at the *yajna-shala* (a hall for yajna), taking a walk on the grounds or even inside the room in which I stay. The descriptor "thousand" in the name of the Goddess is figurative and connotes that the Goddess is omnivoyant, which also connotes omniscience. Surrounding Goddess Lalita in the temple yantra

M. Rao, *Living Mantra*, Contemporary Anthropology of Religion,
https://doi.org/10.1007/978-3-319-96391-4_5

Fig. 5.1 Sahasrakshi Meru temple, Devipuram (Photograph by Mani Rao)

are other goddesses called Khadgamalas. They are the deities named in the Khadgamala-stotra or mantra and may be individually worshiped. "Puram" in "Devipuram" means place, abode or even city; I soon discover, place is also body.

The architecture of a typical Hindu temple borrows concepts from the human form.[3] Vinayak Bharne and Krupali Krusche (2012) point out how a temple layout follows the concept of the seven chakras (energy centers) of the human body, with the deity consecrated at the heart chakra (47–60, 93). Also, "words describing parts of the temple are literal derivations of human body parts"—the temple tower is called *shikhara* (head) and the inner sanctum, the *garbha-griha* (womb) (40). Further, Indian architectural sources of *Vastu Shastra* use the form of a mythical figure called the Vastu Purusha as a blueprint. Discussing the concept, Bettina Bäumer (2001) connects the Vastu Purusha with the vedic Purusha, a cosmic Man mentioned in the vedas whose sacrifice and dismemberment generates the universe. Bäumer quotes from the 12th-century CE Ajitāgama about how the Vastu Purusha is seized by the gods and thrown all at once on to the surface of the earth (37). Thus, in Vastu Shastra, dwellings are carefully constructed as to not hurt the vital joints of this Man. Baumer also finds that temple spaces symbolically enact a male–female relationship: "The temple symbolically represents, and makes spatially possible, the meeting or union between Purusha and Prakriti which symbolically corresponds to the male-female relationship" (37). The Sahasrakshi temple breaks this format. Modeled after a Sriyantra rather than a human figure, the Sahasrakshi temple at Devipuram is as if mapped on the body of a cosmic Woman.

5.2 Hierophany at Devipuram

The founder of Devipuram is Prahlada Sastry who was renamed Amritanandanatha Saraswati after initiation into the Shakta practice of Srividya.[4] In his online blog, Amritananda wrote that at the age of seven, he "used to see divine figures like Krishna, Ganapathy, Hanuman and Saraswati [...] in the patterns of leaves of trees."[5] When he was 11 years old, he had his "first spiritual experience" which he later surmises as a "Jada Samadhi," and which he explains as that "wherein body consciousness is absent and any sense of "I and mine" is also lost when awake" ("Guruji's experiences").[6] Over the years, he heard "humming sounds" and "300 Hz sounds" within himself, which motivated him to meditate. After an MSc and a PhD in Nuclear Physics, Amritananda worked at the Tata Institute of Fundamental Research (TIFR) for 25 years. He writes about himself as a questioning person with an empirical approach: "why should I believe what I don't experience? God is not verifiable!" ("2 Balaji Temple"). As he meditated, he also started to have extraordinary experiences and visions including one of Sanskrit mantras:

> The next night I had felt as if a bomb was placed in my heart and I exploded into bits and pieces, thrown off to ends of galaxies. I saw a blank screen on which about 10 sanskrit stanzas were written. Before I could read the first half of a line, it vanished. I remembered that: it was "Isavasyam idam sarvam". ("3 Explosion 1979")

The line quoted by Amritananda is the first verse from the Ishavasya Upanishad which states that all of this (world) is the clothing of Isha (Olivelle 406). "Isha" means "controller" in Sanskrit and may be referring to a divine entity. One day the same year, Amritananda felt a sensation that began at the base of his spine and moved up along his spinal column to his neck and upward like a "volcano." In yoga, this kind of phenomenon is typical of the awakening of the serpent-shaped *kundalini* from the *muladhara chakra* at the base of the spine to the *sahasrara chakra* at the crown. Alarmed, he turned to Goddess Sarasvati with a prayer—"I realized then that it is most important to seek divine power to help in crisis" ("5 Saraswati 1981"). It is after this that the story of Devipuram begins.

After a vision in which Goddess Bala instructed him to build a home for Her, Amritananda performed a 16-day Devi-yajna, and to his surprise, received three acres of land as a gift. Thirty kilometers and a forty-five minute drive from the port town of Visakhapatnam, and a half-hour drive from the train station of small town Anakapalle, this land was well positioned to become an international hub for Amritananda's followers. Amritananda describes the conception and construction of Devipuram like a collaborative project with goddesses. In the 1981 entry of his memoir, he writes about Goddess Kamakhya:

> It was 12 noon. I heard the sound of anklets. I opened my eyes and saw a huge ball of light in front of me. It condensed into a female figure, her body made of lightnings, bedecked in bridal attire, who spoke thus to me. "Will you do puja to me? I am Kamakhya". ("8 Kamakhya 1981")

Goddess Kamakhya told him to build the Sahasrakshi temple "like a pyramid, with all attendant deities, the main icon being Goddess Lalita on top of Siva creating new worlds of higher harmonies" ("8 Kamakhya 1981"). Each of the Khadgamala deities was seen by Amritananda in meditation and described to a sculptor:

> Then meditation on each deity of Khadgamala, seeing Her form, posture and weapons, sitting with the sculptor and creating a beautiful female form, finishing the structure; all of these activities took 7 years. ("9 Love Power Hladini 1983")

At some stage in the process, Amritananda writes that Goddess Hladini took over. I cannot help but notice that "*hlād*," which means "joy" in Sanskrit, is also the verbal root of Amritananda's civilian name, Prahlada. Bharne and Krusche (2012) describe the key players in the construction of a temple—the *sthapaka* (priest), the *sthapati* (master builder) and *shilpi* (sculptor), all of whom rely on shastras (canonical sources) for guidelines. In Devipuram, Amritananda plays all these roles and takes the place of shastra—even the Khadgamala deities had to be seen by him before they could be sculpted.[7]

Two hundred meters from the Sahasrakshi temple, upon a small hillock, is the Kamakhya-*pitham* (seat, temple) where the story of Devipuram began. Like the well-known Kamakhya temple in Assam, the deity here is a consecrated *yoni*. "Yoni" is a Sanskrit term for the "Shakti" (power or generative center) within everyone, both men and women; in temple iconography, it is depicted in the image of a vagina. In 1983 after a Devi-yajna, Amritananda meditated at the Kamakhya.

> One day, while in meditation he experienced himself lying on the Peetam [pitha], while four others were performing a homa with the flames emanating from his body. And during purnahuthi [final offering] he felt a heavy object being placed on his heart. Awakening from his meditative state, Guruji [Amritananda] was prompted to dig that site. Unearthed from that very spot, he found a Sri Chakra MahaMeru made of pancha-loha [alloy of five sacred metals].[8]

This event seems to occur in Amritananda's mind when he is in meditation, but the physical discovery of a meru proves it is not imaginary. Before the manifestation of the meru/Goddess, the area was an abandoned patch of land. The discovery of the aniconic Goddess is a manifestation of the sacred in a profane space, and an event that makes a sensory experience of the sacred possible—this is a "hierophany," a term made famous by Mircea Eliade (1961) when discussing how sacred spaces are formed.

The immolation described by Amritananda also recalls the scene from the Purusha-suktam (PS), where the universe is created from the ritual sacrifice of a cosmic Purusha.[9] At this ritual sacrifice in Devipuram, Amritananda *is* the "Purusha."[10] In the PS it is the *sapta-rishis* (seven seers) who sacrifice Purusha; in Devipuram, the sacrificers are "four others," and we do not find out who they are. Amritananda's narrative is also reminiscent of another vedic hymn, the Narayana-suktam, where the space within the heart is the location for the presence of the deity Narayana. Verse nine ends with how everything is established in this space (*tasmin sarve pratiṣṭhitam*) and verse ten speaks of the great fire (*mahān agni*) at this location, and at the center of which lives the deity Narayana.[11] *Pratishtha* is a technical term in Hindu rituals meaning "establishment," and a *prana-pratishtha* means that a deity's life force has been established in an image. In Amritananda's narrative, his heart is the site of the pratistha. We can assume a relationship between the "heavy object" and the meru which is found buried at that spot. Not only is Devipuram a manifestation of the body of the Goddess, the Goddess is established in Amritananda's heart and through him, within the community he was soon to lead.

A backdrop to sites of Goddess manifestation is the legend of Sati from the Mahabharata and several Puranas. When Sati's father, Daksha, insults her consort Shiva by not inviting him to an important yajna, a humiliated Sati immolates herself in the ritual fire. Grief struck, Shiva does the dance of transformation (*tandava*) with Sati over his shoulder. To jolt Shiva out of this distressed state, Vishnu hurls his discus-weapon (Sudarshan chakra), severing Sati's body into parts. Each of the sites in India where these parts fall becomes a *Shakti pitha* (seat of Shakti), where the Goddess manifests her power. While Andhra has its share of Shakti pithas, the areas surrounding Devipuram do not feature in canonical lists (Sircar 1950). The case of Devipuram may exemplify for some future scholar how canonical lists reopen to revision.[12]

5.3 Invitation to Cosmic Energies

In our very first conversation, Amritananda suggested that I do a Kalavahana (*Kalāvāhana*) puja—his exact words: "Immersion… Kalavahana." The term "Kalavahana" means an invitation to the Kalas (cosmic energies). This was not a puja that I was to do to the Goddess, but a puja done *to* (the Goddess in) me at the Kamakhya temple. After I was ready, I was asked to sit upon the sacred yoni-pitha. An older woman called Lakshmi and a younger woman called Sirisha conducted the ritual. They began by pouring warm water on my head, and freely smearing such ritual substances as red *kumkum* and yellowish turmeric (*haldi*) on my body along with chanting mantras, just as if I were a deity. I closed my eyes for practical reasons so that the offerings would not enter my eyes. Eyes shut, I listened to the mantras and my body and skin became sensors.

The mantras were primarily structured around the Sanskrit syllabary, each letter ending with an "anusvara" or nasal tone. As the priestess (*pujarini*) invoked each syllable, she also touched particular spots on my body, I knew this was the process of placing syllables (*nyasa*) and the syllable was being placed *in* my body. There were other mantras but I could not remember them; it was as though the puja bath of warm water had washed my memory clean. Back in my room after the puja, I could do little work and no field notes. Every time I closed my eyes I saw Khadgamala goddesses—shapes, outlines, parts of faces, movement. There was a lingering, palpable sense of softness. Surprised at how the Kalavahana puja had impacted my imagination, I wanted a closer view of its liturgy and Srividya rituals; but, my purpose was not personal practice. I expressed my interest and concerns to Prema Reddy, a disciple of Amritananda, who was also a teacher of the Srividya courses at Devipuram. She said I could not simply be an observer in the Srividya course, and suggested that I ask Amritananda. I wrote to Mr. Kandarpa in the administrative office requesting him to ask Amritananda's permission if I could join the course for research; he wrote back in the affirmative. Thus, three weeks after my Kalavahana, I returned to study its liturgy and ritual procedure as a part of a course in Srividya along with three other students.

Unlike me, my classmates were intent on becoming Srividya practitioners. Aryan was an engineer in Hyderabad; Arup, a software engineer in Nasik; and Arul, a welder in Tiruchirapalli. Why did Arul need to come to Devipuram, when nearby places in Tamil Nadu must have plenty of Srividya teachers? "I wanted initiation from the person who has spoken personally to (Goddess) Lalita," he said, referring to Amritananda. Arup was facing problems that seemed insurmountable and hoped Srividya would help. Aryan was inspired by his mother's devotional practice and wanted to learn Srividya rituals and mantras. Across five days, we studied Srividya and practiced its rituals which included mantras for the deities Ganapati, Shyama, Varahi and Lalita. One entire day was dedicated to the Kalavahana liturgy and rituals. Prema, a long-time practitioner of Srividya, knew the mantras by memory and indicated the placement of the string of syllables from the *aksharamala* (Sanskrit alphabet) on the body.

PREMA: *Aṃ. Āṃ.*

GROUP: *Aṃ. Āṃ.*

Prema enacted the placement of syllables on her own body, as we looked at a drawing (Fig. 5.2) and imitated it on our own bodies.

PREMA: No, it's clockwise.

Aṃ. Āṃ. Iṃ. Īṃ. Uṃ is the fifth one, and the last on the side. Ūṃ. Aruṃ. Arūṃ. Aluṃ. Alūṃ. Aruṃ. Arūṃ. Eṃ. Eiṃ. Auṃ. Auṃ is again half, or three-fourths. *Auṃ. Aha. Aṃha.*

Kaṃ. It's in the chest.

"Imagine the petals," she said, as she touched each point on the (imaginary) collar around the neckline, front to back.

Fig. 5.2 Syllable positions—Kalavahana workshop handout

Kaṃ. *Khaṃ*. *Gaṃ*. *Gaṃ* is the one on the, the armpit. *Gaṃ Ghaṃ Jñaṃ*. *Caṃ*. *Chaṃ*. *Chaṃ* is in the back, middle. *Jaṃ*. *Jhaṃ*. *Nyaṃ*. *Taṃ*. *Thaṃ*. We start *Kaṃ* here we end with the *Thaṃ* here. Okay? And then, navel.

Ḍaṃ. *Ḍhaṃ*. Okay? *Ṇaṃ*. *Taṃ*. *Thaṃ*. *Daṃ*. *Daṃ* is on the spinal cord again. *Dhaṃ*. *Naṃ*. *Paṃ*. *Phaṃ*.

And then on the Svadhisthana [chakra]. Six-petal. From the right bottom to the top and from the left top to the left bottom. Yes, goes like this and this.

MANI: Not cross-section like this?

PREMA: No. It's vertical. Until now we went horizontal, now it will go vertical. Okay? So, *Baṃ*. *Bhaṃ*. *Maṃ*. Okay. *Baṃ*. *Bhaṃ*. *Maṃ*. *Yaṃ*. *Raṃ*. *Laṃ*. Vertical, in the back.

ARUP: Left to right, *na*? Right to left?

PREMA: Clockwise. And then, Muladhara [chakra] maybe if I draw…

ARUP: Muladhara is not visible, right?

PREMA: Muladhara is where the garbha [womb] is.

ARUP: Is there any way to touch or something where we have to place the hand.

PREMA: Annh, touch is hard, that's why, you keep your hand on your genitals, but keep your mind inside, end of the spinal cord, tailbone. That is the place, actually.

So the mantras go like this. *Aiṃ Hrīṃ Sriṃ, yaṃ dhūmraciṣe namaha. Aiṃ Hrīṃ Sriṃ, yaṃ dhūmraciṣe namaha. Aiṃ Hrīṃ Sriṃ, yaṃ dhūmraciṣe namaha. Aiṃ Hrīṁ Sriṃ, yaṃ dhūmraciṣe namaha.*

The first three syllables were bija-mantras (seed-syllables), and we were invoking the Agni-kalas at the yoni, and after uttering yaṃ (the sound of the heart chakra), another bija-mantra, paying homage to smoke.

PREMA: If you keep practicing the aksharamala on your body, whenever you say "yaṃ" you know where that is.

In Shaiva tantras and in popular legends, a *kala* is understood as a practical art; there are sixty-four practical arts including dance, music and a number of skills. In the mantras of the Kalavahana, we invoked the Kalas of Fire, Sun, Moon, Brahma, Vishnu, Rudra, Ishvara and Sadashiva. Distinctions between these Kalas were unclear to me—how was Rudra different from Sadashiva, were they not both names of the same deity, Shiva? Each of these had subcategories of what seemed qualities—Preet (love), Vidya (learning), Pusha (health), etc. Sometimes, an entire cluster seemed to exist only so that a syllable was uttered, like "ra" in this line:

> *Agniṃ Dūtaṃ Vriṇīmahe Hotāraṃ Viśva Vedasaṃ. Asya Yajñasya Sukṛtaṃ. Ram Rim Rum, Raim Rauṃ Raha, Ramala Varayūm, Agni Maṇḍalāya Namaha, Agniṃ Āvāhayāmi.*

Had there been no meaningful words at all, it would have been easier to accept the clusters as sound-clusters. At the end, we invoked the Kalas into ourselves—we paid homage to the Agni mandala (the group of Fires), and invited fire-deity Agni to reside in our bodies.

When I asked Prema about the connection between the syllables and the locations on our body, she looked at me quizzically. I rephrased my question: "Say, one mantra has more "ra" sounds, does the "ra" spot in our body respond?" "Yes," Prema shot at once, and then mentioned neurological effects of the mantras. I thought this was unspecific and needing "real" research. While I could accept this as a hermeneutic system in tantra, the painstaking detail with which the Kalavahana process was being taught and learned seemed to suggest a "real" basis. At the next opportunity, I asked Amritananda, "How can I see the syllables in my body?" "Just imagine them," he chuckled, and Prema guffawed. Did that response mean the syllables were *there*, and I could not see them, or that they were imaginary? Conversations with practitioners helped think through this crucial question and the link between imagination and reality.

5.4 Goddess Bala

Mani Prasanna's name had been suggested by a number of practitioners at Devipuram; her home was a ground-floor apartment in a knot of building blocks at the crowded junction of Ameerpet in Hyderabad. An image of Goddess Lalita's eyes on the front door helped identify the apartment quickly. The living room was cluttered with religious ritual paraphernalia, and there were other people about—they did not look twice at me and I was not introduced to them. Mani Prasanna and I sat comfortably cross-legged on a queen-sized bed for the chat, and began a focused conversation immediately; we spoke in English. Frequently smiling, and with a sweet-sounding child-like voice, Mani Prasanna did not seem to mind my direct questions as we talked (Fig. 5.3). I asked her since when she was practicing Srividya, and why, and she said, "No reason. My experience. When I was a child I saw the Mother." Mani Prasanna first saw the Goddess when she was 14 years old. How did she know it was the Goddess? Did she have devotion to the Goddess at the time? Laughing, she said, "Not really, only during exams when I asked for help."

MANI PRASANNA: – When I slept, a woman woke me up and talked to me, I don't know who she was. I was scared and wanted to go back to sleep and I never had any such discussions again. However, whatever happened in my life I remember some things happened in the same way she

Fig. 5.3 Mani Prasanna (Photograph by Mani Rao)

said and whatever I don't remember I realize them at that particular time, when they are actually happening.

Mani Prasanna said that the Goddess told her things that would happen to her, and spoke to her for a half-hour.

MANI: Was she an older lady?

MANI PRASANNA: Around 50 years old.

MANI: Do you remember her form, what did she look like, what did she wear?

MANI PRASANNA: Yes I remember, she was wearing a sari, she was dark. Her hair was open and a lot of jewelry. And I remember the one thing she asked me. She asked – "how would you like Mother to be like/to look like?" And I replied saying I would like to sleep in Mother's lap and chat. And after that I was sleeping actually. I was imagining I was in Her lap. She was saying a lot of things but I don't remember them at all.

MANI: Did she speak for a long time?

MANI PRASANNA: – May be like half an hour, but I was scared.

MANI: Were you sitting and listening?

MANI PRASANNA: – I was sleeping and I was scared. So, closed my eyes and I was wondering what was happening and who was speaking to me. That was my first experience.

At the time, Mani Prasanna said, she did not know the identity of the visitor and only made the connection after a decade when she was visited again, after she met Amritananda. In 2003, Mani Prasanna went to Devipuram with a friend to attend a *homa* for Goddess Chandi. During the yajna, she felt a sensation in her womb.

We did homa, and during that ritual, I had a feeling right here (*places a hand on her belly, a little beneath the abdomen*). After the homa, I felt something was moving inside me. Then I asked Guruji [Amritananda] and he said that I am going to have a girl-child. But it was very funny and silly to me. I did not believe it at that time. But later my pregnancy tests were confirmed and then I believed and changed my mind.

It was not so much the timeline, but Amritananda's prediction or precognition that immediately placed it in the category of divine intervention, or divine will. As such, this occasion was also the birth of a guru-disciple bond; it was in this meeting that Amritananda gave her the Bala-mantra. She began to do this mantra daily, and she was soon visited by Goddess Bala who also gave her a lesson in the theory of the body as a site of mantra.

> MANI PRASANNA: When I was doing the japa of Bala [mantra], I saw Mother again, she came in the form of a little girl and said that she had no one and that she was hungry. And I said, I will take care of you, I am here, your mother. I asked what she fancied, so that I could make her some food. She asked for something and I prepared and fed her. After food…
>
> MANI: All this is in your dream?
>
> MANI PRASANNA: No, not in a dream. In fact. When I was actually sitting. That was my first experience with Bala. Inside our home. I did not know how she got in. So after that…
>
> MANI: No one saw her?
>
> MANI PRASANNA: No, no one was here. I was alone.

Mani Prasanna specifies that she was not asleep and that she fed Bala "in fact." She knows her visitor to be the omnipotent Goddess and yet wonders "how she got in"—a strange mixture of absolute certainty along with the expectations and doubts of a physical world. I thought that this kind of contradiction was a part of the texture of the narrative, and signaled its authenticity. Mani Prasanna's childhood vision had been that of a motherly goddess; ten years later, it is she who plays mother to little Bala and feeds her. Bala claims to have "no one," thus appealing to Mani Prasanna's caring nature and Mani Prasanna tells the Goddess that she will take care of her. The interaction over food creates intimacy; it is something that occurs between the Goddess and the practitioner. After this, Goddess Bala talked to Mani Prasanna about mantra and body.

> MANI PRASANNA: So she was saying then that as to why should we worship the body, why the mantra is required, if you need to go inside your body, every part of your body should be affected by the mantra. Only when that happens, you will be able to see the inside of your body.

Otherwise, the body does not allow anything or anyone inside holding on to a concept called "ego." I was wondering how does a child of three years know all these things?

She told me why the body should be mantra-affected. The body should accept it. Every part of your body is a Shakti-pitham and you need to make those powerful. But your mind does not know that. But it will know when every part that is the Shakti-pitham gets enough power for it.

It was not clear how Mani Prasanna meant "seeing inside" the body? I could think of endoscopes that scanned the inner surfaces of the body, or of instruments with microscopic vision. Because she had talked about her pregnancy, I thought about ultrasonic instruments. But Mani Prasanna was not referring to physical boundaries, and as our conversation progressed, it became clear that when she used the word "body" she did not only mean a physical body, and she had seen syllables in some non-physical aspect of her body. According to Mani Prasanna, every part of the body was already a seat of Shakti, but it was the mantras that helped energize them. This is similar to ideas about the Kundalini and chakras in yoga—every person already has the Kundalini power latent in them, but it has to be activated.

Mani Prasanna leads a campaign to do Kalavahana pujas in many locations of Andhra, from large metros to small villages. When Mani Prasanna and co-pujaris visit a location, they do a hundred Kalavahana pujas for one hundred people daily, five at a time, twenty times a day. This is part of an "empowerment drive," and Mani Prasanna and others believe that invoking the Goddess helps people realize their latent shakti or power. We discussed the Kalavahana puja and the concept of the body as a yantra.

MANI PRASANNA: Once when I was reciting Khadgamala, I saw my body cut into nine pieces. Like a piece here, one here, and here, in a row, like a yantra. So then I got scared and I asked Guruji and wondered what that was.

He said "it appeared that way to tell you that there is no difference between you and the Sri-Vidya. *That is why She [the Goddess] did it like that." Then I understood, when I was told that way.* Then I began looking at myself, and the Sriyantra, and figured out that there is no difference between the body and the Sriyantra. The body is the embodiment, the form of Sriyantra. When we try to understand further, the nine enclosures of the Sriyantra are present in our body too. So then, I learnt that.

MANI: And aksharamala [syllables]?

MANI PRASANNA: I saw the aksharamala. When I saw the body cut, and also when I did (the mantra beginning with) Vasini. You know about Vasini – Kameswari – Modini…so I saw it revolving.

Mani Prasanna was referring to the line from the Khadgamala (mantra) where the eight goddesses of Speech (*Vagdevatas*) are invoked. Within the Khadgamala stotram/mantra, this line begins the worship of the seventh enclosure of the Srichakra.[13] The goddesses of Speech preside over the alphabet and they are credited as the rishis of the Lalita-sahasranama mantra (LS), which means that they were the first to receive the LS and to transmit it to the world. Whereas most rishis are extraordinary human beings, this is one example where *deities* take on the role of rishi.[14] When Mani Prasanna recited the Vag-devata line from the Khadgamala, she *saw* the syllables in her own body. I told her about my conversation with Amritananda.

MANI: I asked Guruji what I should do to see the aksharamala in my body, and he asked me to just imagine …

MANI PRASANNA: It can be imagined. For example, "aṃ," when you imagine "aṃ," you need to imagine the "a" and the "ṃ" (sunna) beside it. You can imagine it being written and one day, even when you don't imagine, it will appear to you. The important thing is, we need to be connected to the deity all the time. If we have to stay connected, we need to find a way. We need to first feel the deity. If you don't feel it, it can't happen. That feeling is the imagination.

I had used the term "imagine" in English to mean unreal or imaginary, whereas Mani Prasanna linked it with an emotional state, with "feeling." This was not a translation issue, but a conceptual difference.

MANI: Imagination is not kalpana [imagination] but bhavana [conception, feeling]?

MANI PRASANNA: Yes. The more you feel Her [Goddess] by you, the closer she comes to you.

MANI: Now, for me, the bhavana comes from the heart, kalpana comes from the mind.

MANI PRASANNA: That is why the mind is not useful in sadhana.

Analyzing South Indian narratives from the 16th-century CE, David Shulman (2012) helps us understand the Indian concept of generative imagination:

> The consequences of imagining in the south Indian style are mostly keyed to a realistic axiology. The world exists, as do the pieces of reality set loose in it by the imagining mind. Pure intellection has little to do with any of this. (285)

It would be another six months before I could even try to suspend that which Mani Prasanna told me was useless in spiritual practice—the mind.

We talked about the purpose of her sadhana, and Mani Prasanna explained how she had changed after doing Srividya. Now she no longer compared herself to anyone else, and had found much contentment (*trupti*). She felt no panic even when she organized large-scale rituals or events, and everything always got done. What was her routine? Mani Prasanna told me that she did *tarpana* (libation) and Kalavahana twice a day—it had become a habit, and it took her ten minutes for the entire ritual and mantras inviting the Kalas. Tarpana is a ritual in the puja where water is poured on to the deity with mantras. If the tarpana is done to oneself, then this action is done at the chakra one focuses upon, by imagining the deity at that location. After three months, Mani Prasanna moved from *bhavana* (imagination, feeling) to an experience.

> MANI PRASANNA: When I was doing that, after three months, I had an experience. When I say "Brahmānām Avāhayāmi," I felt Brahma coming in. Similarly with Vishnu and whatever I was reciting, that particular deity was coming out from that particular chakra. First going inward, looked to me like He was washing/cleaning something, I don't know, and then going in, I could see that. While I was doing it.
>
> MANI: "He" – that means..?
>
> MANI PRASANNA: Brahma, Vishnu.... whatever I was reciting. The deity that I was inviting. So that is one experience with Kalavahana. And then, once when I was doing the avahana [invitation] of Suryakalas, all of a sudden I felt Guruji has come and taken me to the Surya-mandala [solar realms]. He was showing it to me... I felt that.
>
> MANI: What is the Surya mandala like?

MANI PRASANNA: (*laughs*) I don't know. I mean, I don't know how to tell that. Each bijakshara [seed-syllable] like "ka," "ba" was shown to me and how to reach from one to the other. Why is it placed that way, and he was narrating, guiding me through that, is what I felt. I felt astonished that I was looking at the Sun so closely.

MANI: By "Sun" do you mean a jyoti [a light]?

MANI PRASANNA: No, not jyoti, Sun itself. The form. And with "form," I don't mean a human form or something like that, it is light. Not like a lamp, but huge.

Mani Prasanna's descriptions had distinctions between what was imagined and what was "in fact." Yet, she considered imagination as a precursor to reality, and even as a creator of reality. Mantras helped her realize that her own body was a yantra. Another practitioner at Devipuram, Donald, an architect from the USA, visualized his body *inside* the meru (the three-dimensional Sriyantra) when he did mantra-japa.

5.5 Goddess Chandi

Donald McKenna is one of the architects involved with Devipuram's low-cost geodesic housing project for the nearby villagers. We talked late into the evening at the yajna-shala (a room for fire rituals) between the Sahasrakshi temple and the residential hall. The day's mantras and ritual offerings were over, there was warm ash curling in the central pit, and a cool breeze floated in and out of the open-air thatched space. Except for a late bird with something to say, the air was quiet. Don was introduced to the Devipuram community in Rochester, NY, in 1991, by Amritananda's disciple called Chaitanyananda, better known as "Aiyya." Aiyya was Don's colleague at an architectural firm, and Don became orientated to a new subject over work-lunches: "he [Aiyya] would talk about metaphysical things, mantras and energy." I asked if he knew anything about mantras, at the time?

DON: No, I didn't. I had no idea whatsoever. And I started going every week and meeting him for lunch and the meeting started happening at his home and then he said "you have to stay for puja!"And I had no idea what that was!

All of this was new for Don, who was born and raised Catholic, and jokes that he was a "just-in-case Christian"—"I'd go to church just in case they said I was a Jew and I would burn in hell. In my heart I didn't believe that was the case. In my heart, there was always something missing."

> DON: So, on a Friday night, I came and I walked in, into the temple, which at that time was a converted car garage in his home, and there I saw about 25 to 30 people, all with brown skin, all … festively dressed and I sat down to something that I have never witnessed before, which was devotional worship of a nature that really hit me in the heart because these people were totally involved in the worship.
>
> And for the first time in my life, I actually had the idea that God was something tangible, more than something abstract in a way and then it could visit, it could be there and listen and talk to you back.

After the puja, people would ask Aiyya questions, Aiyya would then ask the Goddess and tell the group what she had said. In 1993, Don visited Devipuram and received the sixteen-syllable Maha-Shodashi mantra from Amritananda. When I met Don in Devipuram in 2015, he had been doing the Shodashi-mantra along with a few other mantras for over twenty years. He said his japa was constant, like a "machine."

> DON: Oh it is constant. All my mantras are constant now. It doesn't stop.
>
> MANI: Do you have a svara [tone] or melody for them, are you singing them mentally?
>
> DON: It is more like a chord! It is a distinct chord. It has a color to it. I recognize it by either a color or I recognize it by the whisperings of the chord or by the sound-form that I fall into repeating. But it is like I am echoing what is already there and when I echo it, it makes me focus. I do that a little bit and it basically takes over.
>
> MANI: a resonance …
>
> DON: it is already there. The machine is already running. For example, the machine is running as nun-nun-nun-nun and I repeat it in the same way – nun-nun-nun- un… and so I fall into it. Other than that, the machine is running. When I do Chandi [mantra], every time I walk, [Goddess] Chandi is invoked. So I can … if I start walking…I call them "burning the man." Because every time I would do a mantra, I would try

> to commit it to memory, and I try to get a hundred and eight thousand repetitions as soon as I could.

Listening to the audio-recording later, I was not sure what Don had meant by "what is already there." This is how I understood it at first: Don has done the mantra once. The next time he does the japa of the mantra, he simply repeats the style. Japa has become a habit for Don, so much so that sometimes it feels like an involuntary activity. Some mantras have become associated with some actions, and Chandi has become the mantra he does when he is walking. This is how I understood Don after I had my own mantra-chord experience. Don does the japa constantly at some subconscious level and sometimes becomes conscious of it. Then, when Don does deliberate japa, he matches his utterance to the note that he has heard from within himself. But these accounts of doing mantras non-stop were mundane compared to Don's next narrative about the body as yantra and temple. As an architect, Don was "fascinated" by the Sriyantra, started learning how to draw it and "came to understand the location of the Khadgamala goddesses."

> DON: having some understanding that the *avaranas* [enclosures] were the layers of the meru, coincided with the physical plane and celestial plane, but it also mapped out the various chakra locations of the body, for instance. So I said—ok! I am just going to stand inside the meru and I am going to put my mantra on every single location, all the way up, all the way up. And if they fell close to the right place, I was going to be happy.
>
> MANI: So the yantra is your rosary!
>
> DON: Yes! That always has been.
>
> MANI: And then you turn around after it?
>
> DON: I would come back down. So in the shower, in the morning, I am not kidding you, it didn't make any difference how long I was chanting the mantra, I was in the shower, I would concentrate on all those locations, and if I lost focus, I had to start all over! And I had to go all the way up! And I had to go all the way down.

So Don was "putting" his mantra at ninety-eight points in the three-dimensional pyramidal yantra where the Khadgamala goddesses were located while ascending, and again, at ninety-eight points while descending. "Putting" meant that he was doing the mantra and as he invoked the name of each goddess, he was mentally focused on a particular point of the yantra which was actually also mapped on to his body. He said he did this "a hundred and eight thousand times, or more, for he did not bother to count." I asked, how did he know it was that number?

DON: If you have a single bija-mantra [seed-syllable], it would take me six and a quarter hours to do a hundred and eight thousand in one sitting. And that is giving myself an extra ten or twenty percent.

MANI: You would go boom-boom-boom-boom?

DON: I was diligent to make sure that every recitation was in my consciousness and not just a habit. So you could do like – Hrīṃ, Hrīṃ, Hrīṃ Hrīṃ, Hrīṃ.. you can count how many "Hrīṃs" in a breath, and I would exhale Hrīṃ, inhale Hrīṃ, how many breaths I take in a minute, how many minutes in an hour, but then if I started losing focus, you can do four Hrīṃs for every one Hrīṃ. (*Chants to demonstrate, fast-paced.*) Hrīṃ-Hrīṃ-Hrīṃ-Hrīṃ, Hrīṃ-Hrīṃ-Hrīṃ-Hrīṃ. When I have sixteen in the pace of four. And pretty soon, they are not sounding like Hrīṃs anymore! So, to get your consciousness back, the HrīṃM, as long as you hold the aspiration in your head, and to do that it took extra concentration. And then if started losing focus again, I would do one or two – H-R-ī-ī-M.. and feel it in my mantra and feel it in my body, then I would go "Hrīṃ-Hrīṃ-Hrīṃ-Hrīṃ." Pretty soon, the oscillations, the sound and the vibrations, everything that was starting to happen in your body was so profound that the time went by. The dimensions of the mantra would open up.

MANI: What do you mean by that?

DON: It is a three dimensionality! It is difficult to explain. Maybe it is going into different dimensions, but it is more than visual.

MANI: Inside your mind?

DON: Inside the body! Your body almost ceases to exist. Your body all of a sudden is a location. And in something much larger. And all of a sudden, in a location, you are a speck. You are like an atom. And this Hrīṃ-Hrīṃ-Hrīṃ sounds sending out and echoing back.. I mean there are aspects that are very similar to sonar… all of a sudden I am getting these perceptions of sonar, there is a blackness.

MANI: You are hearing it back?

DON: Perceiving it back! I am not sure I heard it with my ears. The sensation would be akin to hearing but the perceptions were definitely more than the five sense organs. And in that period of time, it also coincided with periods of time I was doing Panchadashi [fifteen-syllable mantra] that packets of information would come to me either in puja or in meditation. Like profound hits, like a torpedo head of all this energy and it would take a long time, days, for to play out on my video tape machine and it was like watching a video tape where it was pulled apart, slowed down so I could digest it.

MANI: Packets of information of the world, your life, or –?

DON: Everything! If I were to look at an individual, there were times when I would be able to look at an individual in not so much of I would look at the person, but somebody next to me said- "what's wrong with that fellow?" I would look at the person and – "he has liver disease! And you know, there is some jaundice in there." I could tell what was going on...

MANI: Without turning to mantra?

DON: Yes.

MANI: But you attributed it to mantra?

DON: Absolutely.

Mani Prasanna had also spoken about seeing "inside" the body by putting the mantra inside. Don's narrative here is similar, except that he lets us understand how going within the body helps the practitioner lose the consciousness of its physical boundaries. Don also notes how the "hearing" is not really a "hearing" and mentions sonar. This point is also brought up by Appaji in Guntur (see Chapter 6) who notes that tantric mantras are subsonic and supersonic (whereas vedic mantras, he said, were sonic). Don's surmise about "packets" of information was graphic.

Since Don did more than one mantra, I asked him if he had found any differences in the practice or results of the different mantras. Here's a summary of what Don told me: Chandi mantra helped improve perceptions, Maha-Shodashi mantra brought an "element of clairvoyance" and with Panchadashi mantra, there was increased physical aptitude, and an "influence over the weather." Was Don attracted to mantras for the *siddhis* (powers) he gained? If he was, these siddhis did not seem self-serving:

DON: But Chandi is one of the things that I would really really love to use, and it invokes automatically when I am sending energy to somebody else that I love and you know I get telephone calls next day, "what did you do? I don't know what you did but it helped me so much." So, it is a very important mantra!

The Chandi mantra "invoked automatically," in response to someone else's need for "energy." Perhaps any association with Goddess Chandi would be altruistic because of the legendary associations of the triumph of good over evil. In the Devi Mahatmyam,[15] when an awe-inspiring Goddess Kali kills the demons Chanda and Munda, she is called Chandi, or Chandika. Don also talked at length about how the Panchadashi mantra had given him an ability to maintain equanimity in the midst of hectic projects that involved multi-tasking. Mani Prasanna had also spoken of equanimity, but she had not specified to which mantra she would attribute that result. Both Don and Mani Prasanna spoke about giving over to the deities, deities as active doers, and of flowing with the Goddess's will.

5.6 Goddess Kali

The will of the Goddess was even more pronounced in the case of Sheela. Practitioners chase after deities, yearning for a response, but in Sheela's account, it was the Goddess who would not leave Sheela alone. I had seen her conduct the daily rituals at the yajna-shala and could tell that she was an insider at Devipuram, but I had no inkling of what lay in store for me. We met in her room in the residential block of Devipuram. Sheela did not know Telugu and I did not know Marathi, so we spoke in English, a language we both knew. She spoke expressively and occasionally used Tamil, Marathi and Hindi words. Sheela has been practicing Srividya for 25 years of which the first 15 years were, she says, "without knowing." She had five teachers, and each of them literally appeared at her door saying that "She"—i.e., the Goddess—had asked them to come and give her something—a mantra, an image or a ritual instruction.

Sheela was fond of bhajans even as a young woman. One day at a bhajan, every attendee received images of Goddess Durga in her lion-rider form (*simhavahini*), while Sheela received a terrifying image of Goddess Dakshina Kali. Goddess Kali is typically depicted near-naked, dancing wildly, wearing a garland of skulls and a skirt made of chopped arms. Nervously, Sheela kept the image of Goddess Kali in a closet rather than in her shrine. At the next bhajans, the woman who gave her the image told her to put it inside the shrine.

SHEELA: I said ok. Because I didn't want to offend her [the woman]. So I came, took out and put it and whatever shlokas [verses] I knew I used to chant them. And one fine day, in the evening, you know after, you lit the lamps, you know, this thing, I did that—(*clears throat*) and suddenly I can see – from the picture – behind the Devi, you know how the uh sun rays come out, like that it started to shine, I mean, glow. I got scared, amma! I asked my husband, you better go and bring that lady home. I don't want to keep it like this.

She continued:

SHEELA: So he went and she came, he brought that amma [lady], she came, and she asked me to get out of the room. We went outside. She shut the door and sat and saw that what it is and that, behind that, there are shlokas [Sanskrit verses], you can see all the syllables.

MANI: What were they?

SHEELA: It was ulta [reverse], na! I couldn't read. So she took out and saw what it was and she again she put it back.

MANI: She took out the … picture?

SHEELA: She took out the picture and she again sealed it.

The woman then reassured Sheela that Kali was only a ferocious form of the compassionate Goddess, and there was nothing to be afraid of. What was the "glow" Sheela saw? Could it be the mantra, which she could not read? The woman had looked behind the picture, as if expecting a physical reason for the glow.

Next, Sheela received the first mantra from Saundarya-Lahari. When she moved to Delhi, one of her husband's colleagues came to meet her of his own accord. Describing the woman at the bhajans who had given Sheela the picture of Goddess Kali, he asked what mantra she had received. Sheela denied receiving any mantra, and he told her, "you got a silent Dakshina Kali [mantra]." Sheela did not know what that meant, so he explained to her that the woman had given her the mantra silently. Sheela said, "To be honest, I never knew anything about all these things. She had given the mantra silently! Not verbally. You know there are different ways of dikshas [imparting mantras]." Obviously, this was not a mantra she could be aware she was practicing. The visitor then told her he had come to give her a mantra and asked her to fetch a pen and paper. He said Devi had put him to this task—"Because that Amma [the Goddess] was nagging me: Go give her! Go, give her!" He asked her to do japa with this *shloka* [mantra], it was the first verse of the Saundarya-Lahari,[16] and promised her that she would have an experience. Sheela kept wondering, "what am I going to see! What is it? Who is going to come? Why he told me?" Nothing occurred for ten days.

SHEELA: So, ten days past. Nothing. (*Laughs*). So when he came I said, "you said I will experience something. But I did not see anybody, did not hear anything…nothing happened!" He started to laugh out loud.

He said, "Vaini! ["sister-in-law" in Marathi] Did I ask you to expect something? Did I tell you to look for something? No, I told you, just do japa. And you WILL experience something. So, stop looking for anything." He told me – just do it. I knew what was wrong and very third day, I got my experience. Immediately I sent my daughter. He was sleeping in the next apartment. I said – "go, go go! Get that uncle, quick quick!" So he came. And said – "yes! Now I can see you have experienced something! Ok, bring that paper and pencil again, next shloka I am going to give."

So ok, the next shloka he gave. Now, I know the trick. DO NOT EXPECT ANYTHING! So, fourth or fifth day, again I got the experience. And I told him and he said "ok, now I think, I have to give you the whole thing!"

I said, "if you are going to dictate, then I am going to write, it is not going to happen. If you have any text give me, I will sit and write it and give it back to you."

The entire mantra came to Sheela in parts, and she was motivated by an experience. When I asked if she would share what had occurred, Sheela was hesitant and said she was not sure if I would "get the picture." "Try me," I said.

SHEELA: So the first time, when I saw, 'ma, I had a thali, a silver plate where I had kept all my .. small small murtis [deity images], and doing puja, and behind you know how its folded like this.. the plate is like this (*indicates the shape with her hands*) so behind the thing when you lit a lamp, you can see the eyes… beauuutiful eyes! I have no words to explain that.

MANI: Devi's eyes?

SHEELA: Beautiful eyes, nothing else…! So that is all I saw first time. So he [the messenger] said – you got a protection. She is protecting you. Till your last breath, you got protection. You don't have to worry, afraid of, about anything. She is always with you. The next one [experience]—I don't want to explain that! This first one—hope you got the picture. So that's all. The second time, I had a different experience. So that's when he gave me all the hundred one [all the Saundarya-Lahari mantras]. That night he took me to the Delhi Shiva temple. So I went there, had darshan, came back.

How did Sheela understand the vision? Her visitor friend had said it meant the Devi was protecting her. Sheela's first vision of the Goddess was that of eyes, and her response was ineffability—"there are no words to express that." As evident from her expressive intonation in "beuuuti-ful," this vision also became a memory that she cherished. The idea that disembodied eyes stare back from a picture can be spooky, and it is the "beauty" and feeling in the encounter that makes it appealing and memorable. Such an emphasis on seeing is consistent with one of the motifs of the Devipuram Goddess, whose very name is "Sahasrakshi."

Sheela declined to share her second experience, but continued with her narrative. She memorized the Saundarya-Lahiri in fifteen days and performed a puja. At this puja, a couple who did regular puja to Raghavendra Swami (a 16th-century CE saint believed to be an incarnation of the legendary Prahlada) asked if they could visit her shrine. She discouraged them, telling them that her shrine was no more than a closet and a table, but they visited anyway.

SHEELA: So they came, both came, she went to open the door and … I had [Goddess] Kamakshi picture. And he came, asked for the karpuram [camphor], he lit the karpuram and did the arati [lamp service] and you wont believe, amma, kumkumam [red auspicious substance] started falling from her lap.

The manifestation of kumkum, a substance used in Devi puja and worn by women on their foreheads, is a kind of synecdoche, but it also becomes a sign of the Goddess reaching out to the devotees, expressing her blessings. This couple then gave her a Srichakra and a single-faced rosary bead (*ekamukhi-rudraksha*) and two Devi-mantras.

Sheela's overall narrative seems eerie because things do not seem in her control. Not only was she approached by strangers and given mantras, one visitor gave her a "silent mantra," which was a mantra that she did not even know she had received. Strangers showed up at her door and asked to see her shrine. Goddess Kali seems to have invited herself to Sheela's shrine, and Sheela is at first reluctant even to let her stay there. Devotion was a part of Sheela's inherent nature, but the motivation to do mantras was fueled by phenomena. If the mantras were on the reverse side of the photo frame, her entire experience was also upside down. How Sheela found her guru was also contrary to the regular flow of events. The normal pattern is that a seeker finds a guru and gets initiated; in Sheela's case, the Goddess came to her and after a long-winded tease, also brought her a guru.

The next part of Sheela's narrative is all about moving to the USA and having regular visits from the 16th-century CE saint Raghavendra Swami who helped her out whenever she was in trouble. Her tone was matter of fact as though she was telling me about a friend or neighbor who would always help her. Next, Sheela met Aiyya in Rochester and through him, Amritananda. On a visit to the USA, Amritananda asked to stay at her home, asked to see this Srichakra and then said they would do the Navavarana puja. Next thing she knew, Amritananda said he would initiate her.

> SHEELA: That day we went from A to Z. One shot he gave me all the mantras—Guru mantra, Ganapati, Subrahmanya, Bala, Laghu Shodashi, Laghu Chandi, Chandi, Ashvarudha… like all those. Total sixteen mantras. And Shodashi [mantra].
>
> MANI: All of them? How will you practice all of them all of them together? One… each one once?
>
> SHEELA: That can also be done, or you take one mantra and do it 108 times, one mala [rosary]. Or you select which mantra you want, and do it.

One day Sheela was cooking and chatting about Raghavendra Swamy to Amritananda, while he sat and watched and listened. On an impulse, she asked him "the million-dollar question."

> SHEELA: "What is your connection between Raghavendra Swami and you?" And I am still cooking and he kept his hand like this (*she placed a hand on her heart*) and said – "I am Prahlada!" That's it 'ma, whatever I was doing, I stopped that and I was standing STILL. I could not speak.

Guruji then said, "Amma, sometimes, when people talk about you, you feel so nice."

As Sheela told her story, her own bafflement was evident. I was baffled too and could make no sense of this complication in the story. The story of Prahlada is also in the Bhagavata Purana and Vishnu Purana. Prahlada is the son of a devout mother called Kayadu and a demon called Hiranyakashyapa. When a pregnant Kayadu is kidnaped by Indra (chief of the gods) and then taken care of by demi-god Narada, the child in her womb (i.e., Prahlada) becomes—unlike his father—a devotee of Vishnu (the preserver, and one of the three major male deities in Hinduism). Finally, in a climactic scene when Hiranyakashyapa challenges Prahlada to prove Vishnu's omnipresence, Vishnu leaps out of a pillar, incarnated as "Narasimha" (half-lion, half-man), and kills Hiranyakashyapa. What was the connection between Amritananda and Prahlada? There was much that was mysterious in Sheela's narrative—she did not disclose all her experiences, and I kept wondering why all of these strange things happened to her. If the Goddess sent Sheela all the regular mantras from within the Srividya tradition, she sent some brand new mantras to Subbarao Kompella, *aka* Karunamaya.

5.7 Goddess Lalita

Since Karunamaya was an established guru with many followers, and I had already heard about some of the miracles in his early years as a sadhaka, I focused on his views about mantra-sadhana in our conversation. Karunamaya had many anecdotes about helping others with new mantras and had developed ideas about vision and the visionary process. I asked about the reports of Goddess and mantra visions—how would one know that a vision was not imagination? Karunamaya differentiated between a memory leak and a vision.

KARUNAMAYA: One is *memory leak.* "I saw Mother-Goddess in a silk sari." Maybe, it MAY be a *memory leak. *

MANI: Do you mean you have a memory of that?

KARUNAMAYA: You have a memory that Mother-Goddess is like that. But then, for a kitten or a baby lizard to come to me and say, *hey man,*

I'm Mother-Goddess, for it to say that, and for me to understand that about it, say that happens, which I have not seen or experienced before, is coming from ...

MANI: somewhere

KARUNAMAYA: ... from somewhere, like an alien message, that is a vision.

Karunamaya's explanation of memory leaks is also proposed by academic scholars including David Morgan (2012) who writes about how visions follow previously seen imagery. To illustrate a vision that was not a memory leak, Karunamaya told me about one of his first visions. After a series of rituals in Tirupati, he did mantra-japa for fifteen days continuously. Then, when he was immersed in japa, (he had a vision that) a guru came up to him, patted his cheek affectionately and said "this is what I want from you." The visit was a commendation. Karunamaya explained to me that "this" referred to his earnest mantra-practice. Five years later, Karunamaya went with a friend to a beach town near the seaport of Vishakatpatnam called Bhimli to visit an ascetic named Yogananda. After some conversation, Yogananda said, "You didn't recognize me, I saw you in Tirupati, do you remember?" Karunamaya remembered at once—"at once, *yadon ki barat*! [a procession of memories]."[17] The verification Karunamaya received from the ascetic confirmed his vision. By contrast, he said, memory leaks cannot be verified.

What allowed a vision to occur? Karunamaya explained that ardent practitioners receive visions. He spoke of "*ardruta*" which literally means "wetness," and is used to convey an ardent emotional state, as when a devotee weeps longingly for a deity. Ardent practitioners receive visions at an auspicious time (*brahma-muhurtam*) early in the morning.[18] Secondly, he explained how visions occurred when there was "no mind."

The difference between ordinary sight and vision is that you don't need to use your eyes. Seeing is in the waking state. Then, 72,000 nerves, mind, five senses when they are all active, you are visible to me. It doesn't have any jnana [knowledge]. By chance if there is jnana [knowledge] also, it is limited. But vision is higher than this. No mind there. With consciousness, without the need of sense organs, eyes are not necessary for vision. They see and they hear too, hearing without ears, seeing without eyes, touch without skin, that is vision.

According to Indian thought, we experience three states of consciousness: *jagrat* (waking), *svapna* (sleeping) and *sushupti* (deep sleep).[19] The fourth state of consciousness, *turiya* (superconsciousness), is when the individual consciousness merges with cosmic consciousness. Karunamaya could have been referring to the dream or deep-sleep state, but because he says there is "no mind," I assumed he referred to a turiya state. His clarification about the involvement of all sense organs in vision matches the internal evidence in Daivarata's mantras (see 3.2). Like Daivarata, Karunamaya was also a perceiver of new mantras. I only knew this because some of the mantras he discussed on his Srividya tutorial videos had been unfamiliar, and even strange. When I asked Karunamaya about these specific mantras, he did not hesitate to describe how they had come about. Here are two anecdotes.

A young woman from Tanuku in Andhra Pradesh began to menstruate, but her periods stopped after a year. An allopathic doctor diagnosed it as a hormonal imbalance. Karunamaya asked the woman's relatives who had approached him with this problem that he had never come across a case like this, but that they could phone after ten days. On one of the days after this, a new mantra flashed in his mind automatically when he was doing the Khadgamala stotram. The Khadgamala stotram, which literally means the "sword-garland invocation," names each of the goddesses according to their place in the Sriyantra. Karunamya's narrative contains a meticulously detailed description of the revelatory process:

> KARUNAMAYA: Then one day while I was doing the Khadgamala – (*quoting the names of the Goddesses in the mantra*): "*Kameśwarī nityaklinne..* Nityaklinna" ... now it must go to "*bherunḍe*" right?[20] Again I read it, "*Kameśwarī ... nityaklinne.*" Again I stopped there. It only goes until there doesn't go forward! "Nityaklinna Nityaklin"—*wait a minute, this is the one. I called them immediately.*

When he was doing the mantra as a part of his sadhana, he was unable to proceed beyond the name of Goddess Nityaklinna.

> KARUNAMAYA: "Nitya" means ever, "klinna" means flow. The one who controls the flow is Nityaklinna deity. *So write it down,* I said. "*Aiṃ Hriṃ Śriṃ Nityaklinnāyai namaha pāhimāṃ rakśamāṃ.*"

This last line was Karunamaya's new mantra.

KARUNAMAYA: We have a new mantra. Here, because it's related to here (*points at uterus area*), putting the hand here (places a hand there) you need to pass the energy, just keep on reciting – how many days? – until you get the periods. You won't believe it, correctly on the eight day!

After doing the mantra, the girl resumed menstruation on the eighth day. Why did he not just recommend a regular mantra, and why did it need to be revised and personalized? What necessitates a new mantra? Karunamaya's response was surprising. He confessed with a shy smile that he wanted the Goddess to give him a special insight: "That's written by some other guy (*Adi yevado rasindi*), YOU [Goddess] should tell me, I should get what has not come until now (*Intavaruku ranadi ravali*). Whether it's just a meaning, or a mantra."

Karunamaya's second example was about a medical emergency. When three-year-old Vaishnavi fell from a bed, a nail went into her brain and she went into a coma; medical doctors in Nellore gave her 24 hours to live. A friend of a friend of a friend of the family phoned Karunamaya and asked him to help.

KARUNAMAYA: I said all I do is puja for Mother. I don't know anything. But, let's see. There is a mantra. It has to be changed. Mother will show. Now, whether that is subtle ego or what …

If Karunamaya is self-indulgent in his expectation for a new mantra from the Mother Goddess, She does not seem to mind. He receives a unique, modified form of the Maha-Mrityunjaya-mantra: "*Jhūm saḥ mām pālaya pālaya tryaṃbakam yajāmahe sugandhim puṣṭivardhanam urvārukamivabandhanān mṛtyor mokśīya māmṛtāt jhūm saḥ mām pālaya pālaya.*" "Mrityunjaya" literally means "victory over death," and the prefix "Maha" means "great"—this is a mantra used to prevent accidents or when a person is seriously ill.[21] Karunamaya then modified it further to make it specific for Vaishnavi by inserting her name in the accusative case to mean "protect, protect Vaishnavi"—"*Jhūṃ saḥ Vaiśṇavīṃ pālaya pālaya.*" Since she was in a coma, the mantra would have to be recited for her by someone else. Karunamaya explained that "*Jhūm*" was an "*amrita bijam,*" "*mrityunjaya bijam.*" A "*bija*" is a seed, and in the language of mantras, a bija is a seed syllable, a syllable that carries potential. "*Amrita*" is sometimes translated as "immortal" but literally, it is "*a-mrit,*" the opposite of death. What Karunamaya means here is that the sound or the syllable "*Jhūm*" is the seed of this latent power of fighting death. He directed that the mantra be recited continually by anyone holding Vaishnavi's hand, and that there be no weeping in her surround.

Karunamaya also shared a narrative about how he gained insight into a mantra's meaning. A woman once asked him why the name of the deity Vishnu was included in the Shuklambharadharam-mantra to the deity Ganesha.[22] At first, he told her that he had no idea, *"I have not studied Sanskrit or the vedas or anything!"* "Then when I was brushing (my teeth) in the USA… Shuklambharadharam!" Subbarao uttered this last word as if he were saying "Eureka!"

> KARUNAMAYA: The meaning is this. Came from inside. "Shukla" means white, white means Brahma. So Shuklambharadharam refers to Brahma. "Shasivarnam" (means) the color of ash. The sign of Maheshwara [Shiva]. Vishnu-Brahma-Maheshwara. These, each becomes evident. "Chaturbhujam" [four-shouldered]. They become evident/recognized because of four vedas. And how is the person who has read the veda? "Prasanna vadanam dhyayet." (*Then he translates.*) He should always be smiling. Anandam. *Sat. Chit. Anandam* [Truth-Consciousness-Bliss, a conventional description of the formless nameless divine]. That's the form you must meditate on. When you meditate on that you won't have an obstacle.

The deity Ganesha (Ganapati) is a remover of obstacles, and Karunamaya reasons his way to such an interpretation. He makes connections between colors and deities—white reminds him of Brahma and the ash reminds him of Shiva. He then combines these deities with the name of the deity (Vishnu) already present in the mantra to derive a reference to the triumvirate in the Indian pantheon of deities—Brahma the creator, Vishnu the preserver and Shiva the destroyer. The reference to four shoulders is interpreted by Karunamaya to mean the four vedas, and these three deities are made known by the vedas. Further, he leaps from this thought to the idea that the reader/chanter of veda is blissfully smiling. There is no apparent logic to the connections made by Karunamaya across the fragmentary nature of the verse. How do the three leading male deities of the Hindu pantheon connect with a mantra that is known to invoke an entirely different deity specializing in removing obstacles? If Vishnu's presence is inexplicable, Karunamaya makes it more so by now inserting two other deities; and yet, for him, this is what the mantra now means.

Moreover, this is the meaning of the shloka as revealed by Lalita. Does this close off other meanings, past and future? I found another explanation in *Bhagavan and Nayana* (Sankaranarayan 2014), a book about the saint Ramana Maharishi and his disciple Ganapatimuni (also see 3.3). When asked the meaning of the Shuklambharadharam-mantra in the presence of Ramana Maharshi, Ganapatimuni said:

> The Muni obliged and proceeded to explain the verse, explaining the words in such a way that they applied to the gods Brahma, Vishnu and Ganapati. 'Here is a great Sadhu. I can explain the verse in relation to him also', so saying, Vasistha Muni began again: "Brahmanaswami [Ramana Maharishi] wears only a white loin cloth, so he is suklambaradhara, he is in consciousness vast, all-pervading visnu, his complexion is pleasing like the glow of the moon sasivarna and he is chaturbhuk—as he has eaten up the four, mind, chitta the memory stuff, intellect and ego – and remains as the Self all the time.' Brahmanaswami said nothing but smiled approvingly.

This explanation begins with a reference to Vishnu and Brahma along the same lines of Karunamaya's discovery. Next, it becomes a reference to Ramana Maharshi. Nowhere in this narrative is any report of an extraordinary experience or vision, nor of any authority vested in this meaning; it comes across as a clever interpretation. In the light of Ganapatimuni's proposal, could Karunamaya's meaning be considered an interpretation that does not erase previous, or preclude later, interpretations? Every seer, interpreter or commentator has a unique interpretation; the mantra itself has not changed and stays an open-text, accruing more possibilities of meanings. As people add their interpretations to the mantras, these become a palimpsest of new perspectives on the mantra, continuing the life of the mantra. It was because Karunamaya described his interpretation in terms of a vision that it became a claim for authoritative meaning.

Did the new mantras simply surface in Karunamaya's mind (or "no mind")? Was there a process by which he had laid the ground for, or become qualified to receive, revelations of new mantras? Karunamaya attributes his methodology to his guru, Amritananda. "Our guru says, if you have a problem, don't pick up a book to look for a solution. Just let it be. It [the answer] will come. That is the real application." There was something hilarious about the process he had shared, and I could not help but comment on that: "I love the part about you getting it while brushing your teeth." Karunamaya chuckled and told me about a mantra he was told by a pundit at Srikakulam, Vemakoti Krishnayaji. Instructing him about the procedures, Vemakoti said, "but, one condition, Subbarao-*garu*, for this, you must say it when you brush your teeth, then it will be effective." Karunamaya was only able to fathom this strange instruction after he got the meaning of Shuklambharadharam. I protested:

> MANI: How?! (*Ala yella vostundi?*)
>
> KARUNAMAYA: Some activities are daily activities. Brushing, excreting, bathing, wearing clothes, putting on a tilakam [sacred mark on the forehead], these are all daily ritual actions (*anusthanas*). Whether you brush with Colgate or Neem twig, it's anushthana.
>
> Now, that which we chant in the puja room that alone is being called anushthana but, in fact, everything that happens daily it's all anushthana.

Karunamaya explains it as a natural and spontaneous expression or insight. This method of letting things emerge naturally is reminiscent of the French surrealists' automatic writing and of Gertrude Stein's experiments with involuntary writing. Gertrude Stein was involved with automatic writing experiments in the Harvard Psychological Laboratory under Hugo Münsterberg. The idea was to deliberately disrupt regular modes of conscious writing and unhook oneself from self-consciousness via distraction to access a "secondary personality" (Armstrong 1998, 197–202). Andre Breton's experiments were similar; he sought a transported state of mind and was interested in the swing between the subjective and objective. Breton ([1937] 1987) narrates how Leonardo da Vinci invited his students to copy their paintings from what they would see when they stared at an old wall for a period of time: "The whole problem of the passage from subjectivity to objectivity is resolved there" (86). What is it about staring at a wall, or such a daily chore as brushing teeth that enables "seeing" a painting or a mantra? Is it that it is monotonous, likely to be conducted in a daze, or just that there is "no mind" involved? I discuss this possibility at some depth in Chapter 7; for now, suffice it to say that somehow, the process of brushing teeth has taken Karunamaya into a state of mind where he finds an answer to his mantra-question, or quest.

The first mantra is as if discovered by him accidentally. Engrossed in chanting, Karunamaya finds himself unable to proceed beyond Goddess Nityaklinna's name in the Khadgamala stotram. This is a mantra he has done for years on a daily basis as a part of his puja routine, and he knows it so well that his utterance usually proceeds smoothly. When Karunamaya finds himself stuck, he takes it as a sign that it is Goddess Nityaklinna to whom he must turn with Vaishnavi's problem. It is as if Karunamaya is taking a walk along a line-up of many deities and finds himself involuntarily stopping when he comes up to Goddess Nityaklinna. At first, he does not know why he has stopped. Moments later, reflexivity and interpretation surface, Karunamaya interprets this abrupt stop and sudden loss of memory as a significant signal that points him toward Goddess Nityaklinna. In the second anecdote, Karunamaya's insistence of a unique mantra reveals an intimate relationship with the Goddess, or an awareness of his own intense devotion. Karunamaya suspects himself of egotism even in the process of finding delight in a new mantra. In these accounts, we do not hear any detail about whether he saw the script of the mantra, or heard the sound of the mantra. In the second narrative we are only told the beginnings of the quest, and the confidence that "Mother will show." Goddess Lalita is credited as the source for his new mantras. How did he know? Karunamaya said, "who else would have told me!" Such a response and relationship with a deity is similar to that of Vasudevananda, a Hanuman-devotee, in Chapter 5.

5.8 Amritanandanatha Saraswati (1934–2015)

In *Understanding Sri Chakra Puja*, Amritananda (2014) explains that there are four traditions in Srividya—samayachara, dakshinachara, kaulachara and vamachara, and writes: "We belong to the first three modes of worship" (91).

> Samayachara means an internal mode of worship and worship with the fire ritual. We do the homas, we do the internal visualizations, whether the external puja articles are present or not we can visualize them and do the entire puja. The samayachara traditions come to us from the Divya Parampara that is through Balaji-Balatripurasundari who is our guru.
>
> From the Siddha Parampara, from Saraswati I have been given the Medha Dakshinamurthi. So the Dakshinachara sampradaya has been given to us through the Saraswati Order. I am eligible for that and those who have taken diksha (initiation) from me are also eligible for that. Here you worship the Sri Chakra. It is a bahia puja. You are worshipping something

outside of you, usually a vigraham (an idol or yantra). However, the suvasini puja is also done. Suvasini is a woman who represents the Shakti, but the puja is done only to her feet.

In the Kaulachara tradition the idol is replaced by a living woman or a man or a couple. You can also think of Her as the union of Siva and Shakti. You can worship Her as a woman, as a man or as both. There is no restriction.

[....]

But the Kaulcahra traditions also come to us through the Dattatreya Sampradaya. Dattatreya is the combination of Brahma, Vishnu and Rudra. He has given his instructions to his disciples: Prahlada, his first disciple, and Parasurama his second disciple. Parasurama had codified his instructions into a Kalpa Sutra. (91)

In this detailed explanation of the modes of tantra that he and his followers are authorized to practice, he attributes the initiations to *deities*—Balatripurasundari, Saraswati, and Dattatreya, thus situating even that within visionary experience. However, when I asked about differences between vedic and tantric revelations, Amritananda confounded the categories, throwing the question back at me.

AMRITANANDA: Also ... (*four-second pause*) There's no essential difference, 'ma. What's seen in meditation ..

MANI: Yes...

AMRITANANDA: may be vedic mantras or tantric mantras. There are also Arabic mantras. Now is that vedic, or tantric?

MANI: (*silence*)

AMRITANANDA When in meditation, I've seen a lot of Arabic *aksharas* [syllables/letters].

MANI: In what language?

AMRITANANDA Arabic language.

MANI: you saw it in Arabic language? (*Pause*). Were they things that are in the Qur'an?

AMRITANANDA Are they in the Qur'an?

MANI: Are they in the Qur'an?

AMRITANANDA I don't know that. I don't know. I've seen some other languages which I can't recognize... hieroglyphics.

MANI: You can't read them ... obviously ... you don't know the script.

AMRITANANDA: One doesn't understand. Say it's in Chinese. I can't read it.

MANI: So instead of hearing the sound, you saw the script?

AMRITANANDA Yeah. Script.

I had read about such phenomena where the vision is in an unknown language,[23] so I was not entirely surprised. However, Amritananda was calling the vision of an Arabic script, a mantra, without access to its semantic *or* phonetic content, and perhaps his counter-question was a way to remind me that categories come later, after the vision. I asked if sound came first, or sight. "Sound," he said, and said that it led to "sight" and was also a form of sight. But:

AMRITANANDA Now, the frequency of visuals are higher than sound frequencies.

MANI: (*Pause*). I see.

AMRITANANDA How much, for sound frequencies, 16000... hertz ... and light frequency...

MANI: So is that the reason why you saw in sight rather than in sound

AMRITANANDA Perhaps. So, this can lead to that and that can lead to this. Both ways.

MANI: So then

AMRITANANDA The bandwidth of sound is small. That bandwidth (of light) is very high.

We touched upon a range of topics in this conversation. Amritananda said that revelations continued to occur even today: "For those who are ready to receive it, it's happening right now." In our second discussion, Amritananda maintained a slightly different pace, taking several moments before he responded to questions. Prema accompanied me on this visit. I opened by asking why we needed mantra, and *whose* language was mantra? He answered after ten suspenseful seconds.

MANI: So why mantras?

AMRITANANDA: (*Long pause*) Why mantras-?

MANI: I mean, whose language is it anyway?

AMRITANANDA: (*Longer pause*) The language of the five elements (panchabhutas).

PREMA (*Irrepressibly*) Adi! [That's it!]

Numerous sources in Indian thinking assert that the world is made of five elements of earth, water, fire, air and ether; they are within and around us. This concept also prevails in the Indian medicinal science of Ayurveda and is expressed in Indian arts. In mantra-theory and practice, akasha, or the element of ether becomes crucial because its attribute is sound; any substance that is only composed of ether can only be heard, it cannot be felt, seen and tasted.[24] As per Amritananda's definition, mantras were naturally occurring sounds within and around us. As we conversed, Amritananda continued to explain that certain mental states have to happen for us to utter a syllable. When we utter a mantra, there are neurological effects.

AMRITANANDA: Even if we say it by the mouth, certain mental states have to happen for us to utter a syllable.

MANI: Okay?

AMRITANANDA: One has to send a signal, lip movements, have to form, have to activate the vocal chords, so there is so much happening inside the brain. And then (*coughs, clears throat*), for example –"*Achyutāya namaḥ Anatāya namaḥ Govindāya namaḥ*" – that's the "Maha Vyadhi Vinashi mantra."

MANI: Mm.

AMRITANANDA: When we say this, the formations excite the brain. That has got a healing capacity. Maha Vyadhi Vinashi mantra. What's in this name, we think. Not the name but what's evoked by us, the neural circuits, its results. Similarly, now, wind (Vayu) has a language. When there's a storm (*toofan*), *Waiiiiinnnnn Waiiiiiiiinnnnn* that's a language too, is it not?

MANI: (*Skeptically*) Mm.

AMRITANANDA: The language spoken by wind. Earth has a language too. The sounds of wings of birds flying. In water (the creatures) that roam. Everything has got a – all these are the languages of the five

> elements. They are all mantras. Nothing's not a mantra. Where they get the value is that some specific neural responses. We pick them up.

Either there are mantras, or there are not—unless both these are true within different parameters. If "nothing's not a mantra," that makes all visions authoritative. Also, it is not as though we hear hymns in the sound of birds flying. I asked if they changed our own *panchabhutas*?

> AMRITANANDA: Our own panchabhutas, and we are responding to them. Ganapati-mantra. The important thing here is *Glau. Ga. Ḷa.* Say if I said *Gaḷagaḷagaḷaga*. Water that flows upon rock, that goes (*he says this in a sing song manner, as though an excerpt from a song*) to *Gaḷagaḷagaḷaga. Gaḷagaḷa Godāri*, ...as it goes (*potunte*) that *Gaḷagaḷa* if we add *Oṃ-kāra* that's *Glau*. So, sounds of nature, which evoke certain images inside us too, they have been placed as mantras. So it has an effect on our subconscious. [...] So what you think becomes subconscious.

Did this mean that the mantras were not communicating with anyone or anything out there, such as deities, and this was all between nature and us? I was trying to understand the scheme. If the elements outside us "spoke" in mantras, and they spoke to the elements which were already mantras inside us, why it was necessary to invite deities which were also mantras to come into our bodies and lives?

> AMRITANANDA: Oh. (*Pause*) There are many of these, ready to invoke the connection between us and the panchabhutas. Called tanmatra s. Tanmatras. Touch, Form, Taste, Smell (*shabda, sparsha-rupa, rasa-gandha*). Only when they are perceived by our sense-organs (*indriyas*) they give us the experience. By themselves they don't.

Amritananda said they were there, but we could experience them via our sense organs *only if we invoked them.* He explained that experiencing and feeling belonged to waking and dream states. A high-speed mental processing occurred in deep sleep, and yogis could become aware of that, it was a state of *jagrut-sushupti* (awake-deep sleep). As dream was an intersection between waking and deep sleep, one had to develop the technique of "lucid dreaming." It was then that one learned to understand what is happening in the mind, and have "some control over what is happening. You're co-creating it." The sense of "I" does not go away. Death was a fourth state. Meanwhile, the world is also having an experience through its *tanmatra s*, and there is an interface between us and the world. What is coming in is "experience" and what we "push back" is action. The interface remained due to the existence of ***upadhi*** (substitution) and hence the difference between knowledge and action.

AMRITANANDA: Because of the existence of upadhi, there is a difference between knowledge and action. When that state is reached,

MANI: Muk—jīvanmu—

My reference was to seekers who attained liberation during their lifetime (*jivanmukti*).

AMRITANANDA: Knowledge becomes action.

MANI: aAHhn.

AMRITANANDA: Asiddhi. How did God create this world, ante! [just like that only], by knowing about it.

MANI: By?

AMRITANANDA: By knowing about it. By thinking about it. By-

MANI: Yeess. By thinking about it. Let there be light and there was light.

I was thinking of the well-known line from Genesis (1:3), and which was also an example in speech act theory. "*A*siddhi" was an interesting concept, not quite the opposite of siddhi (extraordinary achievement / power) but a transcendence of it, a state where no achievement was necessary. Amritananda continued to explain—knowledge, action, past and future, that a child had the language of pain and pleasure, that language forces us to create relationships… I tried to steer Amritananda back to the topic of mantra.

AMRITANANDA: Mantra is the language of nature being perceived by the individual and being interpreted in terms of imagery

MANI: And it has an effect on us?

AMRITANANDA: It has an effect on you and because you are interconnected to the world it has an effect on the world also. You affect the world through-

MANI: to build a bridge between

AMRITANANDA: Setu [bridge]

MANI: between us and — (*looking at Prema*) — Yay! (*Prema laughed, as we had talked about this before coming to see Amritananda*).

AMRITANANDA: Consciousness bridge. Individual to? The world. And there is another bridge also-

MANI: And thought also can do the same function?

AMRITANANDA: yeah.

MANI: as the mantra. Because ..

AMRITANANDA: Thought, emotions. We call the emotions Brahmi Mahesvari Kaumari Vaishnavi.

MANI: So imagine that I don't have the ability to control my thought and emotions, I can have the mantra for the same purpose?

AMRITANANDA: Yes

Amritananda had anchored mantra in nature as well as the individual practitioner, and his ideas followed a similar model for deities.

MANI: How is it that you are into Devi, and somebody else is into Vishnu or Shiva. I mean, how does that happen and why?

AMRITANANDA: Now there are archetypes, right?

MANI: Okay

AMRITANANDA: Unified consciousness can be broken into bits and pieces also.

MANI: Okay?

AMRITANANDA: So there are various shaktis [deities, powers]. So they are consciousness Shakti-peethas [seats, locations of those deities]. That is, rivers, rivers of consciousness, which gives some experiences.

MANI: Okay.

AMRITANANDA: They can choose the vehicle appropriate to them

MANI: Appropriate to them?

AMRITANANDA: (*Smile. Pause*) You are… you are guided by them.

Some weeks later, in response to a written questionnaire, Amritananda wrote that sadhakas began by seeking deities, but later, it was deities that directed practice. Turning to Amritananda's memoirs I found several entries with the ideas he had explained in our conversation. A 1980 entry in Guruji's memoir suggests the idea of co-creation:

> I make the yantra come alive by mantra, repeating it. Now I rediscovered the magical formula of manifestation: repeated intention, till the hazy intention takes a clear shape and manifests over time.[25]

According to this, it is the practitioner whose repetition of the mantra is a repeated intention that manifests the results—whether a deity, or a desired result. If deities/archetypes guide us, is practice a quest to perceive what already exists or occurs, *as well as* to direct the course of events and create outcomes? A Facebook entry by Amritananda a few months before his demise is illuminating:

> I am also understanding the futility of asking for the power of making others see what I see. By the time I get into the others through my will, the visions have changed infinitely. And it never repeats. So what is the point?
>
> They will always be my visions, whoever I happen to be.
>
> At least is there a mantra, yantra, tantra or any process which can give such experiences? No. It is Her choice. By Her I mean the part of me which becomes what I see through my intention.[26]

These statements solve the binary: we find out that the Goddess lets him see through *his* intention. Not only is it the Goddess who decides, She is also within him. There is a similar pattern in descriptions about how uttering syllables activates syllables that are *already* in the body. To use Amritananda's terminology, perhaps this is a process of the "interface" being less rigid. It would also explain how it was that when Sheela talked about Raghavendra Swamy, Amritananda said she was talking about him.

* * *

Seeing is accentuated in this location of the Goddess whose very name is "Sahasrakshi"—my own initial response had been that of having entered Her omnivoyant domain even before I had Her darshan. In the narratives of Devipuram practitioners, seeing is not just an embodied, physical vision, but implies an acknowledgment by the Goddess, an entry into a relationship, and even understanding and insight. Sheela's first vision was that of the Goddess's eyes and her visitors were interested in seeing the image of the Goddess in her altar. Mani Prasanna's description of her own body cut up into triangles reads like a vision at another range, like seeing cells in a microscope. This vision gives her the insight that she is the embodiment of the Goddess, and that the divine resides within.

Some mantra-practitioners here embody deity, yantra and mantra in ways that express their occupations. Don, an architect, meticulously supered the yantra and the Khadgamala goddesses upon his own body, and thus, his mantra-practice would retrace the walk up and down the meru. Mani Prasanna realized that her own body was a temple yantra right down to the details including the placement of syllables—it seems apt that she became a priestess of Kalavahana later. It also seems apt that Mani Prasanna received the Bala-mantra and saw the Goddess in the form of a little girl when she was pregnant and perhaps harboring motherly emotions.

Mantra-practice is second nature to these practitioners. Don speaks about his mantra as if it were his pulse or heartbeat that continues, involuntarily, within his body; Karunamaya calls the Goddess his very life breath; Sheela described a "silent mantra" she had been given—which means she thinks or knows that she was doing a mantra without being consciously aware of it. Just like their guru, Amritananda, Devipuram practitioners seem to have become deeply involved with the Goddess without any apparent reason; and events seem directed by the Goddess. Devotion and surrender fits in with the idea that the Goddess is in charge—Sheela only had an experience when she expected nothing. The Goddess is the key player here, and practitioners realize themselves as her yantras, or her embodiments.

Notes

1. The general meaning of a yantra is any instrument or weapon; in tantra, a yantra refers to a mystical diagram. A "chakra" which literally means "wheel" is also an enclosed shape or form, not necessarily circular, within which a ritual activity occurs.
2. Goddess Shakti is often depicted standing upon a prone corpse, and sometimes this prone figure is that of Shiva. Popular legends offer several explanations for why Shakti stands on top of Shiva. In one version, Shakti continues to be in a rage after killing the evil Raktabija, and when Shiva approaches Her, She steps upon him. Another explanation for the iconography is that Shiva is *shava* (corpse) without Shakti, for Shakti is the animating power of Shiva.

3. There are several modern studies of the principles of a Hindu temple including by Stella Kramrisch ([1946] 1976) and Bharne and Krusche (2012).
4. Renaming marks a transition from one phase of life to another; in religious orders and spiritual practice, it marks a lifelong commitment to the order or/and practice. Prahlada Sastry and his wife Annapurna trained in Srividya with B. S. Krishna Murthy in Mumbai and were initiated (and renamed) after a yajna in Kollur, Karnataka. (Devipuram official website, under "Srividya," http://www.devipuram.com/about-devipuram, accessed 1 April 2015.)
5. Devipuram Official Website under "Guruji's Experiences," accessed 1 April 2015. During my fieldwork, this was a part of his journal entries on the Devipuram official website which was managed by him personally. After his demise, the official website has been revised and Amritananda's journal entries are no longer available. I had downloaded these journal entries on 1 April 2015, and continued to refer to them. The content continues to available on Vira Chandra's blog. (Chandra, Vira. "Guruji's Life Experiences," *Amritananda-Natha-Saraswati* (blog), accessed 2 May 2018.)
6. Ibid.
7. A humorous anecdote circulating at the Devipuram ashram was about a visitor who told Amritananda that his mantras and ritual procedures were not as per the shastras. Amritananda replied, "I don't follow shastras, I make them."
8. As told to Alok Baveja by Amritananda, in Gurujiamrita.com under "Amritanandanatha Saraswati," http://gurujiamrita.tripod.com, accessed 1 April 2015.
9. The Purusha Suktam is also in the Rigveda samhita [1870] 2006, vol. 4, 287–291. A more accessible source is *Veda Pushpanjali* (2000, 109–120).
10. Even though the cosmic "Purusha" has been understood as a genderless, representative figure, i.e., as "Man" rather than "a man," his masculinity is not to be ignored. In verse 5 of Purusha Suktam, Purusha produces the feminine principle, the cosmic egg, "Viraj" and then unites with her.
11. Narayana-suktam is a vedic hymn that is also in the Mahanarayana Upanishad. The portions I am quoting are from mantras 9 and 10 of Section 11 in the version edited by Jacob (1888, 11–12); in the veda compilation handbook used at Puttaparthi called Veda Pushpanjali (2000, 90), these are mantras 8 and 9.
12. Laurie L. Patton (1996) studies a canonical index of deities to show how canon is edited to accommodate changing practices.
13. *Vasini, Kameswari, Modini, Vimala, Aruna, Jayini, Srveswari, Kaulini.* The line from the Khadgamala stotram (*mantra*): *śrīcakra saptamāvaraṇadevatāḥ*

vaśinī, kāmeśvarī, modinī, vimale, aruṇe, jayinī, sarveśvarī, kauḷini, sarvarogaharacakrasvāminī, rahasyayoginī…

14. Verse seventeen of the Saundarya-Lahari also pays homage to the Goddesses of speech, Vagdevatas. This verse is specifically for those who wish to excel as poets as it requests the Goddess for creative powers in language.
15. Devi Mahatmyam, which means "The story of Devi's Miraculous Power" is a popular source in Goddess-worship and is a part of the Markandeya Purana.
16. The three long mala-mantras of the Sri-Vidya tradition include the Khadgamala, Saundarya-Lahari and Lalita-Sahasranamam.
17. An idiomatic expression derived from a Bollywood movie of the same name, which literally means a "wedding procession of memories."
18. Brahma-muhurtam is an auspicious time to meditate and timed at around one and a half hours before sunrise; many people believe this is when the mind is unperturbed, and when the gods and sages actively communicate with human beings.
19. Several sources including Mandukya Upanishad 1.3–5 (Olivelle 1998, 475).
20. The sequence Subbarao is referring to in the Khadgamala mantra: *Kāmeśvarī, bhagamālinī, nityaklinne, bheruṇḍe, vahnivāsinī, mahāvajreśvarī, śivadūtī, tvarite, kulasundarī, nitye, nīlapatāke, vijaye, sarvamaṅgale, jvālāmālinī, citre, mahānitye ….*
21. Maha-Mṛtyunjaya mantra: *OṂ Tryambakam Yajāmahe Sugandhim Puṣṭi-Vardhanam, Urvārukam-Iva Bandhanān Mrtyor-Mukśīya Māmrtāt.*
22. The entire stanza of the mantra: *Śuklāmbhara-dharam Viśṇum Śaśi-Varṇam Catur-Bhujam, Prasanna-Vadanam Dhyāyet Sarva-Vighnopashāntaye.*
23. Robert Buswell (2009, 1068) describes the case of a Korean monk, Chajang, who had a dream in which a great saint bestowed upon him a four-line verse in Sanskrit pronunciation, which he could not understand.
24. Each of the five elements is associated with a particular sensory perception: earth with smell, water with taste, fire with sight, air with touch and ether with sound. This is actually in an aggregating order; therefore, a substance with the earth element may be heard, felt, seen, tasted and smelled; a substance with the water element may be heard, felt, seen and tasted; a substance with the fire element may be heard, felt and seen; a substance with the air element can be heard and felt; and a substance with the ether element can only be heard. Ether pervades space, and it

is this that is the medium of mantra. The materialist school of Charvakas and the Buddhists did not accept ether as the fifth element as it was not perceptible.

25. Devipuram official website under "Guruji's Experiences"—"7 Intelligent triangles 1980," accessed 1 April 2015. See Notes 5.
26. Post on Amritanandanatha Saraswati's Facebook page, dated 13 April 2015, accessed 13 April 2015 and continues to be available as of 2 May 2018.

References

Armstrong, Tim. 1998. *Modernism, Technology and the Body.* New York: Cambridge University Press.

Bäumer, Bettina. 2001. "Puruṣa." In *Kalatattvakosa: A Lexicon of Fundamental Concepts of the Indian Arts*, 23–40. Delhi: Indira Gandhi National Centre for the Arts and Motilal Banarsidass.

Bharne, Vinayak, and Krupali Krusche. 2012. *Rediscovering the Hindu Temple: The Sacred Architecture and Urbanism of India.* Newcastle upon Tyne: Cambridge Scholars Publishing.

Breton, André. [1937] 1987. *Mad Love* (*L'amour fou* 1937). Translated by Mary Ann Caws. Lincoln, Nebraska: University of Nebraska Press.

Buswell, Robert. 2009. "Korean Buddhist Journeys to Lands Wordly and Otherworldly." *Journal of Asian Studies* 68 (4): 1055–1075.

Devipuram Official Website. "Srividya." And "Guruji's Experiences." "2 Balaji Temple 1979." "3 Explosion 1979." "5 Saraswati 1981." "7 Intelligent Triangles 1980," "8 Kamakhya 1981." "9 Love Power Hladini 1983." http://www.devipuram.com/about-devipuram. Accessed 1 April 2015.

Eliade, Mircea. 1961. *The Sacred and the Profane: The Nature of Religion.* Translated by Willard R. Trask. New York: Harper Torchbooks.

Jacob, G.A., ed. 1888. *Mahanarayana Upanishad of the Atharva-Veda with the Dipika of Narayana.* Bombay Sanskrit Series. Bombay: Government Central Book Depot.

Kramrisch, Stella. [1946] 1976. *The Hindu Temple.* Delhi: Motilal Banarsidass.

Morgan, David. 2012. *The Embodied Eye: Religious Visual Culture and the Social Life of Feeling.* Berkeley: University of California Press.

Olivelle, Patrick. 1998. *Early Upaniṣads—Annotated Text and Translation.* New York: Oxford University Press.

Patton, Laurie L. 1996. *Myth as Argument: The Bṛhaddevatā as Canonical Commentary.* Berlin: Walter de Gruyter.

Saraswati, Amritanandanatha. 2014. *Understanding Sri Chakra Puja*. Devipuram, Anakapalle: Srividya Trust.
Sankaranarayan, S. 2014. *Bhagavan and Nayana*, 3rd ed. Thiruvannamalai: Sri Ramanasram.
Shulman, David D. 2012. *More than Real: History of the Imagination in South India*. Cambridge, MA: Harvard University Press.
Sircar, Dineschandra. 1950. *Sakta Pithas*. Delhi: Motilal Banarsidass.
Veda Pushpanjali. 2000. Puttaparthi: Sri Sathya Sai Publications Trust.

CHAPTER 6

Self-Made: Svayam Siddha Kali Pitham, Guntur

6.1 When the Goddess Arrives

No auto-rickshaw[1] driver from the city center of Guntur knew how to get to the temple called Svayam Siddha Kali Pitham and even in the small area of Kottha Pattabhipuram, passersby seemed uncertain if there was any temple on one of the nearby lanes. I found the place finally in a residential block. A typical Indian temple has a tall *gopuram* (gateway), pillars and open porticos on the periphery and an inner sanctum. At this temple, the front door opened immediately into a large, dim hall. The slight glints of the golden arches around the stone statues of ten different forms of the Goddess (*Dasha-Mahavidyas*)[2] along the walls and tiny flames on oil wicks upon traditional brass stands created a subdued effect. There was a calming aroma of such substances used in puja as incense, *ghee* and camphor. I found myself speaking in a low voice to ask about the schedule. Goddess Kali's image was in black stone, decked with flower garlands and upon a pedestal. An unusually large image of a hooded-serpent made of a lighter colored stone was positioned in front of Goddess Kali, facing the visitor. A sense of the hidden pervaded the entire space as though it were a cave.[3] There were objects of utility here and there, some people seated on the floor on thick, cotton mats and some elderly folk on plastic chairs including one woman doing japa, and another, knitting. People and deities both seemed afloat in space.

"Svayam Siddha" literally means "self-made," and the word construction is similar to that of "*svayambhu*" (self-manifested), a descriptor

M. Rao, *Living Mantra*, Contemporary Anthropology of Religion,
https://doi.org/10.1007/978-3-319-96391-4_6

used for Shivalingas that have manifested on their own, i.e., they were not made by people. The story behind the image of this particular Goddess Kali is that She first manifested 600 years ago in the Himalayas during a previous birth of the primary seer of this chapter, Siddheswarananda Bharati, one in which he lived for 300 years. She was carried by Siddheswarananda during his travels, and eventually, was worshiped in a forest near Bhuvaneshwar (now in the state of Orissa). When Siddheswarananda died in that life, it passed on to another yogi. One day in 2001, when this other yogi died, the *murti* (image) of Goddess Kali came as if *par avion* to Siddheswarananda (Ramya Yogini 2014, 5). Right at that very moment, Siddheswarananda was at Srinatha Pitham in Guntur talking to a group of his followers. Witnesses to this event were not difficult to find; among the group was G. Y. N. Babu, who serves on the boards of educational institutions and social organizations in Guntur. He said, "One moment, She was not there, next moment She was there."

I could not help but ask if someone could have carried her in while everyone had their eyes shut? Babu pointed out that they were all awake and alert, listening to Swamiji (Siddheswarananda) talking. Later, when Goddess Kali was moved from Srinatha Pitham to the current location in the Svayam Siddha Kali Pitham, it took four people to carry her… i.e., she was heavy, and there was no way someone could have lugged such a heavy statue without anyone noticing. Babu also told me that Svayam Siddha Kali had been growing in size since that day. Another witness to Her appearance in Guntur, D. V. Apparao, *aka* Appaji, lived next door to the temple. He told me not only about witnessing the arrival of Goddess Kali, but also about a predictive dream. In 1963, Siddheswarananda had given Appaji a *svapna-mantra* (dream-mantra). Doing that mantra sometime in the 80s, Appaji had a dream: "I could see this house, and Swamiji staying in it, and that a deity came here. I told Swamiji about it. *Twenty years later it materialized*" (Fig. 6.1).

6.2 A Poet Becomes a Guru

It was not easy to gain access to Siddheswarananda; he kept a busy schedule. At first, I attended his talks and chatted with his followers. His talks were sprinkled with anecdotes from the epic histories Ramayana and Mahabharata and the lore of the Puranas, snippets of conversations between him and deities and immortal sanyasis, and revelations about the past lives of his followers (some of whom included well-known

Fig. 6.1 Goddess Svayam Siddha Kali (Photograph by Mani Rao)

politicians in Andhra-Telangana). Hundreds of people hung on to his words which were in erudite Telugu. Siddheswarananda is regarded a *mantra-vetta* (a knower of mantras), or one who has mantra-siddhis (powers from mantra). "There is not a deity he has not seen," said one of his followers. Another told me that Siddheswarananda resided in his heart—the Telugu word he used was "*gundelu-lo*," a raw, palpable and anatomical Telugu word for "heart" compared to the softer and more ethereal Sanskrit-Telugu synonym, "*hridayam*."

Accounts of Siddheswarananda's sadhana and siddhis went hand in hand with praise for his poetic achievements. Siddheswarananda was a wrestler and poet by the name of Prasadarao Kulapati before he became a sanyasi. People I met in Guntur spoke glowingly about Kulapati's poetry, especially of his inspired and spontaneous paeans to deities. In his early days as a practitioner, Kulapati visited Jillelamudi Amma (1923–1985) who lived in Jillelamudi near Guntur and who was regarded an incarnation of Goddess Shakti. Kulapati received mantra-initiation from her and wrote a thousand poems on her called "Ambica Sahasri." Appaji spoke admiringly of Kulapati's boldness, and how he would open with the Vairochani mantra at his poetic recitals, inviting the Goddess. There were also those who were nervous about Siddheswarananda's prowess. One informant who wanted to speak to me, but only in confidence, said he had witnessed people possessed by *pishachas* (ghouls or demons) screaming as they sat before Siddheswarananda; after Siddheswarananda wielded his mantra-shakti, they became entirely docile and were restored to their normal selves. My literary friends in Guntur knew about Siddheswarananda as the yogi who gained siddhis by offering blood to Kali. They had read in a newspaper that he had obtained bottles of blood from a blood bank. When questioned, he said that Goddess Kali had asked him to do so and explained his method as pacifist. I was cautioned by such notoriety and assessed him as a person who would not hesitate to break the norm; I was also struck by this act of commitment to a convention of sacrifice achieved alongside modern norms.

Siddheswarananda seemed to share his know-how of tantric techniques and mantras freely, even too freely. Bookstalls at his lectures sold numerous publications with detailed procedures including precautions and risks. In *Mana Samasyalu Mantra-Sadhanalu* (Mantra Sadhanas for Our Problems), Siddeswarananda (2000) recommends mantras to find a life partner, go overseas, cure headaches, correct misbehaving children, increase attraction between a married couple, help sell property faster, etc. There are also mantras for various deities, i.e., mantras that will help gain the favor of those deities, and, under a heading of *Kshudra Prayogamulu* (Wicked Uses), mantras for a range of harmful activities including *māraṇamu* (killing) (57–61). In the preface to *Tantrika Prapanchamu* (World of Tantra), Siddeswarananda (2013) clarifies the dangers of abusing the power of mantras: "Tantric texts also explain that with such abuse the practitioners dig their own graves" (5). He provides examples from popular misconceptions and clarifies them, quoting tantric sources. "The Ucchishtha-Ganapati-mantra is feared; if you do that, they say you will not have children." Then he quotes a stanza from the Rudra Yamala Kavacha Tantra, which enumerates all the benefits of the mantra including progeny (4). Elsewhere, Siddheswarananda reveals how a yogi may conquer death using foreknowledge of the moment of death, and go into samadhi so that the deity of death (*Mrityu-devata*) is tricked (12). How did Siddheswarananda gain authority on the subject of mantra? The answer to this question also gives us insight into the practice of mantras among his followers.

Vadlamudi Venkateshwara Rao, a disciple of Sri Kalyanananda Bharati (1883–1955), was Siddheswarananda's classmate and confidant in Guntur's Hindu College. They continued to be associated as colleagues—Vadlamudi taught Mathematics, while Siddheswarananda taught Telugu. Vadlamudi related some of his memories about Siddheswarananda's trials as a practitioner. We spoke in English and Telugu.

> VADLAMUDI: Extraordinary sadhana. If he sat in the morning he would be at it until the evening. In summer holidays - we were college students - in the summer, if he sat in the room he would come out only in the evening, there would be no food. He would do japa from morning to evening, in the evening he would have milk and some fruit. Forty days. He would do [practice] all night long. Some days, he would get up at two a.m., keeping two pails of cold water outside, take a bath and do japa on *shirsasana* [yoga posture of head-stand]. He took on such a difficult sadhana. *What he is a man [what a man he is]. He did (sadhana) in so many ways.* When he told his experiences. I would think, *ammababoy* [oh my god!], where did you come from!

Vadlamudi said Siddheswarananda began as an ambitious *upasaka* (worshipper) of Goddess Radha-Devi. Radha is a consort of Krishna who is an incarnation of the deity Vishnu, and pure love is her characteristic.

> VADLAMUDI: In those days he [Siddheswarananda] would say, woefully, "the deities are not visible to me" ("*devatalu kanipinchatalledayya*"). And then, one day, when doing anusthanam [daily ritual] he heard, "COME TO MATHURA. Do japa there for a week, you will (be able to) see me." So said Radha.

Vadlamudi quoted Radha's words in a commanding tone and dropped his voice over the last three words, using an emotional, tender tone as though dramatizing it for me. Mathura is the birth place of Krishna and the location of his divine romance with Radha and continues to be associated with legends of Krishna and Radha's presence. Vadlamudi continued the story about how Siddheswarananda then went to Mathura, and did sadhana: "*Seventh day morning, when he started (doing sadhana), She came. Therefrom, he could see the deity. He sees with his eyes open. Doesn't close his eyes. Don't need to close.*" I heard a less formidable story about Siddheswarananda's mantra-connection with the deity Radha from Karunamaya (of Chapter 5, and Amritananda's disciple). Karunamaya told me that Amritananda would send anyone who wanted the Radha-mantra to Siddheswarananda as he had siddhi over this mantra. Siddheswarananda was in a state of permanent Radha-related bliss, fully awake but fully connected to the divine. Later, I shared this information with Sivananda (of Chapter 7). She interpreted this as *Samprajnata samadhi*, a fully conscious transcendent state of bliss. Vadlamudi had innumerable anecdotes—"*Yenni*! (how many!), hundreds of instances." Most of these narratives were in the problem-solution format—the lack of a boy child, an unwed daughter, or an incurable ailment, and Siddheswarananda prescribed a mantra and a sadhana for a stipulated period of time which usually included japa and *homa*. Vadlamudi's glowing praise of Siddheswarananda's sadhana and prowess carried even more weight because he is a guru and visionary in his own right. The author of many books on rituals and mantras, his name had come up repeatedly in my fieldwork among mantra-sadhakas as an authority on Srividya.

Vadlamudi's ([1993] 2013) *Śrī Lalitā Nāmārtha Maṇjūṣa* (Treasury of Goddess Lalita's Names) is a commentary on every name in the Lalita-sahasranama (LS). LS is a long hymn/mantra from an appendix to the Brahmanda-Purana; a sequence of the thousand names of Goddess Lalita and noted for having no conjunctions or particles. These names are considered mantras, and the rishis/seers of this mantra—or these mantras—are the Vak deities or goddesses of Speech. In his book, Vadlamudi presents a number of new mantras for which he provides all details including the relevant rishi. An example is the 114th item titled "Mahā Kāméśa Mahiṣi Mahātripura Sundari."

> There are three mantras hidden in this line where two names come together.
>
> From Mahākāméśamahīśī: Mantra 1: *Oṃ Ślīṃ Mahaḥ Kāmé Kāméśa Daivījagatī Chandaḥ. Śrī Mahākāméśa Mahipyai Namaḥ.* Śrī Śukanandanātha Ṛśiḥ. Daivijagatī Chandaḥ. Śrī Kāmśvarī Devata. Ślīṃ - Bījaṃ. Mahaḥ - Śaktiḥ. Namaḥ - Kīlakaṃ.

From Mahātripura Sundari: Mantra 2: *Oṃ Mahaḥ Klīṃ Sauḥ Tripuré Svāha*. Śrī Śukānandanātha Ṛśiḥ. Paṇktīḥ Chandaḥ. Śrī Tripurasundarī Devata. Mahaḥ - Bījaṃ. Mahaḥ - Śaktiḥ. Namaḥ - Kīlakaṃ.

From the combination of both names: Mantra 3: *Oṃ Mahaḥ Klīṃ Hrīṃ Mahamahiśyai Tripuré Svāha*. Śrī Śukānandanātha Ṛśiḥ. Ūṣṇīk Chandaḥ. Śrī Mahā Mahiśī Tripurasundarī Devata. Mahaḥ - Bījaṃ. Klīṃ - Śaktiḥ. Hrīṃ - Kīlakaṃ. (81)

The details Vadlamudi lists here are called the *shadangas* (six limbs) of a tantric mantra: rishi, meter, deity and *bija* (seed syllable), Shakti (power, i.e., what it achieves) and *kilakam* (spike). Kilakam is the inner syllable of the mantra over which the practitioner must develop familiarity until the mantra becomes automatic. Vadlamudi credits the vision to Sri Sukanandanatha, a disciple of 18th-century CE Bhaskararaya and one of the commentators of LS. There are three seers here: Vadlamudi today, Sukanandanatha in the 18th-century CE and the original seers of the mantra who are the Vak-devatas, the deities of speech.

6.3 An Atheist Turns to Mantra

Another boyhood friend of Siddheswarananda is Potturi Venkateswara Rao, an illustrious journalist and author of numerous publications, who described his journey from atheism to an intense mantra-practice. He attributed the beginnings of his mantra-sadhana to a dream he had "twenty or twenty-five years ago," when "somebody" gave him the *Pranava*, the OṂ-mantra. Vedic sources describe OṂ as the sound in the *akasha* (ether) which is present at the beginning of cosmic creation and remains after creation is dissolved. OṂ prefaces both vedic and tantric mantras and is called an originary source out of which the discrete material world emerges.

MANI: "Somebody" means ... did you recognize the person?

POTTURI: No. I don't know who it was. It was the riverside. Lots of people were moving about. *A sage with his disciples was coming from one direction.* I was standing to one side. I thought, well someone (*yavaro kada ani anukunnanu*). He came near me. Why he came near me I don't know. Having come, *he uttered that mantra in my ears. He kissed me on my forehead.* Why he did that I don't know. I did namaste to him (*nenu dannam pettenu*). He went away. There was no conversation or anything like that. I tried to forget that.

MANI: Who was he?

POTTURI: *He was a rishi. Didn't I say "saint"?* (*He had said "sage"*).

How did he know it was a rishi? I asked if the person in the dream wore saffron ascetic garb (*kashaya*). Potturi said he did not remember, but he was possibly in a "some *loin-cloth,* some matted hair (*jadalu*)." Potturi also wore saffron—a light saffron *kurta* (shirt) over a deep saffron *dhoti* (wrap). Along with a chain around his neck which was a string of pearls but looked like a rosary, he looked like an ascetic himself. The nooks and corners of his study had statuettes of Natarajas, Ganeshas and numerous trophies, all in an unkempt, careless manner, which gave the impression of indifference to a world of representations. As we talked, Potturi emphasized that he could not forget this dream. "I tried to forget about it. But often that mantra was coming into my mind." "For years, I was trying to brush aside. But it was persisting." Six or seven years ago, he mentioned the dream to Siddheswarananda who recommended doing japa of the Pranava (OṂ-mantra). Potturi then began this mantra-sadhana, and on the 30th of March 2015, he had completed three-crore japas, i.e., 30 million repetitions of this mantra (Fig. 6.2).

Since a typical rosary for mantra-sadhana has 108 beads, completing 30,000,000 japas in seven years or 2555 days would mean that he did 11,741 japas daily, or 108 japamalas (rosaries) daily. Potturi said he was always engaged in this activity. "I keep on doing it. I have a japamala, and keep counting. In the bus, in the car, in the train…" Potturi showed me his diary where he notes the number of japas—they all ended in zero. When I expressed surprise over it, he explained that he would count 100 for every rosary, and this was just for easier calculation. He found that whenever he reached a significant milestone, it coincided with an important occasion. When he had done "50 or 75 lakhs," i.e., 5 or 7.5 million, he had darshan at the Tirupati temple with the family, and the day he completed ten thousand rosaries (thirty million repetitions of the mantra, per his calculation) turned out to be Jillelamudi amma's birthday. Why did Potturi wait so long to do this mantra, and how to explain such intensity after commencing this sadhana? Potturi replied, "*I was an atheist. Now I've changed.*"

MANI: How did you become an astika [believer]?

POTTURI: Because of Jillelamudi amma. When I was – in '57, or '58 - I am 81 now – in 1957/58 I lost one child. My daughter. Not even a year

Fig. 6.2 Potturi Venkateswara Rao (Photograph by Mani Rao)

> (old). I was upset. Is nothing in our hands? *Well, I didn't change even then. But someone suggested, including our Swamiji* [Siddheswaranada]. Why don't you see (Jillelamudi) Amma. More for my wife's sake. My father-in-law also suggested. I took her even though I had no belief (*nammakamu*). I told Amma too I don't have any belief. She said: "it's not necessary, son, there's no need to believe." Then many things happened that science cannot explain. Then I thought, there is something. There is something which science cannot explain. Then I started changing. Slowly changing. Even now – not really (believe in) deities – I think we don't know.

Potturi credits his transformation to Jillelamudi Amma, the Telugu saint who had also initiated Siddheswarananda. As young men, Siddheswarananda and Potturi were among the numerous people who visited her and were influenced by her. As he continued to talk about his transformation over the course of his sadhana, he also confessed a deep detachment from worldly matters, and the total lack of desires. I then asked, what was the intention or wish on his mind, when he did mantra-japa?

POTTURI: I am wishing for the end of births (*janma-rahityam*). *I have no desires. By chance if it is so.* Even that I don't know. That there are janmas [that there are rebirths].

MANI: What is "*rahityam*"?

POTTURI: Not being there. *Termination. Of the series.*

MANI: *Moksha* [liberation]?

POTTURI: That's one meaning. That's one meaning. If I think, what is it I've achieved. In this when a stage comes, say 50 lakhs [5 million], 75 lakhs, going to Tirupati and getting god's *darshanam* [seeing the deity] – these kind of things would happen. Coincidence. I can't say that is what will happen. For example when I completed 3 crores I was in Jilllelamudi. That too was not calculated. I went there. (To the) *Samadhi* [tomb].

By "series," Potturi is referring to the series of lives, the cycle of birth and death or transmigration. There was finality in his use of the word "termination"; I tried to interpret it positively, i.e., as a soteriological or salvific desire, but he refused.

Potturi's mantra-sadhana was different from the many others I had been learning about. He took up mantra-sadhana on Siddheswarananda's suggestion, but had received initiation in a dream from a rishi he did not recognize. Over the years, he had found himself transformed, and took delight in serendipitous moments of coincidence. Across decades, he was working for a goal—"termination" of rebirth—that he could never be sure of having achieved. He had been an atheist, and mantra had transformed him to the extent that he considered his darshan at Tirupati as a sacred moment. In our conversation, he had hinted that even though he was no longer an atheist, he still did not believe in deities. I thought it logical that a person who did not or could not relate to a deity would do the OṂ-mantra, a mantra associated with the formless, nameless Brahman, and shared my interpretation with him over email communication. He replied, *"Regarding concept of divinity you are 'correct.'"*

6.4 Experiments with Mantra

Another person with a dedicated sadhana that he said was unrelated to devotion or belief was Appaji. I met Appaji at his home next door to the Kali temple. Appaji's conviction about the efficacy of mantra and *homa* (fire ritual with mantras) was like that of any other mantra-practitioner, but he spoke about technicalities rather than the transported state of devotion or the love of deities. "Homa is the easiest way to approach deities; *parayana* (reading aloud) and japa help in later life, (but) homa is like a surgery." Appaji said that deities were sound forms of mantras, and provided detail. While the mantra produces the deity, a variation in the mantra could result in a different form of the same deity.

> APPAJI: The combination of sounds gives us the shape of god.
>
> MANI: Yantra?
>
> APPAJI: No not yantra just the shape of the god. Kali-mantra *Krīṃ Krīṃ hrīṃ hrīṃ huṃ huṃ* gets you the shape in black –with shulam [spear] and sword – she is coming to support you. But *Krīṃ Krīṃ hum hum hrīṃ hrīṃ* gives us Kali with varada and abhaya mudras [boon and fearlessness mudras], protection.

Appaji spoke with the certainty of a researcher who has documented the results of an experiment. The two different forms of the deity were significant because they indicated different outcomes, even if only subtly different. The first form is a deity who intervenes in the practitioner's circumstance, and the second form is a deity who inspires fearlessness in the practitioner. Vadlamudi had also told me about such an effect and had quoted the *Shaiva Panchakshari Kalpa* (PK) which outlined how different syllable combinations had different results. He told me it was an old manuscript (*prachina grantha*) and did not know if he had a copy. Later, I found a PDF file on the internet—it was a 1914 publication but did not indicate authorship, or if it was an older source that had been transcribed and published. A Sanskrit text in Telugu script, it was framed as a conversation between rishi Agastya, and deity Skanda, who is the son of Shiva. Skanda instructs Agastya in the secrets of the permutations—he utters the mantra, gives it a name and specifies the benefits of doing that mantra.

> Skanda: […]If you do (japa of) "*Śivāyanamaḥ*" it is called Sauṃya-panchakshari, one may do this japa to gain peace (shanti). […] If you do "*hrīṃ*" twice before the Panchakshari, it is the Ajna-panchakshari and gets rid of disembodied spirits (bhuta-pretas). If you do "*Mavayanāśi*" [a permutation of *Namaḥśivāya*] it is called "Sarva-panchakshari" and you get khadga-siddhi [command over knives].

Shivayanamah and *Mavayanashi* are permutations, and we learn from the PK about the strict invariability of a mantra—a different arrangement of syllables has entirely different effects. Such a source gives us an understanding of the kind of information that circulates today, and which practitioners may follow. Compared to a mystical "text" of unknown author and date, a living visionary is considered more reliable. Also, with random sources, one does not know if conventions of antiquity have been adopted for the appearance of authenticity.[4] Appaji related another anecdote about different forms of deities upon doing different mantras:

> APPAJI: In the beginning, Guruji gave a mantra, but he did not tell me what shape it is. He told me, practice it and come and report the shape. OṂ Namaḥ Shivāya was included in the mantra. In the beginning I would see the Shivalinga [aniconic form of Shiva]. A big Shivalinga. Later it started deteriorating and a shape came on top of it. I could see a snake (*sarpa*).

Appaji's experience illustrates that visions may be imagined based on suggestions. If vision may be imagined, understanding may also be misplaced.

> I thought something is wrong with me. Because if you see snakes they say it is sexual, so I stopped (doing the mantra).
>
> Swamiji asked me, what happened, I told him. He said it is Naga-mantra, Nagastra-mantra [snake-mantra, snake-weapon mantra]. I did it for five-six hours in the night-time after nine-thirty. Including smashana-mantra [cemetery-mantra]. I found that I had control over snakes. People would bring them to me. Even if someone hits the snake, if I said the mantra it cannot rise. I started betting with friends. Guruji asked, "what are you doing?" I said, "it's working!" He told me snakes later become planets and then they trouble you, you are playing with snakes. Hereafter you should not use any mantra for your own purpose.

Appaji learned three different lessons from this early experience. The presence of "OṂ Namaḥ Śivāya" within the mantra had become a suggestion that influenced Appaji's imagination and he saw a Shivalinga, the aniconic form of Shiva, where there was none. However, this error taught him the importance of keeping the mind alert and free of influences that would shape imagination in advance of an experience.

Distinguishing between imagination and reality or experience is a major concern of practitioners, and I discuss this point at some length in the concluding chapter.

Secondly, Appaji learned not to be predetermined about the nature of mantras—the mantra that he had imagined related to Shiva was really related to snakes. Thirdly, he learned not to misuse the power acquired from mantra-sadhana. Appaji spoke about the Nagastra-mantra as if it were a weapon to use to subdue snakes. This contrasts with Indian epics where the Nagastra *is* a snake, or a snake-weapon used against enemies. "Astra" means a "weapon" and in epics, heroes and heroines activate or animate their weapons with mantras when unleashing them upon enemies. On the sixteenth day of the Kurukshetra war in the Mahabharata, one of the warriors, Karna, tells his charioteer Shalya that he has a weapon which takes on the form of a snake, proving deadly upon impact. In this speech, Karna speaks about how he has worshiped his Nagastra weapon, saving it for the special occasion. Karna and Appaji both treasure their Nagastras, anticipating some future use. In the Mahabharata, Karna promises his mother Kunti that he will only use the Nagastra once against his brother Arjuna. Karna's charioteer Shalya advises Karna to aim the Nagastra at Arjuna's chest, but Karna aims at Arjuna's neck. Krishna, who is Arjuna's charioteer, lowers the chariot, and the weapon topples Arjuna's crown instead. Just as Karna wastes the Nagastra, Appaji wastes the Nagastra-mantra.

In *Naga Sadhana* (n.d.), Siddheswarananda writes that mantras related to snakes are used to cure skin diseases and some other ailments. Appaji misuses the Nagastra-mantra when he targets snakes for amusement. Siddheswarananda warns Appaji that the snakes will take revenge on him after they become planets in their future lives—this is another theme common to the Mahabharata, and to beliefs in the Indic tradition about karma and transmigration. In the concept of karma, it is the individual who is responsible for his or her own fortunes and misfortunes; past misdeeds have repercussions, and good behavior is rewarded. Somewhere along the cycle of births and deaths, today's downtrodden can become tomorrow's avengers—hence the imperative to be ethical and conscientious. Mantras fit into this scheme by helping intervene in karmic justice, and that is also why working with mantras is fraught with risks. Appaji spoke about a deity he had invoked, and an unforeseen outcome:

APPAJI: (Goddess) Pratyangira has no shape. It is a flame. People say she has a lion-head, because "*sahasrasiṃha-vadane*" [thousand-lion-face, the description in hymns]. They worship her to help in several things. I don't believe it.

MANI: Huh?

APPAJI: Pratyangira is mainly to give suffering to enemy. We used to do Prayojika homas [goal-oriented homas]. Once someone came and asked for Pratyangira homa. I did it. Three days later he came back and said that five people died in a car accident in his enemy's house. From then on I don't do it unless it is compulsory. I felt I was instrumental. Is it to kill the enemy or to kill the enmity? We don't have the right to kill.

Appaji spoke anxiously about this experience. I interpreted the point about the lack of a shape as a marker of the ferocity or malevolence of Goddess Pratyangiras; was She so negative that She did not even have a shape? Appaji's conviction about the efficacy of mantras was not just a happy innocence for he had dealt with the responsibility of agency. An analogy Appaji gave me was that of a knife—we can use it for surgery, or we can use it harmfully. So it is the practitioner who has to have the discrimination; by contrast, deities are less discriminating.

Appaji's assertion about *bhakti* (devotion) and mantras was rational. If mantras and rituals produce results, there may be no need for bhakti. If deities are indifferent, there would also be less reason to idealize them and perhaps even less justification for bhakti. Moreover, if mantras *created* deities, perhaps that also reduced the status of the deity, and put the control and power in the hands of a practitioner. Appaji's comments indicated how he considered deities instrumental:

APPAJI: Even physical creations, comes in tantra-shastra.

MANI: Materialization?

APPAJI: Yes. 99% is already manufactured. They touch it once. Then when they want it the deity gets it for them. All right, I can even say the name. It is (Goddess) Matangi. She can do it. She will get it [i.e., the object that is materialized].

Goddess Mathangi is one of the *Dasha-Mahavidyas*, or the ten forms of Goddess Shakti. Appaji's lack of devotion did not make him irresponsible; on the contrary, he was very conscientious. Because a mantra is potent, a practitioner has the responsibility to not misuse the mantra. Appaji also emphasized the role of the mantra-practitioner's will:

> APPAJI: In fact, 80% of the job is done by sankalpa [intention/wish]. If you come to me for homa, I believe the distance should be less than three feet. Easy to transfer thought. So if you have a purpose, I make the sankalpa on your behalf. My mind must be clear. If I get another thought, I say, not now, come back later.

6.5 Devotion as Investment

While Appaji distanced himself from bhakti, Swami Vasudevananda was devoted to the deity Hanuman.[5] A part of Siddheswarananda's ascetic order and reputed to be clairvoyant, Vasudevananda told me that he has not studied Indian astrology and said he barely knew basics about the planets; in fact, it was Hanuman who spoke in his ear. "If you tell me your name and birth-constellation (*nakshatra*),[6] soon as you tell, then He comes into my ear, tells me everything (about you)." How did he know it was Hanuman at his ear? Vasudevananda said, "Know? The one for whom the *upasana* (worship, service) is, He would speak, who else? I am an ordinary person. But at *that* time, He. Everything is His." Vasudevananda used the word "*ayana*" a respectful form of the third person singular pronoun in Telugu. We spoke in Telugu, and he occasionally used English words.

Vasudevananda began his journey as a mantra-practitioner at the young age of thirteen years when his paternal uncle gave him the Naga-mantra. Why? "Well, it's a village, snakes, *vipers*, they're plenty. And my uncle was getting old and wanted to pass it on. After I learned it, first for some five or six years, I *stock-piled* japa, then I started to put it." What does it mean to "stock-pile" a mantra? Vasudevananda clarified, "If we have to go to a bank we need money in the *account,* right?" Before he could use the mantra, he had to have earned and accumulated the shakti of that mantra in his mantra-shakti "account." The idea that mantra-shakti is a reward for service or penance and that this reward is like credit which can be stored for future deployment has many precedents in Indian epics. In the Mahabharata, rishi Durvasa gives Kunti a mantra with which she can compel any deity she chooses to father her child. She uses this mantra at once to invoke Sun, who fathers Karna, and then saves the mantra for future use. Having already heard Appaji's narrative about how he tried to subdue snakes, I visualized Vasudevananda in front of a snake-basket attempting to petrify a snake. However, the Naga-mantra was entirely different from the Nag*astra*-mantra, it was used to heal people suffering from snake bite. Vasudevananda spoke about extracting snake-poison with this mantra.

VASUDEVANANDA: No. The poison. With the mantra it comes out.

MANI: Out?

VASUDEVANANDA: Out.

MANI: After it has bitten

VASUDEVANANDA: Yes

MANI: After it has bitten, with the mantra—

VASUDEVANANDA: —then it is cured, he gets up and goes home. When it bites he has no *sensation, unconscious.* So if a mantra is put, then they, wake up a little, and then after an hour, they do namaste and go.

Vasudevananda said it could take fifteen minutes for a Naga-mantra treatment. Exactly what did he do in those fifteen minutes? Did he do mantra-japa? Vasudevananda said, "Uhn, japa, and blow," and blew twice in quick succession to demonstrate, "*allaaa*" (like that). These were procedures his uncle had taught him. The mantra was uttered upon a "turayi," i.e., a white cloth that was knotted and tied to a specific part of the patient's body. "If the bite is on the right side then (we tie it) on the left hand. If it has bitten on the left hand, then (the cloth is placed) on the right leg. *Alternation.*" Every day, four or five villagers would be bitten by snakes and come to Vasudevananda for mantra treatment. There was also the mantra called "Garudaṃ" which was more powerful than the regular Naga-mantra and which he "took out" in more serious cases. (Note the verb here, which suggests that a mantra is a weapon or instrument taken out of an arsenal.) Soon, villagers would bring him sick infants, or cows that did not give milk, and Vasudevananda would put a mantra and give *vibhuti* (sacred ash), and the problems would be solved.

In 1970, when Vasudevananda was in college, he received a handbook in the mail from an unknown addresser. Opening it, he found that it was the Hanuman-Chalisa, a hymn in the language Awadhi with forty stanzas honoring the deity Hanuman believed to have been authored by Tulsidas, the 16th-century CE saint. The handbook also listed results of chanting the mantra 11 times, 108 times, and so on. Vasudevananda began to the Hanuman-Chalisa 11 times daily for two years and became an arden devotee of Hanuman; he would go into a trance when he sang bhajans.

> VASUDEVANANDA: In bhajans during a Hanuman song, I would get *punakam* [a possessed state]. In those days, five or six people would hold me. Tight. It would come, intense.

His transported singing caught the attention of someone who sought him out and gave him mantras including the Hanuman-mantra and the Rama-mantra, which he also began to do. Why did Vasudevananda simply do these mantras given to him? Vasudevananda simply shrugged his shoulders as though to say he had no idea. Inducted by his uncle into the practice of mantras at an early age, perhaps Vasudevananda did not have the occasion to question his practice.

After ten years of doing the Hanuman-Chalisa, Vasudevananda began to have extraordinary experiences during mantra-sadhana: "I would get an experience (*anubhuti*) when I was doing japa, like this (*draws in front of his eyes, horizontally*) a *focus, light,* of intense brightness would come." Moving his hand from left to right in front of his eyes, he dramatized the phenomenon: "*Ilaaaa* (like th*aa*at) it would come and go away. Like th*aa*at (*again gesturing*), a Shivalinga would come." In 1995, he was told by a guru that he had (done) lots of *upasana* (service) and that he had "Vak-shakti," i.e., the power of the word, or whatever he said would occur. Vasudevananda was surprised—"Is all this shakti in me? I would think I have nothing! (*Laughs*). It developed like that." Even though he had years of experience helping others with the Naga-mantra, he never considered that as his shakti, only as mantra-shakti. A single recitation of the Hanuman-Chalisa takes around ten minutes, and a practice of eleven daily recitations even for two years is no mean effort. Vasudevananda's mantra-practice continued for an entire decade before he had encouraging visionary experiences and it was *twenty-five* years before he even thought that he had extraordinary powers. This was a long-term investment that had yielded dividends. Many Indian legends feature devotees who have proven their devotion and then feel it's time to cash in on their investment. The story of 17th-century CE Ramdas from Bhadrachalam in Andhra demonstrates such a reckoning. Originally named Kancherla Gopanna, he was a state employee who collected tax revenue from the publics and diverted it to the construction of a temple to his favorite deity, Rama. Songs that Ramdas composed in prison are popular in Andhra, film made in 1964 (and remade in 2006). A legend- nal song) that begins "*Ikshvaku kula tilaka*..." enu- he has given Rama and family. The song ends with you get these goodies from your father-in-law?"[7] ity to see Vasudevananda's clairvoyance at work ed after a couple whom I knew, mentioning a problem y known—I thought—to a handful of people including myself. When I let them know what Vasudevananda had asked, they expressed a wish to consult him and gave me their horoscope information. Vasudevananda's comments were stunningly accurate. He recapitulated accurate information about them, and asked if the woman in the couple is a devotee of the deity Rama (—this was accurate), and told me to tell her to drop Rama and catch hold of Hanuman instead—Hanuman would put in a reference for her with Rama, and it would solve her problem. He then gave me some *vibhuti* to take back to them, and to ask them to smear it daily, for forty days, on their foreheads. They did. Their problem was solved.

6.6 Persistence Pays

Many practitioners do not have a special relationship with a deity at the outset, and they embark on mantra-sadhana because they face problems they believe cannot be resolved any other way. Lakshmi, a retired teacher from Visakhapatnam, was denied her pension due to some bureaucratic tangle and fought back with mantras. This practice became a full-time engagement for five years and with progressively increased hours spent in japa and homa until Lakshmi was, she said, "exhausted." Many years before Lakshmi faced this problem, a sanyasi had given her the Hanuman-mantra, but she had not done it in earnest. In 2005, when she approached Siddheswarananda with the problem, he asked if she already had a mantra. When a guru gives a mantra to someone, other gurus hesitate to intervene; when Lakshmi insisted that Siddheswarananda give her another mantra, he gave her a "combination" mantra which revised her old mantra. He told Lakshmi that she had to first gain control (*vashamu chesukuni*) over the deity Ghantakarna before she could win Hanuman's favor and asked her to do a hundred thousand japas and a set of rituals (*purascharana*).[8]

How would Lakshmi know she had control over Ghantakarna? Lakshmi said that if she *saw* Ghantakarna, she would also have control over him and then she would get Hanuman also. A purascharana usually works in proportions—a routine of 100,000 japas goes along with 10,000 offerings (*ahuti*) with mantras in a homa, followed by 1000 libations of milk over the yantra (*tarpana*), 100 libations of water over the yantra (*marjana*), and food (*bhojana*) for ten people. Lakshmi began to do these rituals with the aim of seeing Ghantakarna. She said, "only if you do all this you will get the right (*adhikara*)—well, having the right doesn't mean wonders occur, you simply get the right to ask for a favor from the deity, you've earned the eligibility (*arhata*)." This extensive practice yielded no results, and Lakshmi went back to Siddheswarananda to discuss the lack of progress.

Siddheswarananda then told her she had lots of obstacles from her previous life, and that she really needed to do the Vijay-Ganapati mantra. Ganapati is the deity who clears obstacles. Lakshmi began this mantra-japa intensely. "I did 3,000 daily. Sometimes even 5,000. I sat and did without moving. 5,000 japas means nearly 50 rosaries." Lakshmi has a friend and confidante, Dhanalakshmi, with whom she had traveled to visit Siddheswarananda. Dhanalakshmi felt so sorry for her that she wanted to join forces, and Siddheswarananda approved. About the collaborative mantra-practice, Dhanalakshmi said, "it's like putting ten sticks together, stronger than one stick." Lakshmi said, "you can pass on *fifty percent* of the practice to another person." After this set was completed, Siddheswarananda told Lakshmi it was not enough, she had a lot of (bad) karma, and needed to do homas with at least 2,000 offerings with mantras daily. Disappointed but persistent, Lakshmi stayed home and did her sadhana for three months. She was at the end of her energy:

> LAKSHMI: I was done for! I used up all my shakti. I was exhausted. We did forty days. Then when Swamiji came in Chaturmasya [a season for rituals that begins in June] to Visakhapatnam he said we should all do the homa for (the deities) Kali (and) Kala-bhairava for the good of the world. Then, Lakshmi [Dhanalakshmi] said, "don't become *desperate,* we are all doing it, you too come and do it, even if hard or pointless." So I too went, I used to do a private job, I had no pension, I had so much difficulty, I would finish my job and run there and join them.
>
> DHANALAKSMI: Nor would we eat, just take tiffins.
>
> LAKSHMI: And when doing that Kali Kalabhairava homa, I came to know that a little, step by step, it [pension-appeal] is moving. Then again I began Vijay-Ganapati (mantra) at home. One day, what I did, on a Tuesday, I did homa, it was 4.30 in the evening, I said, Ganapati-deva, I have done a lot,

> I must get a phone call that all my papers are through—and I got a phone call, at once!—saying "Madam, your papers are through." We went and told Swamiji, he said, "very happy, you have achieved it (sadhincheru).

Lakshmi thought the first mantra had not worked because it had not really been from Siddheswarananda—"I told him I was doing it [Hanuman-mantra] and he *changed* it (to the combination-mantra) and gave it back to me." But the Ganapati-mantra worked well, and Lakshmi knew it was working because she had numerous extraordinary experiences and felt sensations of the mantra in her body. She spoke about this mantra when discussing distinctions between her experiences of mantras:

> LAKSHMI: I did all these (mantras), sometimes I do eleven rosaries, or I turn (the beads) 108 times and let it [the mantra] go. But the one mantra I held on to was the Vijay Ganapati mantra. What Swamiji said, do any one mantra seriously. Even if you do all the mantras, hold to one deity only. It seems that the deity thinks, well, the other one is handling this so I don't need to … so to this day I do Vijay Ganapati mantra. Because of that I have had LOTS of experiences. Because of that mantra, while doing japa, the vibrations in the body, I cannot describe it, from beneath from the earth too, Ganapati is the governing deity (adhishtana-pati) of the root-chakra (muladhara-chakra). He keeps pushing upwards.
>
> DHANALAKSHMI: That's correct, today as I did that, I felt it
>
> LAKSHMI: At the Nadi Ganapati (temple).
>
> DHANALAKSHMI: From the spine it crept up.
>
> LAKSHMI: It is He [Ganapati] who is pushing. Oh He pushes, how He pushes, illaaga illaaga illaaga (like this, like this, like this), the vibrations.

Eventually, Lakshmi did not appeal to Ghantakarna nor to Hanuman, but to Ganapati. As Lakshmi described her physical sensations, Dhanalakshmi corroborated them. They had both been doing japa at the Nadi-Ganapati temple in Courtallam, a temple that has become famous for the living *nadi* (pulse) of the stone image of Ganapati. This is at the Maunaswamy matham (religious center), now under the leadership of Siddheswarananda. The story goes that when this image was installed and ritually animated, some skeptics commented disapprovingly about the inordinate time and expense over a mere stone idol. Siddheswarananda's predecessor, Maunaswamy, refuted this charge.

Medical doctors were invited to test the claim, and when they checked Ganapati's image with a stethoscope, they recorded a heartbeat. Since then, this temple became known as the Nadi-Ganapati temple.[9]

Siddheswarananda's use of the word "*sadhincheru*" is telling—literally, it means "you achieved it," and shares the verbal root with sadhana. We see in this narrative how sadhana is much more than practice; it is a rigorous effort toward an achievement. Siddheswarananda had told Lakshmi, "fight it!," and it was a five-year long fight. Lakshmi's narrative illustrates how difficult mantra-sadhana can be as well as how people are willing to take on its challenges. A practitioner who undertakes mantras to solve a problem is motivated by hope, and works within the framework of a few beliefs—karma, the powers of mantras and deities to counter karma, and that a focused effort can solve unsurmountable problems. Lakshmi did not regard this effort as excessive, she said—"intense sadhana pleases the deities and only then the job gets done, and sometimes the task is difficult, because it has been accrued from karma of previous lives." Repeatedly over those years, Siddheswarananda advised Lakshmi that she was fighting her own karma. "You caused much suffering to someone in your last birth. Now if your body suffers, they will be contented. So make your body suffer, and your karma gets reduced. Your sadhana gets reduced." Lakshmi did not know how to understand this concept, and asked Swamiji: "I don't know what is my past life, I don't know what's the next life when I die, now all I know is this life, and for me to hold on to some karma that I supposedly have from before, what do I do? What can I think about something I don't know?" Lakshmi also asked Siddheswarananda to look (into her past) and tell her what was her obstacle. Siddheswarananda declined and told her that as she continued to do japa, she would automatically get visions about the extent of her previous sins, "just like one saw a movie reel."As her sadhana progressed, Lakshmi did get numerous clairvoyant visions, some of which she patiently shared with me, but none about her past life.

One of her anecdotes was about an experience in a trip to Vellore. In her meditation that day, within minutes of starting her japa, she saw water, and inside the water, a Shivalinga. "*Inta* [this big] Shivalinga" (*spreading her hands to indicate the massive size*). She had the same vision that night and commented about it to Dhanalakshmi. The next morning, her friend's brother visited and told them about a temple in the area called "Jala-Kantheswara Lingam," a Shivalinga in water. Lakshmi interpreted this as a call from Shiva:

> He was telling me, "I am here, you come." When we went – what (size) I had seen, that was what was there. It seems it was once inside water, there was also a plank to get to it. Water all around, and Shiva inside. Now there is no water. The priest told us when we asked him. What to say about this? I did not imagine it, right? I didn't know there was a temple there, right? When I told Swamiji he said it's a divine experience, when you do japa, you get experiences like that.

Siddheswarananda told Lakshmi to ignore such experiences and to stay focused on the mantra sadhana until she was more advanced. As discussed before, while phenomena help ratify progress, they are also to be ignored for transformational results.

Lakshmi's and Dhanalakshmi's practice did not stop after this. They continued to do mantras for Kali, Kala-Bhairava and Radha-Krishna. Sometimes these were for friends in trouble, sometimes for the general well-being of the world (*loka-kalyanam*) and in general for their own future well-being. They told me about pilgrimages to such places as Varanasi and Brindavan, each time choosing a destination that was related to their mantra. Dhanalaksmi said, "We did Kali-Kalabhairava (-mantras) and went to Kashi, when we did Anjaneya (Hanuman-mantra) we went to Rameshwaram, (we did) Radha, (and went to) Brindavan." Some of the mantras they received were at their own behest, some were given by Siddheswarananda, and some mantras were offered by him to volunteers. Dhanalakshmi spoke about the feeling of love (*prema-tattva*) in the Radha-Krishna mantra that both of them experienced when they visited Brindavan.

> DHANALAKSHMI: Radha-Krishna mantra is sattvic (pure, light) - body feels happy. Krishna is an incarnation of Vishnu whose characteristic quality is love and he is usually depicted with his lover Radha. The love-play of Radha and Krishna is legendary in the location of Brindavan.
>
> LAKSHMI: But if you do Kali-mantra and Kala-Bhairava mantra, it is not like that. They are both – even to look at are ferocious – they are really not ferocious. It is to scare enemies. (They are actually) embodiments of peace. We get courage, we get confidence. Kali and Kala-Bhairava mantra we get josh [vibrance]. When you do the Hanuman-mantra or Vijay-Ganapati mantra, you have no fears.

Lakshmi's narrative also illustrates the crucial role of the guru in mantra-diksha. She was unsuccessful when she did a mantra that had not been given by her current guru and had to change the mantra. Practitioners consider their guru as the person they have access to and who has direct access to deities. These gurus are believed to have succeeded in their sadhana and are now willing to help others make similar progress. Canceling old karmas for future well-being is also a part of the soteriological endeavor, because only when the karmic "account" is nullified, a person is free to leave the cycle of birth and death.

6.7 After Many Lives

If Lakshmi's past lives were troubling, Ramya Yogini's past lives were glorious. In *Mahimānvita Yogi*, a book about Siddheswarananda, Ramya (2014) also describes her own past lives. I translate a few representative lines:

> 5,000 years ago, my name was "Shyama," I was Radha's friend. After Krishna went to Mathura, Radha-devi went away, to do penance (tapas). Then, I've come to know, I did service to Siddha-naga. When that birth was completed, I went by the name of "Hiranya-Devi," I was Siddheswari-devi a family-deity. 3,000 years ago, I was (by the name of) Nagavali, the wife of a Brindavan gentleman called Pravarasena.
>
> After that, by the name of "Anuradha," I was Bhuvaneshwari-devi, a family deity. In the 6th century, I was a virgin-goddess in the Himalayas. At the end of that century, due to the curse of a great sage (Maharshi), I was born in the Buddhist Shakhya-clan. During delivery, (my) mother died because of a tiger; I, who grew up among monkeys, was released from the curse due to a Siddheswara yogi called Padmasambhava. As "Bhemle Sakhyadevi," Padmasambhava recognized my Vajra-varahi-shakti (extraordinary powers). Due to the Vajra-Bhairava sadhanas done by him, I got a body as brilliant as Indra's bow. (67–68)

Ramya's narrative is well within the framework of past-life stories one hears in India, and is no indication of missing modernity—if qualifications in sciences count toward modernity, Ramya is a medical doctor. Further, she told me how she received mantras directly from the deities Kali and Kala-Bhairava.

> RAMYA: In my 16th year, Swamiji [Siddheswarananda] gave me the Kali-mantra. I would sit in the temple in front of the image (*vigraham*) and do japa. One day in the evening, a deity came out of the vigraham and made me hear a mantra.

Ramya waved her hand in the air as she said this, enacting the movement of a form stepping out of the deity image.

> MANI: What did she look like?
>
> RAMYA: Semi-transparent.
>
> MANI: Was it the same mantra as that which you were then doing?
>
> RAMYA: I cannot tell you that.

When an image is consecrated as a deity, that deity resides in the image; the consecration ritual is called *prana-pratishtha*, which means "establishing of life-force." I assumed that the semitransparent figure who stepped out of the image was Goddess Kali. Ramya did not say it was Goddess Kali who gave her the mantra, only that *a deity* came out of the image and did so. Later in the conversation, Ramya told me that not all visitors are deities; often, it is a representative, someone lower in the hierarchy of the world of deities. Thus, an image of a deity may still function as a portal through which deities enter the world of humans. Ramya did not say the figure uttered a mantra. She said "*mantram vinipincindi*," which means "she had me hear a mantra." Although Ramya was forthcoming about the phenomenon, she was secretive about the mantra itself. Practitioners tend not to divulge mantras they are doing, as though doing so would take away some of the power gained from that mantra. In this instance, my probing was poor etiquette, despite the excuse of research. I knew that a practitioner would not divulge a mantra gained after arduous sadhana; on the other hand, if it was meant specially for Ramya's progress in sadhana, it would be of no consequence to anyone else. Ramya had received the Kali-mantra from Siddheswarananda, so I guessed it was the japa she did as she sat in front of the deity image; therefore, the next mantra she received from Goddess Kali was probably not the Kali-mantra.

The second occasion Ramya described followed an identical pattern—she was doing japa in her room when the deity Kala-Bhairava appeared and gave her a mantra.

> RAMYA: In the Chaturmasya Diksha [a religious event] at Shravana Paurnami [a seasonal festival when initiations are done] one early morning, I could see before me, (the deity) Kala-Bhairava. He gave me a mantra. That mantra should not be chanted when you are in the householder life-stage (*grihastha*).

MANI: What did he look like?

RAMYA: Kala-Bhairava is a ferocious form of Shiva. Just as it says in the (hymn) Kala-Bhairava Ashtakam… red hair, red eyes, in a drunken state and dark. But deities can appear in any form they choose.

MANI: Did you know for sure this is Kala-Bhairava?

RAMYA: Yes.

MANI: You just knew it?

RAMYA: Yes.

Ramya only clarified the appearance of the deity in response to my question, but she did not need to rely on appearance to recognize that this was Kala-Bhairava. In interviews, I found that practitioners sometimes expressed doubts whether or not they had really seen a deity, but they never expressed doubts about the identity of that deity. A sense of certainty and of knowledge, understanding or insight seems to be at the heart of the vision, which is a visual form of this insight. At Nachiketa ashram (see Chapter 7), Nachiketananda tried to help me understand such a conviction. He said, when we see a person in a dream, we tend to *know* who it is even if s/he may look like someone else—it is similar with visions in meditation. Thus, the sensing mind can see through false appearances. Recognition implies a prior knowledge of the object, and Ramya's recognition of Kala-Bhairava cannot be explained except perhaps through one of her own narratives about her past-life connections with deities.

Ramya explained that receiving this mantra from Kala-Bhairava was transformative—"I was changed by the mantra"—it was after this that she took sanyasa (ascetic orders). Ramya brought up the issue of credibility on her own:

> After five-six days I went to Swamiji (and said) who will believe this! This is my personal experience, people will say it is hallucination. (People will say) we are doing sadhana for years, and how is it, this young girl says Kala-Bhairava himself came! Swamiji said, you ask Kala-Bhairava that question.
>
> After that Pournami-Diksha [initiation on full-moon day] on the eight day, we did a homa. Everyone was there, Kanta Rao, Poorna Swami … Swamiji suddenly said, look under the fire, Kala-Bhairava wants to give you something. A rudraksha[10] [a rosary bead], it came out of the fire. Caked in mud. Moon-shaped single-faced rudraksha (ekamukhi rudraksha).

A sadhaka and an official, Poorna Swami, confirmed this account with me later. Ramya showed me her gold neck-chain with a large single-faced rudraksha bead pendant. A single-sided rudraksha is said to cultivate a preference for solitude. Ramya said she had told me this story to illustrate how response does come from deities. "If we ask, it reaches them and they react. Especially faster if you are doing their mantra."

After Ramya received the mantra from Kala-Bhairava that early morning, she was restless to report this to Swamiji. In deference to his schedule, she could only speak to him after nine in the morning. Concerned that she might forget the mantra—"after all, it's not as if we have pens and papers under our pillows" she said, smiling—she began to chant it for a couple of hours. When she went to see Siddheswarananda, it was he who asked her first about the episode. By then, she was all set to take ascetic orders—"By then, the choice was made. When the deity himself comes and gives you, what is there to worry about!" I asked her if that was the *niyama* (the discipline to follow when doing that mantra), or had she lost interest in *grihastha* (householder life) after chanting the mantra?[11] Ramya's response was not about making any choices—"I was just like any other 25-year old Brahmin girl. I had no idea this is how I will change. Transformation happened on that day. A change came about. It cannot be described in words." The opposition of "sanyasa" to "grihastha" in this context was a reference to a life of celibacy and renunciation, instead of a regular life of marriage and children.

Ramya's experience of mantras as transformative went along with a sense of responsibility. Like Appaji, Ramya felt that a practitioner needed to be discriminating and not use mantras for destructive purposes—"if one reaches a certain stage, that won't happen." This was also a pragmatic approach, for the deity was ultimately in charge. Ramya shared an anecdote, withholding names, about a mantra-adept who tried to use his powers against another mantra-adept. The deity punished the practitioner by stripping him of all his powers. Whereas Appaji's narratives focused on the mechanics of mantras and his discoveries, Ramya's narratives were about engagement, transformation and relationships with deities. "It's not just the mantra, but the *bhavana* (feeling, intention). We have to think of the bond we want from the deity." The vision of a deity or a fulfilled wish is only a beginning. "Experience is not only about the darshan of deity … when the job is done, there is the realization, the sense of gratitude." Ramya offered an alternative point of view to Appaji's idea about indiscriminate deities—"with mantra-sadhana, one can do anything that is normally impossible, but I will add one clause, i.e., if the deity wishes it." It was not adequate to have an intention, the mantra-practitioner was not in command, he or she was only a supplicant. I shared the example of the Pratyangiras homa Appaji had told me about, where the matter had got out of hand. Shrugging, she said:

> RAMYA: We cannot say how the deity will solve the problem, we cannot ask for specific suggestions. It is Her decision how to protect. We can ask them, we can beg them. So, for example, (Goddess) Pratyangiras. Self protection = destruction of enemies. So if we ask for protection, who knows how She will solve the problem. She protects, She gives wealth, it is unpredictable how She will solve the problem. We can take a problem and put it in front of the deity.

I asked Ramya if deities understood the intentions of mantra-practitioners.

> MANI: Say two people use the same mantra, and they have different purpose, (do) devatas understand?
>
> RAMYA: Yes.
>
> MANI: Then why mantra at all, why not just intention?
>
> RAMYA: Can do, (there's) nothing against it. It is just that mantra is the shortest, easiest, fastest way. Easily possible. If we take the formless it takes time to concentrate, but if a mantra, it is fast, energy. High voltage energy.

Many mantra-practitioners in this research assert that mantras can be substituted by intentions. In particular, Chapter 7 raises this question in the context of those who practice silence instead of mantra, and I discuss this in more depth in the concluding Chapter 8. How does a practitioner know which route to adopt and do all practitioners stand an equal chance? Ramya listed—"Three things, our sadhana, *samskaras* (impressions/habits)[12] of past lives, and *guru-kripa* (the favor of guru) all of these create a relationship with deity." Thus, all practitioners are not equal—"some may see the mantra-deity after a lakh (100,000) of japa, others may get there with only the turning of one bead." Ramya gave the example of Ramakrishna Paramahamsa, who only had to do one mala (rosary), and the deity of that mantra would appear. The concept of transmigration is an integral part of the journey that is mantra sadhana. Some arrive at sadhana in their current life with a long credit earned in previous lives, and some may even have to reverse debts or negative credits from previous lives. After reaching a certain point where results begin to occur, a practitioner's successes came "faster." "After one mantra devata is seen, it's faster, seeing other mantra devatas."

I asked Ramya if it bothered her that mantra helped people intervene with nature and the natural course of things. She could not fathom why anyone would not want to change their situation, if they did not like it? "If Nature is perfect," I began, and she interjected, "I would say balanced, not perfect."

> RAMYA: Mantras are for using, we are not disturbing Nature, what human beings have done to Nature, we are getting it back.

This topic also came up in my discussion with Siddheswarananda. He gave the example of a river—"Don't feel it as a disturbance. It is not a disturbance at all. If a river is flowing will the river feel bad that "hey, he's taken my water!" Not at all. There is shakti in Nature. It is not an interference. Nature seemed inexhaustible, and generous. Ramya told me about a woman who did a mantra-ritual for her daughter who was afflicted with skin disease. She "extracted" the disease into red water colored with auspicious, red *kum-kum*, and was supposed to pour it upon the roots of a tree, i.e., back into Nature. But, this water fell upon her foot, and within days she had the same disease on her foot. In this anecdote, not only did the mantra extract the disease, but the extracted disease had to be redirected into a substance or receptacle that had the power to absorb and nullify it. Since the water fell on the foot, the foot became infected; had it been poured on to the roots of a tree, it could have been absorbed by Nature. Narratives like these in my fieldwork often pushed my credulousness, and I would withhold my reactions and try to think about what the narrative illustrated about mantra.

6.8 Calling Deities

Siddheswaranada spoke in a soft and gentle voice and answered my questions patiently. My main questions were about deities—do they exist, and if they do, where do they live, what do they look like and how did they relate to human beings and the world? Do they exist within us or outside

Fig. 6.3 Swami Siddheswarananda Bharati (Photograph by Mani Rao)

us? There was nothing speculative or hypothetical in the response. Siddheswarananda told me that the gods have *tejas-shariras* (bright bodies, or bodies of light) and that they had shapes similar to us (Fig. 6.3).

> SIDDHESWARANANDA: They are outside, they will come inside if asked. Air is outside, it is also inside. Because it is there, doesn't mean it cannot be here. Deities, they have shapes, they have realms, they have places, living spaces, they come into us sometimes, if sadhakas call. Anyhow, since the human body is just like a deity's body, that there are deities in it is a kind of a truth/reality. But really, they exist, *they are separately there, they exist, with lives, with bodies,* but those bodies, we cannot see, cannot be seen by our physical eyes, only with divine eyes, they are there, they will be there, they will be there in all the realms.

Siddheswarananda used the Telugu/Sanskrit word "*sharira*" for body; this word does not refer to the material body only. An Indian concept is that a human being has many bodies or sheaths (koshas) of which the physical is one. Here, Siddheswarananda is speaking about the bodies of deities, and he notes that they cannot be seen by the naked eye.

He continued, quoting from the Puranas—which are narratives of gods, kings and genealogies dated to the 1st millennium—and listed the various kinds of otherworldly beings.

> It has been stated clearly in the Puranas. The *suvarloka* [heaven]. *They will be there* with bodies made of light. In the region below that there will be vidyavaras, apsarasas, yakshas, rakshasas [different beings] they are all in *bhuvarloka* [middle regions]. We are in the *bhuloka* [earth]. If they are called, if they are called by those capable of calling them, they will come. *It is their will and pleasure.* If they are pleased they can be seen by us. This is a truth. The Greek philosopher Plato said once, there is divine creation in divine realms, this human creation is only an imitation of that. *It is only an imitation.* So, they are there. Looking at those bodies, Brahmadeva [the creator] created these bodies just like that, devatas [deities], anyone at all.

Siddheswarananda quotes from Puranas as well as Plato and intersperses these with his own assertions—"really, they exist," "this is a truth." He said that the deities have human-like forms, as pictured in Indian legends.

> SIDDHESWARANANDA: "Why do you think these bodies are like that, two legs, two hands, they have them like that. Since when do they have that? *From unknown times, unimaginable.* So, each time the creator Brahma "*yathāpūrvam akalpayat*" [imagined/created the way it was before]. *It was like that before, he's doing that* [....]
>
> *This human creation is only an imitation of that.* Among people, people who want to make themselves full of the divine, they imagine/feel the deities within and *they will make it real.*
>
> So. They are there, they will be there, they are in us, if we ask them to come into human beings they will come, if we call them they come. Among people, people who want to make themselves divine, they feel the devatas and "they will make it real." (Fig. 6.4).

When I protested that there were many versions of legends, he told me that all the versions were true, they had simply occurred in different yugas.

If deities are already inside us, why do we need to place them at different locations of our body or bodily space as in the Kalavahana puja at Devipuram? Amritananda had said one had to simply imagine the

Fig. 6.4 Puja to the deity Kala-Bhairava (Photograph by Mani Rao)

syllables (which are also deities) before one could see them, and his disciple Mani Prasanna had iterated the same point.

MANI: I see. Now, when we do nyasa [placement of syllables on the body] that we ca…ll (Siddheswarananda echoes, "yes call") the deities into us… is that kalpana [imagination]?

SIDDHESWARANANDA: Kalpana only. Whatever you consider, whether deity is there or not, at first you don't know. You do the mantra. You try to see the deity. *First you imagine. That imagination becomes true.* (MANI: I see). It is your personal affair. They are doing their own thing. But, you frame a body by your imagination. They will come into that frame, when you prepare. So, if you imagine/create (kalpiste) appropriate situations for them to come, they will come. What "kalpiste" means

> is you do so because of your shakti. And what's the shakti, it's the mantra. *Imagination.* Mantramu, bhavana [Mantra, ideation/feeling]. Mantramu, bhavana. Both these should go together. You should keep doing the mantra. One should *imagine* how the deity is (yatla untundo). Even if you don't imagine, the deity comes, because of the mantra. But if you *imagine* she/it will come a little faster. You prepare a frame.

Siddheswarananda's point stresses imagination and ideation, just like the Devipuram practitioners. The practitioner had to do the mantra with feeling, use her imagination, and sooner or later, the real visionary experience would occur. Was that the only way to have a visionary experience? What about sudden experience of gnosis? I gently broached this matter too.

> MANI: Now, between us and that realm, the mantra, like a bridge, say ...
>
> SIDDHESWARANANDA: yes
>
> MANI: Without that, is there a way to make a connection?
>
> SIDDHESWARANANDA: Yes it is, yes it is," in sadhana, without mantras (mantra-vihina).

Siddheswarananda then talked about how human beings and deities became distanced from each other.

> At the beginning of creation, deities came to earth, they lived here. After some time – they [our ancestors] told (us) in the Puranas – on the banks of the Devika river. After they lived here, some among them felt "let's stay here." (MANI: huh). Felt let's stay here. And at first there were contacts between these and those above. Those [deities] used to come and go, these [i.e., deity-friends of deities] used to go, but after staying here for a long time, in their descendants, the earth's atomic particles got into their bodies and they could not go up. When they called, they would come. After some time, some ages, when *thousands of years, lakhs of years* passed, them coming when these people called stopped.
>
> Now some of those with shakti among them said, *Ayya* [Sir], you're not coming when we call, before when we said "come Mahendra" you would come, now you're not, humans need you, our shakti has become weakened (MANI: I see), so how will you come fast? Then, when they said that, (they said) we'll give you mantra, if you do that mantra, we will come.
>
> All the mantras – they have been given by the gods to human beings. Mantras— they are not created by people.

Siddheswarananda used the word "up" to indicate the realms of the deities—whether this was sky, heaven or simply a better place; according to him, it had been lost to human beings. Luckily, there was mantra.

* * *

The narratives of this chapter illustrate how mantras are instrumental, and used by practitioners to connect with deities to achieve some goal. Mantra-sadhana calls for dedication, stamina and endurance. Even though devotion is evident in the discussions on Radha-mantra and Hanuman, mantra-sadhana here seems arduous rather than joyous. Practitioners are willing to wait for years, even without the motivation of extraordinary experiences, to see the results of their endeavors—Vasudevananda waits for ten years, "stockpiling" his mantra. The astounding numbers quoted by practitioners represent the inordinate effort they have put into mantra-practice.[13] These numbers are the equivalent of investments, and the results are as if earnings, or a return on investment.[14] The concept of mutual exchange is common in Indian religious practices, especially in vows and pilgrimages where the suffering of the devotee or pilgrim builds religious merit. This is not a debt, but a forward payment, and it tends to go along with an expectation. Narratives of feats of mantra-repetitions suggest that the goal is extraordinary, and it is really the practitioner who takes the credit for achieving results, even though they may say that it is the deity who does the favor. After practitioners gain experience and become seasoned seers, they have access to deities and begin to play the role of mediator, helping other practitioners. Here too, some practitioners seem to in a position of power, as though the deities have no choice but to respond to mantras—Appaji was more sensitive to questions of risk and responsibility because he placed the onus of achievement upon himself. By contrast, Vasudevananda and Ramya were more relaxed because deities decided the outcomes.

Mantras are considered instruments for both good and evil purposes. The goals of practitioners are varied—Lakshmi wants her pension, but Potturi wants nothing by way of material benefits. Transformation occurs as a direct outcome of mantra-practice for Ramya and Potturi. Vasudevananda and Appaji use their expertise and access to deities to help others. All the practitioners regarded mantras, and mantras in rituals, like surgical weapons to combat diseases—Appaji used the term "surgery," Vasudevananda spoke about taking out poison with the mantras, and Ramya's anecdote of the skin disease also seemed to excise the diseased skin with mantra-empowered water. Practitioners were conscientious about not misusing mantras, but the very tenor of Siddheswarananda's literature made it clear that there was scope to put mantras to destructive use.

This was not an environment where mantra-sadhana was just done by rote; there was a methodology of trial and error, and a process of discovery. Siddheswarananda had refrained from telling Appaji the identity of the Nagastra-mantra. He did not give Lakshmi answers to her questions; instead, he told her to persist with her sadhana and she would be able to see her past lives "like a movie reel." When full-time disciple (and disciple across lives), Ramya, asked how she could prove she had been visited, Siddheswarananda redirected her to Kala-Bhairava, and told her to ask him directly. Each one of the practitioners was a seer in his or her own right, working with an experienced seer-guru.

Notes

1. An auto-rickshaw is a commercial three-wheeler vehicle, an inexpensive mode of transportation in India compared to taxis.
2. "Dasha-mahavidyas" are ten deities who are forms of Goddess Shakti. They are Kali, Tara, Tripura Sundari, Bhuvaneshvari, Bhairavi, Chinnamasta, Dhumavati, Bagalamukhi, Matangi and Kamala.
3. In Sanskrit and Telugu, *gupta* (hidden) and guha (cave) are both derived from the verbal root "guḥ."
4. For a book about yoga written and published in 2013, a Sanskrit scholar was hired to write sutras (aphorisms) in Sanskrit in order to give a semblance of authenticity to the work.
5. Hanuman is the son of Anjana and Vayu (God of Wind). In the Ramayana, he plays a key role by helping Rama cross the ocean to rescue his wife Sita, who has been kidnaped by Ravana. Hanuman's devotion to Rama and Sita is legendary.
6. "Nakshatra" is a term from "jyotish (Indian astrology)" referring to the "lunar mansion" in the sky through which the moon passes at the precise moment of birth. A lunar mansion is one of many divisions of the sky through which the moon travels; each mansion is identified by a prominent star. This is similar to the concept of zodiac signs which are based on the apparent path of the sun through the sky in relation to the constellations. Nakshatra helps calculate the positions of the planets at that particular time.

7. Using a refrain, "Oh Ramachandra!" each line enumerates a gift that Ramdas has given Rama. The first line: I gifted you a good-looking, glittering plume with which you proudly go about. Do you think you inherited all this treasure? The last line: Did you inherit all this treasure? Did your father, King Dasaratha, gift you all these ornaments? Or, did your father-in-law, King Janaka, send them to you, Oh Ramachandra?
8. Ghantakarn is depicted as Vishnu's gatekeeper at the Badrinath temple in the Himalayas. Searching for a single textual source more valid than others proves futile, as there are many sources and versions of this story. One source is the Harivamsha, a supplement to the Mahabharata. Here is the version Lakshmi told me: Ghantakarna's devotion to Vishnu was so intense, he could not tolerate it when other people remembered Shiva and attached bells to his ears so that he would not hear Shiva's name. Ghantakarna also refused to worship Rama, and this was unreasonable, for Rama is actually Vishnu's incarnation. The next big event in Ghantakarna's story is a battle with Rama's devotee, Hanuman; they fought long and hard with no outcome. Vishnu personally visited when they were locked in battle; he explained to Hanuman that Ghantakarna was his devotee, and explained to Ghantakarna that Rama was really his own incarnation. At the end, Ghantakarna acknowledged Hanuman's superiority and became his devotee.
9. This narrative is widely reported in Telugu publications, in hagiographies about Mounaswami (the first pontiff of the Peetham). It is also on the official Siddheswari Peetham website siddheswaripeetham.org: "Sri Sidhi Ganapathy known as Nadi Ganapathy," accessed 3 May 2018.
10. Seeds of the Rudraksha tree (*Elaeocarpus ganitrus*) are used in rosaries. The most popular rudraksha is the five-sided panchamukhi.
11. To say "sanyasa" and "grihastha" is often a euphemism for a celibate and non-celibate life.
12. This is a part of the concept of transmigration. It is believed that people retain the impressions from their experiences of one lifetime and carry them over into their next life. These impressions may be manifest as tendencies or characteristics of their personality.
13. Not all practitioners approve of such feats—Swami Madhavananda at Thogutta (see Chapter 7) called such practitioners "leaf-counters."
14. Such a practice is common in Hindu and other religious traditions—the tougher the pilgrimage, the more desirable the journey and the more rewarding the outcome. The concept of mutual exchange is also in vedic yajnas, where the gods are fed and in return they look after the order (*ṛta*) of things in the world. The concept of dāna (charity) in exchange for religious merit is prevalent in many religious traditions; the Christian practice of penitence and indulgence is also comparable.

References

Ramya Yogini. 2014. *Mahimānvita Yogi—Swami Siddhesvarananda Bharati* [A Yogi Full of Miracles]. Guntur: Svayam Siddha Kali Pitham.
Siddheswaranada Bharati, Swami. 2000. *Mana Samasyalu Mantra Sādhanalu* [Mantra Sadhanas for Our Problems]. Visakhapatnam: Lalita Peetham.
———. 2013. *Tantrika Prapancamu* [World of Tantra]. Visakhapatnam: Lalita Peetham.
———. n.d. *Naga-Sadhana* [Snake-Sadhana]. Visakhapatnam: Lalita Peetham.
Vadlamudi, Venkateswara Rao. [1993] 2013. *Śrī Lalitā Nāmārtha Maṇjūṣa* [Treasury of Meanings of the Names of Lalita]. Vijayawada: Metro Printers.

CHAPTER 7

"I Am in Mantra, Mantra Is in Me": Nachiketa Tapovan, Kodgal

7.1 The Ashram at Nachiketa

Eighty kilometers to the south of Hyderabad on the highway after the Balanagar crossroads, stay peeled to the left side of the road. Take care not to miss a milestone on the roadside with blurry lettering: "Rangareddyguda." Turn left at once into a narrow dirt road and past the railway crossing and then keep going ten, or maybe fifteen, or maybe twenty kilometers past some fields and Banjara[1] villages of Potlapalli, Kallepalli and Thirumalgerry. Then ask anyone, "*ashram*?" Follow directions and you will see it soon enough—a red-walled boundary and large iron gates that are shut (Fig. 7.1). If you have a phone number, you can get someone to open the gate for you. On forty-five acres of land here, there is an ashram that does not charge visitors to stay, a large temple with no set schedule, and a primary school with free education. The school is called "Veda Vyasa Vidyalaya," after Vyasa, the revered seer of Hindu tradition accredited with the compilation of vedas and the authorship of the epic, Mahabharata. The main guru here is a maverick sanyasi, Swami Nachiketananda Puri, who tries to convince his followers that they are their own gurus (Fig. 7.2).

After some preliminary chit-chat, Nachiketananda took me to "Ma Yoga Shakti Pitham," a sprawling temple made of a reddish stone. There was no one there except three kids at play, and who ran toward us, screaming "*OṂ Namaḥ Śivāya*!!!," and hurled themselves on to Nachiketananda with the liberty of familiarity.

M. Rao, *Living Mantra*, Contemporary Anthropology of Religion,
https://doi.org/10.1007/978-3-319-96391-4_7

Fig. 7.1 Nachiketa Tapovan ashram (Photograph by Mani Rao)

Fig. 7.2 Swami Nachiketananda Puri (Photograph by Mani Rao)

I learned that the temple was inspired by a story about how Swami Vivekananda brought together concepts of a church and a temple for the Ramakrishna Mission Belur Math. Ramakrishna Paramahamsa (1836–1886) was a Bengali tantric saint reputed for his devotion to Goddess Kali, and his disciple Vivekananda (1863–1902) is credited with promoting Indian spirituality internationally. These role models set up a syncretistic framework—a mixture of bhakti, yoga and advaita Vedanta (non-dualism) that one finds in pan-Indian Hinduism.

On the temple walls, there were reliefs of *yogasanas* (codified yoga postures), mudras (codified hand gestures), a japamala, Ardhanarishwara (half male and half female, a composite form of Shiva and Parvati) and sections from the Sriyantra. Circumambulating the main temple on the outer platform, we crossed small temples of a strange assortment of deities set into turnings and corners. Nachiketananda explained that these deities had been chosen for their connection to the *chakras* (the energy centers) of the body—the deity Ganesha empowers the *Muladhara* chakra, the deity Rudra empowers the *Manipura* chakra, the deity Balaji the *Swadhisthana* chakra and the deity Krishna, the *Anahata* chakra. The three main temples inside are also a part of this chakra progression—Ramakrishna, Kali and Shiva relate to the *Vishuddha* chakra, *Ajna* chakra and the *Sahasrara* chakra, respectively. Yoga treatises explain these as the seven energy centers which are activated as the *Kundalini* energy rises. Worshiping these particular deities, therefore, is a way to systematically direct attention to one's own energy centers.

When we approached the Ramakrishna temple, Nachiketananda asked if I was willing to sit in the Ramakrishna temple to meditate, as we could continue our meeting after that. Even as I found it an odd request, I thought he must have his reasons and agreed. He asked me to close my eyes; as he muttered a Kali-mantra, I felt the sensation of his hand over my head. Nachiketananda's low, intense voice reverberated in the empty hall. He said I could stay inside the temple as long as I wished, asked me to keep my eyes open, and closed the heavy, temple door behind me. My conversation with Nachiketananda later that day was just as off the grid as the ashram space; he disrupted the very definition of a mantra. We spoke in English:

> NACHIKETANANDA: Any syllable, any letter, you take, it's a mantra. The sound is mantra. It is through my experience, what I am speaking. Anything is. Even, you frame a very big sentence, it's (a) mantra. You

don't have anything to contemplate, it's still a mantra. So, it is not something particularly, when like it is written in the shastras so and so it is called as mantra. There is nothing like that. So mantra could be anything. Even just gazing at something. Is the process of that mantra. So something happens. That is mantra.

MANI: So the function of mantra is…"something happens"?

NACHIKETANANDA: Yeah, it takes you from one shore to other.

MANI: I see?

NACHIKETANANDA: It is like a vehicle. Mantra is a vehicle. See, you came all the way from Hyderabad in a car. That's a mantra.

MANI: Wouldn't you call that a "yantra" (device)?

NACHIKETANANDA: There is in Mahabharata somewhere…"There is not a single root which cannot be used as medicine. Similarly there is no syllable which cannot be used as a mantra." (*He quoted this in Sanskrit*).[2]

MANI: Then, why can't a Bollywood song be a mantra?

NACHIKETANANDA: Who said not?

MANI: Can it be?

NACHIKETANANDA: Yes, it is!

At the time, I was disappointed by Nachiketananda's stance on mantra. Perhaps sensing my response, Nachiketananda urged me to meet his disciple, "Mataji," who, he said, was the person to speak with about mantra. A few weeks later, I met Mataji Paramahamsa Swami Sivananda Puri at the founder and trustee Vasundhara Reddy's home in Hyderabad.

7.2 Ocean of Mantra

Nothing like my imagination of a motherly or elderly Mataji (mother), the sprightly, and even impish, 25-year-old Sivananda (Fig. 7.3) had a lot to say about mantras—mantras were her *raison d'être*. She was ten years old when she received her first mantra, the Panchakshari (five-syllabled mantra *OṂ Namaḥ Śivāya*), from a wandering *sadhu* (ascetic). In her late teen years, Sivananda became the disciple of Nachiketananda, who introduced her to *kriyas* (yogic practices), but it was japa that

Fig. 7.3 Swami Sivananda Puri, Navaratri 2014 (Photograph by Mani Rao)

engaged her fully. During mantra-japa, she would often slip into the state of samadhi sometimes for twelve hours at a stretch. I learned later from Vasundhara that Sivananda's meditative states and some attendant phenomena created both consternation and concern in their group; Sivananda's had also been the subject of cognitive research at S-VYASA university in Bangalore. Our conversation progressed fast; within the first ten minutes, she told me she was receiving mantras from *siddhas* (celestials) who visited her. We spoke in English and Telugu.

SIVANANDA: It was so intense, the japa, though I did the yogic practices, I used to really listen to the celestial sounds. It was in my right ear, it used to go on all night sometimes. Such beautiful mantras. It was like no one can chant. No one can chant. So my faith in mantra was established. Now I am in mantra and mantra is in me.

I focused on what I could probe further. What was the language of the mantras? "They would all be in Sanskrit," she said. What kind of mantras were they? "Vedic mantras, but in a different tone (*svara*) altogether." Sivananda was referring to the *udatta* (rising), *anudatta* (falling) and *svarita* (mixed) tones integral to vedic mantras; the mantras she heard were vedic but not in vedic svaras.

SIVANANDA: Sometimes in a female voice, male voice. Sometimes the voice was so different and I used to be so excited and I used to get up in the night and I used to start my sadhana. I had such beautiful visions about mantra. and now also…

MANI: Visions about mantras… meaning?

SIVANANDA: Yeah, you can even see mantras. Oh.. it expresses in a different way to each individual. It is not a rule that everybody should hear it, everybody should see it.

MANI: So you think mantras are .. somewhere else.. which is .. also here?

SIVANANDA: No, I felt they are in the universe, They are in the cosmos, I myself got tuned to it. And I reached to the frequency where it was there. And I just was like… that's what now also.. it… I find that… no words to express mantra. It is my life. That's how I define it.

Sivananda said she was listening to celestial sounds "almost regularly, every day, whole night"—these were mantras as well as music.

SIVANANDA: Yeah Music. Different musics. Sometimes I used to hear drums, veena [a stringed instrument]— it is not the veena that I hear usually, sometimes I hear Sanskrit mantras, chanting and chanting…I never found it in any texts or Upanishads also, such a beautiful.. someone is chanting.

Together with hearing these sounds, she also had dreams where she was taught mantras and mudras by siddhas.

SIVANANDA: Then I have received so many mantras in my dreams. And I started doing. Then I also saw siddhas in my dreams. They would teach me different mudras and initiating me different mantras. Suppose I would practice one mantra, clearly what I have to do and not do, how.... They would tell me how to do..

MANI: What would they look like?

SIVANANDA: Initially they would come in the human form, sometimes, like a light, sometimes like transparent bodies, sometimes, like half the body, it was all different.

MANI: So they also have access to the mantras and ... they are using it...?

SIVANANDA: In fact they are always chanting mantras. And they are always looking for right disciple whom they would initiate. I was initiated by different sadhus in my dream. So I was initiated into one mantra and I was asked to practice it for 21 days and after 21 days another mantra would be ready for me to practice. So it is a sequence of mantras.

Sivananda said that she was given different mantras each time, and they could be "sometimes three words, one word, one sound, yeah sometimes one sound, two, sometimes three, four, five, sometimes *Ashtakshari* (eight-syllable mantra, *OṂ Namo Narayaṇāya*)." She then talked about the set of rituals she was engaged in, and I asked from where she got the procedures. She replied, "I don't know. I didn't read any shastras [religious books]." Sivananda's comment about not reading shastras was said simply, without pride or apology. I guessed she had read popular spiritual literature, for she used such terms as "cosmos" and "celestial sounds" in conversation, but her responses were based on her own experience. Why did a mantra need to be done hundreds of thousands of times? Why did her visitors care if she had done her mantras or not? What was the relationship between mudras and mantras? What was her motivation for japa? What did she mean by "mantra is in me, I am in mantra"? Was this just an expressive way of saying she was immersed in mantra-sadhana? I had many questions, and when she warmly invited me back to Nachiketa ashram for Navaratri, I accepted.

7.3 Openness to the Divine

Navaratri, which means "nine nights," is a pan-Indian festival dedicated to Goddess Shakti who has a different form and name on each of these nights (and days). The nine goddesses, configured differently in different regions and traditions in India, are Siddhidatri, Shailaputri, Brahmacharini, Chandraghanta, Kushmanda, Skandamata, Katyayini,

Kalaratri and Maha-Gauri. Each day is also associated with specific colors—people may follow these themes for the clothes they wear on those days, or how they dress the Goddess. Rituals for these nine nights and days are guided by the astrological calendar (*panchanga*) which is based on the movement and favorable positions of the stars and planets. Shailaputri's day has *Ghatasthapana* which establishes the pot that *is* the Goddess, Katyayini's day has the Sarasvati puja, and the eight day (*ashtami*) has the Ayudha-puja which is a ritual honoring instruments from tools to vehicles. At Nachiketa, everyone waited eagerly in the mornings for the temple doors to open, revealing the appearance of the Goddess on that day. I found a Telugu brochure in the shelves of the backroom of the temple which was a useful guide to the forms and personalities of the goddesses. The goddesses have distinct forms—Shailaputri rides a cow, carries a trident in the right hand and a lotus in the left hand; Chandraghanta rides a tiger, has ten arms and carries a sword, trident, mace, pot, lotus and bow. The details were either gleaned from, or corresponded to, the Sanskrit hymn called Navadurga Stotram.

Every evening at the yajna-shala, there was a homa led by Sivananda. She used different mantras on each day of the homa, and sometimes, would repeat lines without a fixed pattern. She seemed to have some counting scheme, for she used a little rosary in her left hand. Her rendition of the Kali-mantra was particularly piercing. As she chanted, the syllable "*krīṃ*," her voice was sharp, audible over and above the group. All of us chanted in pace with her, and when she stopped, we quickly stopped too. "*Krīṃ svāha - krīṃ svāha - krīṃ svāha - krīṃ-svāha krīṃ-svāha krīṃ-svāha krīṃ-svāha krīṃsvāha krīṃsvāha*"—it went on like this, and with each "*svāha*" the people closest to the fire offered the kindling dust (*samidha*) to fire-deity Agni.

During homa on the day of Goddess Chandraghanta, a teenage girl called Anu began to breathe heavily, rocking her body. Those who sat next to Anu moved, clearing space for her. When the very last movement of *krīṃ* began, she lay back and began to do a series of mudras. Anu's movements were graceful, slow and smooth, like a dance. Vasundhara walked across to the opposite side and began to take photographs. Occasionally, some attendees turned their heads to watch Anu; others carried on as before, chanting along with Sivananda, and making offerings to Agni with each *svāha*. My phone camera did not capture very much in the late evening light, so I put it away and watched. After homa, Sivananda continued to sit, eyes shut, hands in the *chin* mudra, where the tips of the thumb and forefinger touch, expressing union with the divine. The whites of her eyes began to show. There was pin-drop silence in the yajna-shala. Anu continued to do mudras. Sivananda's face grew darker. As the fire began to subside, someone added kindling, and Agni lingered.

Some days later, when we were in Hyderabad, I asked Sivananda, "Is Anu aware?" She said, "No, she doesn't know what she is doing, you can tell, her eyeballs are completely still." The other person who was present, Mr. Reddy, said, "It must be *samskaras* (past-life impressions), maybe she goes into a trance and then the past-life memory surfaces." I looked toward Sivananda. She disagreed, "No, she is responding to the mantras, she is so accepting, it is beautiful." Reviewing the video of the incident later, I noticed that Anu's gestures were slower than the mantras, but kept time with their punctuations. I asked Sivananda if she knew which mudra was in response to which mantra. She nodded.

I met Anu some weeks later for an interview. Did she know what she was doing? Anu responded, clearly: "*Yes.*" She said she did not know if she was *conscious* but she knew she was doing mudras. Sometimes she could hear what was happening in the environment. No, she was not asleep. No, this was not the first time. The first time she began to do mudras was at Navaratri homa in 2013. She was in meditation during the homa and as she continued to sit after the homa, her hands started moving on their own, doing mudras. She had meditated since she was very young. "I know what I am doing. I do new ones each time. I don't know why I do them. They [hands] move without my thinking." I asked if she had tried to stop them. Anu said, "No." I then tried to discuss the mudras. She said she did not know what mudras she was doing, and that Sivananda had told her they were the mudras done by Ramakrishna.

Can we classify Anu's state during the homa as "possession"? Janice Boddy (1994) provides a broad definition: "an integration of spirit and matter, force, or power and corporeal reality, in a cosmos where the boundaries between an individual and her environment are acknowledged to be permeable, flexibly drawn, or at least, negotiable" (407). In her anthropology of Tamil rituals, Isabelle Nabokov (2000) concludes that the personality of a possessed ritualist is ruptured, and permanently changed. But Sivananda spoke about Anu's state as a healthy, positive response to mantra. There was no hint of a possession by some other entity; the mudras simply expressed Anu's personality favorably. Moreover, Anu did not disclaim responsibility—"I know what *I* am doing." Frederick M. Smith's *Self-Possessed* (2006) helps understand Anu's collected response. Discussing possession in tantra, Smith includes devotional states in his study and illustrates how *avesha* which is possession or entry becomes connected to *bhava*, an emotional expression of intensity and longing described by bhakti poets (355). He also differentiates between bhava and avesha:

> The difference between āveśa and bhāva seems to be that āveśa is a state of "open" absorption, in that the elements of the experience as well as the identity of the experiencer can shift in different directions, while bhāva denotes a specific experiential state in which the identity of the experiencer is not necessarily threatened. (355)

Smith's broader proposal in the book is that the very notion of the self in South Asia comes with the idea of porosity and permeability. Anu's state during homa fits Smith's description of bhava. We do know that bhakti is on Anu's mind, for she attributes her response to her *deep feeling* for Ramakrishna, and Sivananda had *endorsed* this connection by telling her that these were the same mudras done by Ramakrishna. Researching this further, I found in the public domain, photographs of Ramakrishna's spontaneous mudras (see Fig. 7.4).

What interpretation might Anu have of the phenomenon? I probed gently—did Anu know why this might be happening? Perhaps I was looking for such emic explanations as past life; however, Anu said she had no idea and had already said she did not know if she was "conscious." Anu would have been exposed to such basic terminology by exposure to the talks of Nachiketananda, who often advised practitioners how to bridge the conscious and unconscious. A variant of Pranayama breathing taught at Nachiketa is called "Nachiketa Chaitanya Kriya." Nachiketananda tells practitioners that this will wake the body and mind, but also help link the conscious and subconscious parts of the mind. If this is practiced at night before going to sleep, he says, one stays aware of realizations that one has in the dream-state.

There are, of course, a number of ways to explain the phenomenon. A psychoanalytic interpretation would attribute it to some repression surfacing under pressure. A cultural anthropology may find in this a case of cultural cultivation and nurturance. While these explanations would not be invalid, they would not help understand why Anu performed or chose to perform mudras, and how the mudras matched the mantras. Moreover, Anu only did the mudras when Sivananda did homa. She told me that she did not close her eyes in school group meditations as she

Fig. 7.4 "Ramakrishna at Studio"[3]

was scared this would happen again, and others would think badly of her. This, I thought, was evidence of authenticity; it implied that she doubted if she was in control, or/and that she did not feel safe enough to slip into a mudra-state in her school environment.

Mudras have a long tradition of denotative meanings and prescriptive usages in the Indian tradition, and in Hindu rituals.[4] One of the most visible mudras in Indian culture is that of folded hands, which accompanies greetings. Some mudras popular in iconography of deities and sages are the *abhaya* mudra (conferring fearlessness) and the *varada* mudra (conferring boons). Explaining the significance of mudras to tantric rituals, André Padoux (2011) provides a definition from the Mahanayaprakasha—"[mudras] *make known* the nature of reality" (67).[5] Here, mudra is understood ontologically—a deity with the power and inclination to protect *expresses* this inclination with the abhaya mudra, and this inspires fearlessness in those who approach the deity who has that mudra. By "essential nature" is meant the natural physical expression. A simpler way to understand this concept is to think of closed-eyelids as the mudra of a sleep state. *Yoginihridaya* (YH) 1.57–71, translated by Padoux (2013), describes how the divine energy takes the form of nine mudras during the process of creation. Correspondences between mudras and mantras, mudras and deities, and mudras and chakras are codified in various manuals of tantra.

A compendium of mantras called *Mantramahodadhi* (Caturvedi 1981) which means the great ocean of mantras, and which I found at the homes of many practitioners in Hindi and Telugu translations, explains the term "mudra" as derived from the verbal root "*mud*"—to rejoice—because the practitioner who does mudras makes the gods happy and is released from sin (23). Mudras are done in rituals because the natural is considered a link between the physiological and psychological—one leads to the other. Just as an emotion, thought or psychological state is believed to be naturally expressed in a mudra, doing the mudra is believed to lead to that psychological or emotional state.

According to Sivananda, Anu was responding to the mantras; but Anu believed it was a connection to Ramakrishna—it is possible one of them knows better and it is possible that both are correct, especially if Ramakrishna was also responding to mantras when he did those mudras. It is clear that Anu *likes* herself in the state in which she does mudras as she does not try to stop herself, and we do not know if she can stop herself if she wishes to. Anu's fear of meditating in other spaces tells us that she is not, or not entirely, in control of her response. Why does she only do mudras during homa? There could be two reasons for a specific link to the occasion of the homa. A homa is known among practitioners to be an occasion when deities are invited, and present. It would be reasonable to assume that Anu's mudras are not, or not only, for the people at the homa, but for the deities present. Such a speculation makes sense of why this phenomenon only occurs during homa. In this explanation, Anu's performance becomes her paean to the divine. Like a poem, it is intimate, but it also presents such intimacy to the public eye for appreciation, empathy and to underline a shared life. It would also be a little embarrassing for her with her cohorts, like a confidential communication found later to have been actually in full public view. The second reason could be Sivananda's presence during homa. When Sivananda is center stage in samadhi during homa, Anu stays with her, although on the ancillary stage. If Sivananda was in a state of bhava in connection to Goddess Kali, it would be a well-matched response for Anu to express the bhava of the Kali-devotee, Ramakrishna. Anu's response illustrates the inexplicable power of any of a range of factors: guru, deity, homa, mantras, the sacred location and even the festive occasion. The artistry of the response is to Anu's credit, and gives her a special status. As a person who can respond to the occasion by expressing herself so elegantly, Anu enjoys the favor of, as well as is open to, the divine. Such an understanding would accommodate and appreciate why Anu is eager to own the identity of the state in which she does mudras automatically.

7.4 Repetition of Mantra

I too had a mantra that Navaratri—the Durga-mantra, "*Dum Durgāyai Namaḥ*." After some days of doing this mantra, I asked if I could change to a Kali-mantra. Sivananda said, "no, it must come naturally." "Natural" and "spontaneous" are also ideals in the middle of all the discipline of sadhana. I understood this as referring to transformation—if a mantra had its effect (physiological, psychological) then the practitioner would be ready for another mantra/deity. Everyone who was at Nachiketa ashram during Navaratri was engaged in sadhana. Typically, this would involve the continuous repetition of mantra and participation in the daily pujas. When there was no group activity, practitioners would disperse to different parts of the ashram to do their sadhana, sometimes for hours—under a tree, inside the temple, or in their own rooms. While their posture (if they sat in public view) seemed like meditation, that was not the term at Nachiketa to describe what they were doing. Sivananda did not use the term "meditate"—she said, "If anyone says they are doing meditation, I don't believe it … meditation is spontaneous (but), japa we can do." Our questions sometimes took on the form of a dialog; I was looking for answers, and she was probably checking to see if I knew the answers.

MANI: How much japa is needed a day?

SIVANANDA: If you're able to do ten minutes of japa seriously, that's enough.

MANI: Why do I have to do japa with a mala [rosary]?

SIVANANDA: Because that's when you understand about the mind. Let me tell you, if you want to achieve success in japa, mind is the tool.

SIVANANDA: Focusing on breath and doing japa – what is the difference?

MANI: With breath I'm aware of my body. With japa I'm in the mind. (*Sivananda nodded*).

MANI: How does japa bring on bhava?

SIVANANDA: The moment you say Krishna, all the lila [divine play] of Krishna is right in front of you. Japa is like an ocean.

The idea that the name of an object represents it is rudimentary; but, in Sanskrit, the noun "*naman* (name)" is related to the verbal root of "*man*" which means "to think," "remember," "believe." S. K. Ramachandar Rao ([1991] 2008) in *Lalita Kosha*—a compendium of Goddess hymns with a commentary that I found many practitioners referring to—has a clear explanation of how "name" connects with the object:

> Nāman" in Sanskrit is derived from the root "mnā" meaning that which serves the purpose of repeated employment (abhyāse); mnāyate abhyāsyate yat tat nāmaḥ. It is commonly used as a designation (abhidhāna), a denotation (ākhya), an adoration (sambhāvanā), and invitation (āhva), a description (lakshaṇa), or a symbol (saṁjñā). There is a secondary meaning which signifies mind's inclination towards an object (namayati, namyate anena vā); the mind bends towards what the name points to. As a devotional device, the name reveals the deity, the aspects of the deity and the relevance of the deity to the devotee. (26–27)

Names are not only representative, but also descriptive—they function as adjectives even though they are nouns. The name of the deity is associated with the primary characteristics of that deity, and events in the life of that deity add to names to the deity. When Kali vanquishes the demons Chunda and Munda, she acquires the name "Chamundi," and to address and invoke her by this name means invoking that particular warring Goddess. It is also why, when sadhakas become seers, their names are changed—it is not only to signify a change of status, it is because *they* have changed irreversibly. Thus, Prahlada Sastry's name was changed to Amritanandanatha Saraswati, Prasadarao Kulapati's to Siddheswarananda Bharati, Viswadeep's to Nachiketananda Puri, and Bhavani's to Sivananda Puri. Further, names are considered existential links to objects. Thus, when names are given to new-born babies as per Indian astrology (*jyotish*), they are selected for the syllables they contain which help balance the negative effects of the particular combination of constellations associated with the time of birth. Sometimes, misfortunes are remedied by changing the name. Repeating a deity's name does not require the knowledge of Sanskrit. In fact, there is the implication that the simplicity of repeating a name belongs to a decadent era; at the same time, such minimal requirements are appreciated for the egalitarianism implied. Moreover, the ease of repeating a name-mantra in heartfelt devotion is contrasted to elite scholasticism. In the words of Guntur's Vidyasagar Sarma, a scholar and a follower of Siddheswarananda:

> Mantras are anantam [without end]. Every letter is a mantra. What is the Dattatreya bija, it is 'Da.' What is the Durga bija, it is 'Du.' That is also a maha-mantra. You don't have to struggle hard, in Kali Yuga, just remembering the name (is adequate). Hare-rama hare-ram -rama-rama-hare-hare, that is a maha-mantra. Durgadurgadurgadurga, that is a maha-mantra. What's not a mantra?

7.5 Transported by Sound

Sivananda regards mantras ontological like in early Indian thought—mantras are sounds available in the universe and we simply access them. She was also insistent about the primacy of sound over visual form: "The source of everything is sound. Without sound no form takes place." In one of our conversations, I complained that I was only seeing Indian gods in my sadhana, but no Greek gods, and wondered why that was so, considering I was equally literate in Greek as in Indian mythology? Sivananda seemed very amused; she laughed, and then responded, attributing it to the mantras.

> The god also is created by the sound. I have SEEN like that, through my eyes, when I am chanting certain mantra, how it is taking first a gross body, gross level, it's forming some circles and triangles and all, and then it is turning into a particular form of... let's say I am chanting Panchakshari. [....] So it is just, the sound is just transforming AS a Shiva. And when I am chanting a Devi, Kali-mantra, or any mantra, it is just y'know, the form goes so beautifu...
>
> I - first when I discovered this I was very fascinated. I said how come it happens like that. So I wanted to test myself. So I sat, you know, nights I would sit. Now also I enjoy nights you know because no one will be there. And I see how it happens...

Sivananda's experience of mantra-sound is similar to that of other practitioners who reported deities as sound forms; but different in that she spoke about "catching" the particular frequency of mantra.

> SIVANANDA: See, my voice is so gentle. But when I chant mantra, without my notice I understand there's something is happening to me. What happens I do not know. I catch certain frequency. I just wanted to tell, that mantra, when we chant, it has certain frequency. And if we can catch to that certain frequency, just you are in that mantra. That frequency is so wonderful if you can catch. That's it, if you can tap that …

Having heard Sivananda chant during homa, I understood what she meant by "certain frequency." At the time, I also thought it a part of her performative skill, an enacted utterance rather than something that happened involuntarily.

> MANI: Do you think that is related to performance?
>
> SIVANANDA: No, it's not related to performance. Many people think that it is related to performance … Just start that frequency and everything changes. The tone changes, that outer consciousness which is there, that completely .. you are a little aware of.. maybe you are aware of 5%. If you keep chanting even that reduces, and what happens is that mantra gets stopped. Suddenly. You are, it is.. you are going to that frequency, you are in that frequency. When you are settled there then everything drops. Even the loud voice, whatever you are chanting, suddenly it stops. And you are in it. You catch up to that frequency so quickly, just, you are established in it. So this happens through loud japa.

I asked if this discovery of the frequency of a mantra only occurred during loud repetition. Sivananda replied that it also occurred during silent japa.

> SIVANANDA: Aaan no, it occurs when you say it silently also. When you say it loudly, the nervous system gets so vibrant, so activated, and then when you say mentally, along with nervous system, there is a smooth, it is smooth activation, and then you switch on to different planes.

Sivananda explained at length about losing body consciousness and then being transported on to other planes. I could understand the first part, for that also occurs with engaged and focused activity, but not the latter—what did she mean by "different planes"? *Where* was one transported to? Sivananda described an episode when she had traveled somewhere with others at Nachiketa and visited a temple. They had not eaten for hours and were hungry; when she sat down in sadhana, she forgot her body—hours passed by and she had had no hunger. She said, "once you go to the *anandamaya kosha* (bliss-filled sheath), it is another world out there. There is yet another world beyond that too, void." In Indian thought, the body is regarded a conglomerate of sheaths or containers, of which the physical body is only one. The physical body is called *Annamaya-kosha* (food-filled sheath) because it is nourished and sustained by food. The next sheath is the *Pranamaya-kosha* (breath-filled sheath); this is the sheath where the vital life force circulates. *Prana* means breath *and* something that animates the breath, of which the physical part is air; chakra activity is located at seven spots along this sheath, and that is why *pranayama* is an important part of yoga. The next sheath is the *Manomaya kosha* (mind-filled sheath) and this is also the sheath in which we dream, and where the impressions of our experience are sifted and sorted—perhaps this is equivalent to the English term "subconscious." The next sheath is that of the *Vijnanamaya kosha* (wisdom-filled sheath) where intelligence, discrimination, learning and language reside. This ordering of sheaths is not hierarchical; Vijnanamaya is not "above" Manomaya—all the sheaths penetrate each other. The final sheath is the *Anandamaya kosha*, the sheath of bliss.

Such a conception makes it possible to think about shared selves—a sheath becomes a shared platform upon which all sorts of information could possibly be shared, exchanged and communicated. This also dispenses with the problem of physical boundaries, for what is outside the physical sheath may be inside a mental sheath. It also solves the problem of existential reality of deities—and if mantras and deities are realities *within* us, they would also be accessible to everyone. So I asked Sivananda, "In what *kosha* is mantra?" "*Vijnanamaya kosha*," she said, completely unsurprised by my question, and then, "it takes you to the *Anandamaya kosha*." An early source that discusses how a hierarchy of beings are in a state of "ananda (bliss)" is the *Taittiriya Upanishad* 2.98 (Olivelle 307). Devatas (gods) are described as enjoying a state of bliss numerous times that of the material bliss enjoyed by a human being. As she spoke about how mantras are in the vijnanamaya kosha, a bridge to the anandamaya kosha, I also understood how she meant what she had said in her very first interview, that mantra was *in* her. Nachiketananda, however, had a different technique for being transported.

7.6 The "No"-Mantra

Up until the time that Geetha saw what she saw at Nachiketa, she had never had an "experience," except perhaps vaguely, once. She had gone to Uttarkashi, a pilgrimage place in North India, with a group of practitioners. At a Shiva temple, when sitting under a Bilva tree (known to be sacred to Shiva) she did slow-japa according to Nachiketananda's instructions. Nachiketananda asked the sadhakas to first mentally "scream" their mantras to help quiet the mind before doing slow-japa of their respective mantras. Geetha felt a range of sensations during this japa. The entire left side of her body, from head to toe, tingled, and she felt her heartbeat everywhere on the left side, her face tingled and "the whole ear was vibrating ... as if something was going to come." Scared, she opened her eyes. She said it could have been the fear of losing the life she knew.

Geetha confessed that japa had always been like "a mechanical exercise"—"you have to do it, it's part of your puja, and because your guru's asked you to do it, so you do it." Such actions conducted mentally before embarking on a japa as offering a flower to the guru, or lighting a lamp, were all done in a routine manner. "You go to work after the puja, right, so already you are switched to the next ...(appointment)." We chatted about the difficulties we faced in our sadhanas. I said that sometimes, when I did or said something that appeared loving, I also chided myself for I knew that it had risen from my sense of good behavior and had not surged from a genuine feeling of love. Geetha could not agree more—she said "yes! sometimes it is just pretending." But the sadhana she did at Nachiketa in May 2014 was anything but posturing.

In May 2014, Geetha was struggling with some problems, and turned to Nachiketananda for help. He asked her to do a two-day sadhana of silence (*mauna*). This was not just about staying silent externally, it was inner silence too. For two days, Geetha was to stay inside a room and *not think*. If she had a thought, she had to say "no" to it; her mantra, simply, was "no." She would keep her eyes open, but downcast. There would be no communication with the outside world and no reading and writing materials at hand. There were one or two exceptions—a short prayer to Ramakrishna that she could read twice a day, and a clipping of an article written by Nachiketananda titled "the witness in you." She was to go to the temple on the evening of the second day, but sit at the back without making any eye contact. How can one not "think"? Nachiketananda (2015) explains:

> The moment we try to understand with our mind, mind comes in and SELF disappears. Then we start experiencing the mind and soon get carried away by the mind's play without witnessing the mind. (29)

Nachiketananda then details a "focusing" and "defocusing" technique, at the end of which one can defocus from the body as well as the mind. He also differentiates between "vacuum" and "silence," calling vacuum "a state of inertia" contrasting with silence which is a "state of activity." How does one know if the mind is silent or vacuous?

> In silence, one can sense or judge a situation, whereas in vacuum one is completely helpless and unaware of results. Silence soothes the body and mind, goes deeper within to communicate with the soul, whereas vacuum jolts the body & mind and dances on the surface, making more noise. Silence sends very soothing and inspiring waves in the spine, whereas vacuum sends shivering waves through the spine. Therefore, it is important for one to know the difference. Silence makes us feel charged, vacuum drains our energies. Vacuum sucks, silence fills. (29)

Thus, the silence in which a mantra is heard and out of which an intention can create results is not an empty mind, it is a mind in suspended stillness.

Geetha was able to engage wholly in inner silence: "Absolutely no thought. Once or twice it would come I would say no." She was not hungry throughout this period. She had some visions, of a script (*lipi*) but could not read it. She had some other visions, but they were restful and not extraordinary. It was toward the end of the sadhana, on the second evening at the temple that she saw the Goddess. Sivananda was engaged in a puja in front of the Kali temple, and Geetha saw a little girl walk into the inner sanctum.

> I saw a little girl in red – pavada [long-skirt] and blouse – walking in – I could see. Into the temple. And then I knew that - later on I saw the *kalasham* [sacred pot] was the same red color. She was wearing the same dress that they had put on the kalasham. I got scared a little.

A *kalasham* is a particular arrangement of a brass pot with a coconut, which stands in for the Goddess, and is decorated and worshiped as the Goddess. From where she sat, at the back of the temple hall, Geetha had not seen the kalasham and did not make the connection until she saw the kalasham later. I asked her for more detail.

> MANI: Can you describe? Did you see her face? Did she have a *jada* [long braid]?
>
> GEETHA: Yes. She had long hair. She was well-dressed, as for a wedding. Face glowing. And you will (know) immediately, I could see that she was not a, not a human child at least, I mean the things that, you will know, right, that she is a kid – I didn't feel that - that you want to cuddle and all, she was not like that, it was a different thing I felt.

I had heard about Geetha's experience from Sivananda too. She made a connection that was not in Geetha's narrative—"I was calling Her, doing the *ahvanam*-mantras (invitation-mantras), and Geetha'*ma* saw Her come." When I asked Geetha about the mantras, she said she did not remember any in particular. Mantras only feature in the next part of Geetha's narrative. After everyone left, Nachiketananda beckoned Geetha to the Ramakrishna temple and did some mantras over her head and behind her head. He asked her to sit there with eyes shut as long as she wanted, and to open her eyes only when she felt ready. Geetha described what happened:

> GEETHA: After some time I opened my eyes and looked at Sri Ramakrishna, and, he was, like, alive, face, face was live. It was not marble. It was a person's face. And, his lips, he had opened his eyes, and I could see him blink, and his lips uh were moving. Again, after a couple of seconds. I couldn't stop crying. I lost it after that. Really, really wonderful.

Geetha said she had felt "immense joy." It was not the kind of joy one gets from achievement or other things. "This was totally different, a different kind of feeling," and she has never had a similar feeling ever after that either. How did Geetha interpret her visions?

> MANI: What do you think was the purpose of letting you have this vision? Whoever, whatever caused it … was it some kind of sign or something?

GEETHA: See my (business) partner is a Christian, she calls me "doubting Thomas." My trusting instinct is low. Social with everybody but still don't let anybody come close. If anybody tells something I always take it with a pinch of salt. So His reasons would have been, uh, the way of telling me that it is possible for me to achieve it. That I can also realize God during this lifetime. That was something, like, I wasn't sure, I think I was postponing it to my next birth (*janma*). Which .. I think.. this was one way of saying, yes I can also see, and it is not necessary that I should work and do sadhana – I still believe that I have to work, that I have to do sadhana for anything– but still, that I can also get, some, get this kind of boon without actually working for it!

MANI: Does the vision lead to *moksha* [liberation]? What does it do in itself?

GEETHA: Nono, no. No. It doesn't lead to any moksha, definitely not. But then, it.. at least, reinforces faith, no? Somewhere. Because, we say we have faith but I think, it's quite, it is more like a fear than faith. More like fear .. because you think He will strike you when it's necessary so I have to be good and that kind of a thing. From fear to faith is (a) big leap, actually. I think.

MANI: Faith in what? Faith in existence of Devi and Ramakrishna?

GEETHA: Faith in existence of God. I believe in … God being formless, but, us, we need to make some..thing out of Him, so we give Him an image. So, that we can, we can realize Him. This is not an experience, right, we are not experiencing God, we are seeing Him. So seeing Him is different, and maybe experiencing is different. It was an external thing, whatever I saw, was external, it was not something internal.

Geetha distinguishes between an external and an internal experience. Seeing deities in their physical form is "external," and she speculates that there must be an entirely different "internal" experience that occurs. Why was she making such a distinction? Geetha said, "There should be a change, no?—in the person once you experience God?" Geetha expects that transformation ought to occur when one experiences God and she expects this to be something internal. Geetha is also aware of her own transformation and that she has moved from fear to faith. Her initial motivation for the intense sadhana of inner silence had not been soteriological. At the outset, she had specific worldly problems (which she did not share with me, and I did not feel it pertinent to ask). I asked if this sadhana had also addressed the problems she had been facing. She said her problems persisted, but now she had an entirely different attitude toward them; she had arrived at an acceptance of her situation and she had never again been overwhelmed by any situation.

If numerous practitioners had invoked and seen deities with mantras, and some had said that they saw how mantras produced the sound forms of deities, Geetha had visions without the help of any mantra. Whereas some practitioners acknowledged that intention or a directed thought was as equally powerful as a mantra, Geetha had visions in a state of thoughtlessness. Geetha's mantra was "no"—either this made the phenomena of her sadhana entirely random and accidental, or confounded the effort of all other practitioners. So I probed the idea of sankalpa (intention). Sankalpa is an active and dynamic intention that may be different from the meaning of the words, and a sentence may thus have a sankalpa as well as a meaning. In the case of mantras, even when there is no meaning, there is usually an intention. Geetha had no mantra and "no" for a mantra, but she may have had a sankalpa. Had she *wanted* to see the Goddess? "Absolutely not," said Geetha. Moreover, she added, she did not think herself worthy of it and had not done anything to deserve it. The vision of Ramakrishna was because of Nachiketananda—"I think he knew. That kind of a vibration he set up or something like that." If Geetha had no sankalpa, did Nachiketananda have a sankalpa *for* her? The role of the guru-seer and the significance of the place come to the fore in Geetha's experience. She specifically visited the Nachiketa ashram and undertook a sadhana given to her by Nachiketananda. I asked Geetha if she thought Nachiketananda and Sivananda had changed after *their* experiences. This was an apt question for Geetha because she has been acquainted with Nachiketananda and Sivananda from the time before they became ascetics and gurus.

> GEETHA: Definitely. They may appear to us as if they are not, they are like y'know, with us, but they are in a totally different dimension and world, the world they live is totally different ...to the world we are in.

7.7 Guru-Disciple Bond

Navaratri tends to deliver a bounty of phenomena for sadhakas at Nachiketa. Twenty-two-year-old student and researcher Maheshwari, *aka* Mahi, described a series of visions during Navaratri 2015. The first was a vision where she returned to an empty yajna-shala after doing japa in the temple and saw several people there including an ascetic sitting in Sivananda's seat doing homa. She felt his presence after she circumambulated fire-deity Agni, bowed, and got up.

> MAHI: Stepping into the yajna-shala I felt there are people sitting and doing homa.
>
> MANI: You felt?.. You saw?
>
> MAHI: I felt. As soon as stepping in. Somebody is there. Doing – some - ritual. Felt that way. After one circumabulation (*pradakshina*), after bowing and getting up, you know Mataji's table [seat] where she does yajna, on that table a sadhu [ascetic] is sitting and doing yajna. I bent, and as soon as I got up, that I felt. I did not see his form. But I am very much sure that he has... matted hair.. he is very.. a big personality. And near him too, there are people. This I found. This is one incident.

The second incident was during japa at the Kali temple. She saw a man sitting inside the inner sanctum, doing homa. She described his precise location: "Here's the statue of Ma [Mother Kali] here's the homa-kunda [fire-pit], he sits at this angle." She knew there was no homa-kunda at the Kali temple, so she wondered if this had been her imagination and consulted Sivananda, who confirmed her vision as reality. A third incident was her vision of a crowded inner sanctum, except these were not standees.

> MAHI: Then, what happened, as soon as I closed my eyes, you know Amma's statue, right, there, from the ceiling, people were hanging. Not people. Celestial bodies, Mataji told me later. But I used to feel that presence on the corners. They'll be doing sadhana. This corner. That corner. In fact, in Kali-amma's inner sanctum there were lots of ascetics, I felt. Later I asked Amma [Mataji], lots of great people are coming to do sadhana, she said yes, in Navaratri lots of celestial bodies are coming to do sadhana.

Could Mahi's vision of people hanging from the ceiling be a "memory leak" (see 5.7) from exposure to Indian temples, where numerous gods and demi-gods crowd every inch of crown molding on pillars and temple exteriors, holding up the edifice? Mahi too suspected her imagination, but she took Sivananda's word as final. She described how close she felt to Sivananda, and how she would answer her whenever she had any need. Searching for the right words to use, Mahi said, "Maybe Mataji becomes present in her energy form." Mahi was a Masters student of Yoga Consciousness in Bangalore, and her thesis was based on intervention-research into mantras, so I was more persistent than usual in asking for clarification.

> MANI: What do you mean "energy form" and you can feel her "energy presence."
>
> MAHI: What that is…mm.. In my entire eyes Mataji comes. In my mind, in my eyes. I am looking like this [i.e., physically], I see Mataji. Like that. I used to feel her like that.
>
> MANI: But that's imagination, right? While looking normally, suddenly, to come…
>
> MAHI: Nonono. That *feel* is entirely different.

I urged Mahi to explain this "feel," this difference between imagination and reality. Mahi's response was that it was to do with retention of memory.

> MAHI: There's a LOT of difference. Because, in imagination, we just imagine and we forget. For a fraction of moment it will be there. But when I feel, that comes from within.
>
> MANI: Imagination does not come from within?
>
> MAHI: Imagination comes from thoughts …
>
> MANI: "Within" doesn't mean thoughts?
>
> MAHI: "Within" does not mean thoughts.

According to Mahi, imagination not only came from thoughts, it was not retained. On the other hand, she spoke about feeling as if it were in the category of perception. I asked if thoughts too did not come from within us.

> MAHI: Thoughts do come from within us, but I would not have understood it is Mataji. But I used to feel her, "she is with me." Now how to explain that, I am not getting. But that is definitely not imagination. Because whatever doubts I had in me, I used to get the answer from that. I know I don't have that capacity. I know – for ordinary Mahi – that shakti [power] is not in me. Something is energizing me.

Mahi's certainty that Sivananda is with her is based on "understanding"—a word she uses like cognition or recognition, and this has a certainty and lasting impression contrasted to "thoughts" that are fantasy-based and insubstantial, forgotten. Mahi has also received mantras during japa. At Navaratri 2015, during japa—"suddenly a voice. I got one mantra." Mahi does not recall if it was a male or a female voice, nor any other detail. This was a syllable mantra, and after consulting Sivananda, she did thirty roasaries of this mantra. This occurred a second time:

> MAHI: The other day also a mantra came. A bijakshara. I did thirty malas that day. Mataji told me to continue that. But the next day I continued (with my regular mantra). Because what (mantra) Mataji gave, that will remain like that only. I don't know what God is but I see God in Mataji.

7.8 Diksha

Diksha establishes a relationship between practitioner and teacher, disciple and guru, aspirant and seer; the mantra *is* that relationship, and even referred to as a *sutra* (thread, connection). Diksha is also considered an integral part of the rubric of mantra-sadhana. In *Tantric Tradition*, Agehananda Bharati ([1965] 1970) writes: "a syllable or a collection of syllables constituting a mantra is no mantra at all, because a mantra is something imparted personally by a guru to a disciple" (106). Can mantra-diksha be compared to *aksharabhaysa*, the ritual marking the beginning of literacy for a young child? In aksharabhaysa, a guru draws the first letter of the alphabet and the child traces over it. When I aired this analogy to Sivananda, she agreed, but said, "similar, but different; like purva-mimamsa and uttara-mimamsa." She was giving these systems of philosophy as an example to explain external rituals vs. inner observance—purva-mimamsa is the hermeneutics of vedic rituals, and uttara-mimamsa expounds the oneness of *atman* (soul/self) and *Brahman* (God/formless divine).

My mantra-diksha from Sivananda happened at the Nachiketa yajna-shala. It was morning, and the fire in the *homa-kunda* (fire-pit for homa) from the previous night had subsided. The ashes were still hot. Sivananda picked up a long fire iron, pushed it into the pit to extract some *vibhuti* (holy ash) with its tip, and then smeared it across my forehead with three fingers. Then I bowed for *pada-namaskar*, i.e., touched her feet, and I felt her hand *writing* or scrawling something in the air just over the crown of my head. (I had expected her to whisper in my ear—just like in popular depictions of Gayatri mantra initiations.)

Months later, I found that I could recall the texture of Sivananda's voice at the moment of initiation. If I did the mantra in the same tone as she had first uttered it, my japa became focused. Perhaps the practice of whispering is not about secrecy, but about privacy and creating a quiet space; the voice of the mantra-giver becomes imprinted in the memory of the mantra-receiver, a memory that works as a model. Mahi told me that in her diksha, Sivananda had whispered the mantra in her right ear.

Sivananda said she initiated some practitioners in the Panchakshari mantra because she had the "authentication" for that. Was this like gaining siddhi (mastery) over a mantra, or gaining control over that mantra's deity? I remembered that Karunamaya had said, if anyone wanted the Radha-mantra, Amritananda would send them to Siddheswarananda. Like professors at a university who specialize in different subjects, or different deities who are in charge of different qualities or tasks, different gurus could be adept at teaching different mantras.[6] Later that week, Sivananda spoke about someone who did not want the Panchakshari, she wanted the Shirdi Sai Baba mantra. Sivananda obliged, but six months later, the woman returned, telling her that she was getting visions of Shiva. I joked, "so it doesn't matter what mantra you give, it's really the Panchakshari in any guise?"

I was to discover that the *sutra* or connection between initiating seer and initiated sadhaka was not just figurative. When I went back to the USA for a month in October 2014, one evening, I remembered Sivananda intensely during my sadhana. I was shocked that night to receive an email from her in which she wrote, "I experience your call." When I met Sivananda after I returned to India, I asked her, "*where* did you experience my call?" Smiling, she said, "in the heart." Some weeks later, after Shivaratri celebrations at the ashram, when I took her leave, I joked that I would "call" her and she would have to "call back." Smiling sweetly, she nodded. Nachiketananda, who was standing with us, misunderstood what I had said, and reassured me—"yes of course, feel free, you can call her, you have her number, right?" Sivananda and I screeched in laughter. I teased Nachiketananda—"Oh Swamiji, that would be *so* clever of her, to call back if I called her *phone*." In the two weeks that followed, I only had a focused japa session twice. Both times, as soon as I got up from my sadhana, my phone rang, and it was her. Such responsiveness had something to do with my decision to embark on sadhana without ulterior motives. Sivananda had anyway complained about my research to me and said I would not make progress if I was asking questions and taking notes all the time. She also commented on my recorder, but I could not not fish out my recorder when we suddenly began to have conversations about mantras.

7.9 Inner Silence and Anahata

There were some basic observations I had noted from mantra-sadhana. When I did japa aloud, after I became familiar with the utterance, I found myself comfortably entertaining other thoughts; the memorized mantra could flow without error from my vocal chords, and did not require my full attention. This was not just due to the simplicity of syllable-based mantras; I found that I could parrot any mantra once I was very familiar with it. Mantra done aloud blanked out external sounds but not my internal noise or thoughts. When I did mantra silently, I could silence other thoughts. If I could hear inaudible mantras when my thoughts ceased, it meant that thoughts were like sound, disturbing and interfering with sounds at wavelengths not normally audible. Don't we refer to this idea when we say, "I hear you" (to mean "I understand what you really mean") or as when we say "Please stop talking, I can't hear myself think." The well-known definition of a mantra is—*mananāt trāyate iti mantra*—"that which comes from the *manas* (mind) and protects, that is a mantra." What if it also meant "that which protects you *from* the mind"? I began to regard a mantra as a *yogasana* (steady yoga-posture) of the mind. Perhaps it is in such a quiet environment that a focused sankalpa (intention) can be "held," with or without a mantra.

I was given my brief about inner silence on the evening of 19th July, 2015. I was to have no thoughts, and only do my mantra—i.e., the mantra in which I had been initiated by Sivananda. I asked, "is mantra not a thought?" "Yes," said Sivananda, "but consider it a good thought." She then gave me my routine: (1) Nachiketa Chaitanya Kriya (a breathing exercise taught by Nachiketananda; (2) Bhramari (humming of the "ṃ" sound as at the end of the *OṂ* mantra); (3) Pranayama-mantra (japa of my mantra along with in-breath and out-breath). There was another routine I was given as a way to warm up before I began japa: (1) *OṂ* (9 times); (2) *Hrīṃ* (9 times); (3) *Raṃ* (9 times); and (4) Guru prayer with visualization of favorite deity. Pranayama-mantra meant I had to do my mantra while I breathed, i.e., all day long (when I was not doing my repetition of mantra with the japamala, or when I ate or did anything else that would make such a practice impossible). We went over the inhalation and exhalation detail. "When I walk," I said, "I do the mantra in four steps. If I fix it to my breath, is that not too … fast?" "No," said Sivananda, "half the mantra in, and half out." I tried it. She said that when I breathed slower, the mantra had to be slower.

I tried some of it that night. I tried silent utterance as though I was greeting the deity of my mantra. I imagined that the deity sat before me, and then I said my mantra, but that felt absurd, especially when I repeated it as though the deity had not heard me the first time around. And if I simply uttered it, I felt a little bored by the routine. I was also not able to visualize the deity of my mantra—the only imagery that came to mind were from television serials or calendar art, and I did not warm up to those images. While I was unable to visualize the deity, I was able to visualize my guru, Sai Baba. I was also able to reproduce, mentally, the memory of Sivananda's tone when she gave me diksha. I reported these efforts to her the next morning. She said the routine I had been given was not compulsory, and it was only there to help me. If I felt focused, I could go straight to the japa and pranayama-japa. I handed over my backpack which had my laptop, phone, recorder and a couple of books. It was my way of demonstrating that I was sincere and meant it when I said I would cut myself off from the external world completely. I kept a scratchpad and pen with the commitment that it was only to help me communicate with her, and only when absolutely necessary.

The first day was somewhat chatty, i.e., mentally. I could focus, but if I was not watching my breath, my mind would slip into streams of thought. If my eyes were closed, a series of visuals would take over. Sometimes I found myself dwelling on personal matters as though this was a time in which to solve problems and make plans. I also dwelt on research questions but would catch myself immediately, and stop the thought process. If my eyes were open, the blank staring at objects became stressful. When I went on a walk, I could focus on my pranayama-mantra, but if I did not have conscious focus, everything I saw was really a topic: what the birds were up to, the texture of sand, the arrangement of stones, activities of ants, shapes of trees. I would come up with smart observations I could use later in my writing. The mental chattering wore off in a couple of days and I became more focused. As my focus on the mantra increased, I seemed to have forgotten how to sleep, or sleep forgot me. I did not yawn once, I was never tired and my energy levels were high. If I slept, it seemed brief, and I would be woken up all of a sudden with the sound of OṂ in my right ear. This happened on the very first night of the silence. It was the same sound I had heard in Puttaparthi over a decade ago. *Anāhata*. I jumped up from bed and stepped out of my room and into the terrace. It was pitch dark. Then I sat up in bed for the sadhana. After some hours, I lay back and slept, but woke up again. Again the terrace, and finding that it was still night time, and then the sadhana. I kept the curtains at my window open. Hours seemed to pass before it was dawn. And that was how I knew that I must have first woken up at ten or eleven p.m., or midnight.

When I woke up on the second night, I did not expect it to be daybreak, I just settled into listening to the anahata or doing the mantra-pranayama. That week, I was always jolted awake by a loud anahata. It was mainly in the nights that it was clear, first in my right ear, and the next day I could move it from my right to my left ear by willing it. Two days into the silence, I heard soft music. It was on this same night that I felt and heard a whirring or rotating motion within my chest, at the center. I was startled, and the whirring stopped after a few moments. Over the next couple of days I distinctly saw bright sparks or rays between my brows, to the left, light flashing around both my eyes. On the second or maybe it was the third night, when I sat up, listening, I became anxious. Some fragments of conversations with Nachiketananda and Sivananda about the kundalini played on my mind. The anahata would not let up, and I was uncomfortable. Then—and I somehow stumbled upon this—I began to use the anahata tone to guide my japa. This was a discovery that made me fully engaged in the japa. In that same session I also began to do the mantra-japa in a rather high tone (and all of this was mental, silent). I then felt, or knew, that a group or choir did the mantra with me, and I was doing it with them. Then, when I stopped, I *heard* a group continue the chanting, and the mantra was actually *in* my ear, and instead of saying the mantra, I was *listening* to it. I also heard the mantra in my heart. My mantra-japa had suddenly changed. Once, when I was listening to the japa, the permutations of the syllables in the japa changed automatically, and I saw my mental images also change. Then I heard a melody, like temple bells or like the musical instrument *jal-tarang—tun, tun, tun, tun, tun*. I could not tell where this music was coming from. And I could not remember how many days had passed. I was restless and I had also begun to try to remember what I was going through. I tallied the breakfasts—*upma, daliya, idli, tamarind rice*, and then *upma*—that meant five days had gone by. It was probably on the sixth evening that I had the best focus of all the days. The rosary flowed on my fingers, effortless, and the anahata was blissful. My *maunam* (silence) came to an end that day. I wrote the two gurus a note: "*maunam samaptam*" (end of silence).

In the debrief conversation with them, I told them about hearing the mantra within. Nachiketananda exclaimed, "*that* is *ajapa*!" Ajapa is when the sadhaka does not do the japa, and when it occurs involuntarily from within. When I imitated the *tun-tun* sound, Sivananda and Nachiketananda looked at each other, laughing. "Chakras!" they said, in unison. When I heard these sounds in later sadhana, I identified them as the bijakshara sounds of the chakras. I asked about the rotating chakra, and they said it was normal activity of the prana (life breath). I asked, was it related to kundalini? No, they said, I would have been able to tell if it was the kundalini, for that is inside the backbone and will feel like it is burning up the spot when it rises. I was relieved as well as disappointed. Sivananda was thrilled that I had figured out mantra frequency and reached the state of ajapa, and I felt I had finally taken a dip.

* * *

Are mantras discrete sounds, or any sound anywhere? Are they naturally occurring sounds received by seers, or can they be composed by humans like movie songs? Nachiketananda and Sivananda had different points of view, but it was one of definition. Even though Nachiketananda seemed not to care for mantras, and his technique of "no"-mantra seemed a counterfoil to Sivananda, he had used mantra at the Ramakrishna temple both with Geetha and with me. Nachiketananda's methodology of "no"-mantra was an alternative to Sivananda's methodology of mantra. Either way, both gurus focused on a practice of arriving at a stage of stillness that would in turn be receptive—to deity, vision or any revelation. In *Kathopanishad* 1.20, Yama the God of Death asks young Nachiketa to choose a boon. Nachiketa asks, "*asti iti eke, nāsti iti eke*"—which I translate: "Some say it is, some say it isn't" (Olivelle 1998, 379). Commentaries over the centuries have interpreted this question to refer to the *ātman* or the self (translatable as "soul")—thus, the question would mean, "some say there is a soul, some say there is no soul." Yama tries to dissuade Nachiketa from wanting to know if it (the self, or soul) exists, but Nachiketa insists this is the one and only knowledge he seeks. Reconsidering the two distinct approaches of Nachiketananda and Sivananda, I reinterpret this question in the context of mantras—"some say it is, some say it isn't."

Sadhakas at Nachiketa looked upon Nachiketananda and Sivananda as seers and as ideals, and saw themselves as seekers. Could it be possible that my experience was imagined? I did not think so, and my experience only took me deeper into mantra-sadhana. I also began to see Sivananda and Nachiketananda as researchers. That first day, I had heard breathing in the Ramakrishna temple; it was just behind my right shoulder, and quite close to me. Afterward, Nachiketananda asked about my time at the temple and I duly reported the breathing incident or phenomena. He simply noted, "many others have experienced that"—I had no idea what investigations of his own were served by my experience.

Notes

1. The name of a nomadic people from the northwest India, now settled in other parts.
2. The entire line: *Na akśaraṃ mantra rahitaṃ, na vā mūlamanauṣadhaṃ, ayogya puruṣaḥ nāsti yojakaḥ tatra durlabhaḥ.*
3. "Ramakrishna at Studio," photograph of Ramakrishna, taken on 10 December, 1881, at the studio of The Bengal Photographers in Radhabazar, Calcutta, India.
4. Mudras are also used in yoga and dance arts; an early documentation is in the classical text on dance-drama, second-century CE Natyashastra compiled by Bharata.
5. The definition: "*svarūpajñānapanarūpaṃ mudrā-samsthānam.*"
6. Buhnemann's (1991) essay describes some of the procedures for choosing a mantra, based on the practitioner's name and astrological sign.

References

Bharati, Agehananda. [1965] 1970. *Tantric Tradition.* New York: Anchor Books.

Boddy, Janice. 1994. "Spirit Possession Revisited: Beyond Instrumentality." *Annual Review of Anthropology* 23: 407–434.

Bühnemann, Gudrun. 1991. *Bulletin of the School of Oriental and African Studies*, University of London 54 (2): 292–306.

Caturvedi, Sukadeva, ed. and trans. 1981. *Mahidhara's Mantra Mahodadhi.* Varanasi: Pracya Prakasana.

Nabokov, Isabelle. 2000. *Religion Against the Self: An Ethnography of Tamil Rituals.* New York: Oxford University Press.

Nachiketananda Puri, Swami. 2015. *Sadhana.* Hyderabad: Nachiketa Tapovan Trust.

Olivelle, Patrick. 1998. *Early Upaniṣads—Annotated Text and Translation.* New York: Oxford University Press

Padoux, André. 2011. *Tantric Mantras: Studies on Mantrasastra*. London: Routledge.

———. 2013. *The Heart of the Yogini: Yoginīhrdaya, a Sanskrit Tantric Treatise*. New York: Oxford University Press.

Ramachandra Rao, S.K. [1991] 2008. *Lalita Kosha—Being a Collection of Texts in Sanskrit Bearing on the Cult of Lalita wih an Introduction and Translation of the Thousand Names*. Delhi: Satguru Publications.

Smith, Frederick M. 2006. *Self Possessed—Deity and Spirit Possession in South Asian Literature and Civilization*. New York: Columbia University Press.

PART III

Conclusions

It remained in shruti, *the detailed part, it was never written anywhere.*
—Swami Madhavananda Saraswati

CHAPTER 8

Understanding Mantra Again

8.1 Anchored Spaces: Mandalas

The three locations of mantra-sadhana in this fieldwork had different approaches to mantra. At Devipuram (Chapter 5), mantras were a part of interacting with and developing a relationship with a deity. The mood here was devotional; like their guru, Devipuram sadhakas expressed surrender to the Goddess. In Siddheswarananda's group (Chapter 6), mantras were primarily used to surmount problems and empower oneself. A self-made guru with a self-made (*svayam siddha*) deity encouraged followers to be dogged until their penance bore results—mantras here were instrumental. At Nachiketa ashram (Chapter 7), the goal was soteriological—mantras were a part of the process to attain a state of mind in which the practitioner achieved a visionary experience, gaining faith or confidence in the guru and the divine. Yet, across the three spaces, there were many commonalities in the understandings of mantra, deity, visionary experience and how such experience creates authoritative sources. There were also links between the locations and one of the active links was me—as I traveled on research, I would refer people to each other or share narratives; sometimes a question from one location would find an answer at the other.

I had not expected, in today's digitally connected world, to find mantra-sadhana anchored to physical locations. Practitioners who lived far away made a point of traveling to the place where their guru was located. Such a location is regarded as a point of convergence, a *sangam* (meeting

M. Rao, *Living Mantra*, Contemporary Anthropology of Religion,
https://doi.org/10.1007/978-3-319-96391-4_8

place) for visible and invisible influences. A well-known example of such a location is the Triveni-sangam in Allahabad, the confluence of three rivers Ganga, Yamuna and Sarasvati—Ganga and Yamuna are visible, and Sarasvati is invisible, or mythical. Sadhakas go on pilgrimages to sacred locations (*tirtha*), expecting such hidden imprints, and they situate themselves at these locations as claimants of a legacy. Whether a temple with a consecrated deity, or a *samadhi* (tomb), sacred locations are aids to mental concentration, as well as spaces for *darshana*—to see, and be seen by, the deity and/or guru. Sadhakas would comment about how a *kshetra* (field or location) was potent and how extraordinary phenomena tend to occur there. It was as though the history of sadhana at that location had the capacity to attract deities, or as though deities too had habitats, and habits.

How may one think about such anchored spaces of mantra-sadhana? A term that communicates shared ideas is "world"—a *weltanschauung* or world view; however, such a term would not cue in a sense of the sacred. Instead, I propose the term "mandala." "Mandala" has a long history of association with mantras. Rigveda-samhita (mantra-collection) is organized in "mandalas," a term that may be translated as "chapters." This is linked to the idea of lineage—five of eight Rigveda mandalas (mandalas 2–7) are mantras attributed to lineages of specific rishis. In non-vedic ritualistic contexts, mandala refers to a specific diagram or structure. Mandalas are not regarded as the creations of human artistry, but as images of cosmic origin and holding universal significance. There are also various etymologies for "mandala" in tantric literature. Güdrun Buhnemann (2003) notes a religious etymology from Kularnava-Tantra 17.59: "it is called maṇḍala because it is auspicious (*maṅgalatva*), because it is the abode of the group of Yoginīs of the Ḍākinī, and because of (its) beauty (*lalitatva*)" (13). She also notes Jayaratha's commentary on Abhinavagupta's Tantraloka which explains "*maṇḍa*" as "essence" and "*la*" from the verbal root '*lā*' [to take] (225). A twentieth-century thinker who repurposed this term is Carl Jung. Jung (1971) called mandalas "archetypes" which "signify nothing less than a psychic center of the personality not to be identified with the ego," and thought they had alchemical properties (362). Such a definition aligns with my thinking about the material and mythical spaces shared by mantra-practitioners within which an intense process of transformation occurs.

8.2 Primary Sources

When we refer to ideas from centuries or millennia ago as ancient or early sources, we mostly associate them with a few influential individuals—Bharata on aesthetics, Bhartrihari on philosophy of grammar, Jaimini and Shabara for vedic hermeneutics, Sayana with vedic commentary, Shankara's advaita, etc. Similarly, ideas and practices in mantra today can be traced to charismatic individuals with, and reputed for, visionary experience. They are our contemporary rishis, and they may become teachers or gurus for other practitioners.

Mantra-sadhakas are existentially linked to the guru-seer who initiates their sadhana. Sometimes, sadhakas try out a range of gurus and practices until they find the one that suits them. Prema at Devipuram had done Mahesh Yogi's Transcendental Meditation and found that it did not work for her; it was when she met Amritananda that she knew she had found her guru. After sadhakas enter an intense sadhana, they tend to keep to their own circles, mingling closely with others who have the same guru. The guru becomes the source of their information and is often their interpretive lens as well as a messenger. Mahi accepted Sivananda's confirmation as evidence that her visions were true. In Don's narrative, we hear about how Aiyya at the Rochester temple takes questions from the sadhakas, asks the Goddess, and reverts with answers. When Lakshmi told me that she had asked Siddheswarananda to inform the Goddess about her plight, I asked her why she expected him to play messenger? She replied that Siddheswarananda had said he was like a postman (mailman) for sadhakas. A number of sadhakas discounted their own abilities and devalued formal education—Vasudevananda was reputed for his insight into the past, and made recommendations for the future, but said he had not studied *jyotish* (astrology); Karunamaya prescribed "new" Sanskrit mantras and intuited meanings, but said he did not know Sanskrit; Mahi said she found answers beyond her acumen; sadhakas gave the credit for their abilities to their gurus and deities.

The relationship between a guru and a disciple seems to be that of mutual consent. Gurus hesitate to intervene when another guru is already involved. At Devipuram, visitors fill a form with the name of their guru and note if they have already been initiated by anyone. Lakshmi thought the first mantra did not bear results as it was a modified form of a mantra someone else had given her. The identity of my guru was a vital part of my first conversation with any sadhaka or guru. When I recounted to Sivananda and Nachiketananda a dream about Sai Baba that I thought significant, they commented that I had been initiated by him. Loyalty was an issue in my initial interaction with Sivananda until I realized that there was no competition, only collaboration and learning. Gurus too have to prove their worth and be tested. It was when Sivananda passed her test that I felt inclined to go to the next step. It is only when Amritananda's prediction comes true that Mani Prasanna discovers him as her guru.

I probably gravitated to Nachiketa as it aligned with my sensibilities, and emphasized yoga and meditation rather than elaborate and intricate rituals. However, I came to appreciate the mandalas of Amritananda and Siddheswarananda and recognized that their particular visionary experience/s made them authoritative sources. This understanding shaped the methodology of my research (see 3.3 for a discussion about the relationship between practice and theory). Sadhakas with visionary experience often become gurus and guide others, revising old, and instituting new, forms of practices. While early sources may not be accessible or comprehensible to the general public, numerous publications by visionaries are in circulation serving as guides for religious practice. Scholars study early sources that have been transcribed but often neglect contemporary sources which are already in circulation among practitioners, and will eventually be transcribed and even canonized. Realizing that individual authoritative sources are continually in the making also directs our attention to the individuals behind hallowed sources.

On public occasions, it is not often that one finds more than one guru on the same stage and such occasions seldom include conversations about practice; if conversation between gurus occurs in private meetings, the public is rarely privy to it. Then, research like this across mandalas also helps the flow of information among practitioners. But such a role for a visiting researcher also makes one wonder about the lack, or apparent lack, of collaborations between practitioners. Why is it so important to those who seem to learn something from visionary experience that they did *not* get it from secondary sources? This may simply be the relentless honesty of the practitioners, and some of them may be ill-equipped to engage in scholastic debates. They may also recognize that they are their own evidence, unfalsifiable, and this can place them in a vulnerable position. From the perspective of a scholar, however, even the claim is exciting, for it is a comment about currency. Just as the discoveries of science are revised when new information is found, perhaps primary sources access and reveal new information. And knowledge may always be in a state of revision.

8.3 Relating to Deities

Some practitioners in this fieldwork insisted on an equivalence and relationship between mantra and deity. Sivananda talked about seeing a deity in the process of being formed while she did a mantra, specifying that it was an optical vision, through her eyes. On another occasion, she explained the relationship between mantras and deities by equating mantras to seeds, and deities to trees. Appaji spoke about different forms of the deity produced by different sound combinations. This is identical to ideas in early sources—Sanjukta Gupta (1989) explains the sequence of the relationship between image and sound: "it is the sonic form of the god which is primary, since the designating epistemologically and ontically *precedes* the designated" (230). Are deities *more* than sound-forms? In this fieldwork, even those who said mantras are the sound forms of deities specified if their vision was that of a mantra *or* a deity. The idea that deities are *only* sound forms produced on the spot is not admissible if deities are also seen without mantras. Ramya Yogini received mantras from Kala-Bhairava and from a figure that stepped out of the image of Kali; Vasudevananda heard Hanuman and many others saw deities. Seeds produce trees, but trees produce more seeds too. If mantras produce deities *and* deities give mantras, perhaps mantras produce deities who subsequently dispense mantras.

When I asked Sivananda about the predominance of Indian deities in my visions (—why not Greek?), Sivananda proposed that deities are *formed* by mantras and that I had done Indian mantras. This explanation is like noting that Peepal trees are rounded and firs, tall—both are natural forms, and it is the distinct seeds, also natural forms, that give rise to distinct results. The second explanation provided by sadhakas is that the production of the deity form is a *collaborative* process. A 1981 entry in Amritananda's memoir quotes Goddess Saraswati from his vision: "We are really ageless beings. We can appear to have any age. I can be 9, 15, 18, 33, whatever age *you wish to see me* with any time" ("5 Sarasvati 1981," italics mine).[1] The idea that the sadhaka's wish and imagination is incorporated into the rubric of deity visions resolves the question about how mantra and deities can be ontological and yet within the cultural idiom. Even though it is practitioners who have the vision, they often speak about it as though they have been treated to a "showing" by the deity. Is this a convention, or an expression of love and surrender? But there is yet another possibility—responding to a question I sent him in writing, Amritananda noted that the initial progress depends on the sadhaka's endeavor and imagination; eventually, it is deities who direct the practice.

The very notion of "inside" and "outside" assumes a physical boundary for the self and becomes invalidated the moment this boundary is redrawn. In *Self-Possessed*, Frederick Smith (2006) explains the idea of the self in Indian conceptions as "permeable layerings and boundaries," both of which constantly shift and mutate" (10). The concept of "koshas" also explains how these layers mutate. If mantras and deities are in the vijnanamaya kosha, a shared platform, they are, as Siddheswarananda said, both outside and inside. Also, if the vijnanamaya kosha is a part of our self, and we share it with every one else, it resolves how individuals may be separate in one part of their selves, and connected with other people via another part of their self. This is not unlike Carl Jung's idea of the collective unconscious, where archetypes become accessible across collectives. Jung notes such connections as hereditary, whereas the Indian concept of the vijnanamaya kosha is universal.

Why would deities make appearances and give mantras to sadhakas like in dumb-charades or as calling cards? Are they eager to be spoken to via mantras, are mantras their "code" or "language," are they compelled or obliged to do so because they exist because of, or benefit from, mantras? There would be no way to know (nor would I get a deity to sign an informed consent form)[2] ... sadhakas said mantras are the fastest way to reach and please a deity. Those who received mantras from deities did not mind describing their visitors, but they rarely shared information about what mantra they had been given as if it were a pact of secrecy. By contrast, those who received mantras in response to problems usually had one main deity they had a relationship with and who was given credit for the vision. Karunamaya does not already have a mantra when he is asked for one, and waits for Goddess Lalita to reveal this. In Karunamaya's and Vasudevananda's narratives we are asked to assume that it is Goddess Lalita and Hanuman who are responsible for their visions, because those are the deities with whom they have a relationship. Siddheswarananda had said that mantras were given to us by deities to call them, and sadhakas speak about calling deities with mantras—just like ultrasonic whistles used to call birds. (Like birds, if deities also had habitats, it would make sense to go to specific locations to find them.)

Sadhakas say that deities play decisive roles in human affairs, and have the power to intervene on their behalf. They did not discuss deities beyond the context of their own lives and practices—even the narratives of the three gurus did not go as far. One way to think about this is that mantra-sadhakas only receive visions of deities in relation to their needs; they do not have insight into the lives of deities beyond that relationship. If there is new lore in formation about the lives of gods and goddesses, I did not come across any and saw this as a proof of authenticity of narratives of experience.

Why do mantra-practitioners trust deities? How do they know that deities are not giving them nonsensical or false mantras? An over-enthusiastic language learner is an easy target for practical jokes, and it is easy for a mischievous friend to teach them the wrong words. Might there be a joke in showing Amritananda an Arabic mantra, and a tease in giving Sivananda series after series of mantras for endless japa? Devotion and earnest sadhana then seems the logical way to oblige—or embarrass—deities into reciprocating with generosity and kindness. Another possibility could simply be that deities have no need to be malevolent, because they are *happy*. Sivananda said that mantras were in the Vijnanamaya kosha and help the practitioner travel to the Anandamaya kosha (the sheath of bliss) *where deities live*.[3] In Taittiriya Upanishad (2.98), deities enjoy multiple times the "ananda (bliss)" that can be enjoyed by human beings (Olivelle 1998, 307).

One of the initial challenges in overcoming adversity is to identify the deity who can help. Once identified, as Siddheswarananda said, it is possible to please the deity with suitable mantras and homas. Karunamaya's process of identifying Goddess Nityaklinna, and Lakshmi's journey away from Hanuman and toward Ganesha, are examples of how sadhakas find their way to the appropriate deity. Sometimes, a sadhaka gets affiliated to a deity from the beginning, as did Sheela (see 5.6). When sadhakas talk to each other, or talk about another sadhaka, they tend to include information about the associated deity—somewhat like knowing lineage or party membership. One such account I heard was about a renown politician and movie actress from Tamil Nadu who worshiped Goddess Pratyangiras—the information was offered as an explanation of this politician's long and tenacious career.

Distinctions between deities seem crucial to practitioners, even when they are forms of the same deity. The Kali-mantra calls on Goddess Kali, and the Durga-mantra calls on Goddess Durga—therefore, the surprise when Shiva responded instead of Shirdi Sai Baba. Even when sadhakas do japa of a syllable, the syllable is the deity (and all the letters of the alphabet also have iconic representations called *mātṛkās*). Contrasting with the cute (although powerful) Goddess Bala, were goddesses Varahi and Pratyangiras—Varahi is depicted with war armaments and a sow's head, and Pratyangiras, with a lion's head.

The relationship between mantras and deities in this fieldwork may be summarized by these options: (1) Mantra produces deity *or/and* (2) Mantra invokes deity *or/and* (3) Mantra is deity (4) Deity gives mantra. If the mantra produces a deity, it can also continue to invoke that same deity. Thus, the first option includes the second, and the third option is really a combination as well as an explanation of the first two options. But, though a deity may be created/invoked by many mantras, a mantra refers to one deity. Also, deities respond even without mantras, therefore they are not dependent on mantras.

8.4 What Is Vision?

The seer of a mantra usually refers to the person who *first* perceived the mantra. What about all subsequent seers of that same mantra, i.e., all those who perceive that mantra later? When a guru gives a mantra, it is understood that s/he is a seer and has the *authority* to give this mantra. Here, the guru-seer is a perceiver or receiver and also a mediator between deities and the world. As I sat in Siddeswarananda's visiting room, I heard him tell people on the phone that he would "look" in his meditation the next morning and find out what was the problem. Here, vision does not come across as miraculous, dependent on a deity, but as a deliberate activity within his control. People who had come to consult Siddheswarananda expected him to *see* their past lives (thus understanding the root of the problem), or discover which deity needed appeasement, or find out which mantra would solve their problem. I also heard Amritananda tell a visitor that he would consider his problem when in meditation and revert. Sivananda said people approached her with all sorts of questions, but she did not know the answers in her waking state. These remarks indicate that extraordinary vision is not a permanent state, but a capability.

Is Vision Visual?

In *The Embodied Eye*, David Morgan (2012) discusses the visual and material nature of visions. Asking if mental and visionary phenomena belong to visual culture, he quotes W. J. T. Mitchell who distinguishes between "picture" which is material, and "image" which is an "immaterial motif that floats in thought like a Platonic essence." Morgan concludes that seeing is distributed across mental and material domains and illustrates how external images find their way in to "fix" the apparition (186). Visions of deities described by mantra-sadhakas are evidently visual, especially when they describe such detail as form and color. Ramya said Kala-Bhairava looked just like in the Kala-Bhairava Ashtakam (a hymn)—either she was influenced by the hymn or both the seer of the hymn and Ramya had a similar vision of Kala-Bhairava. Such descriptions do not mean that the object seen is also physical. When sadhakas use the word "body" they are not necessarily referring to a physical body. Sivananda had responded to my question about the appearance of siddhas by saying they were *transparent*. Siddheswarananda said that the subtle bodies of deities are attracted to the fire in lamps and yajnas because they are filled with light themselves (*jyotirmaya sharira*). In general, we can assume that vision connotes a form that is perceptible, but not that it is material. Vadlamudi talked about how Siddheswarananda can see deities with his eyes open, and Sivananda emphasized that she saw a deity forming with her eyes. Such comments suggest that an optical vision is even more extraordinary than the vision of the mind's eye. Mantra-sadhakas who reported dream visions acted upon these visions just as one might with an optical vision—e.g., Potturi did millions of mantra-japas based on an initiation in a dream. If anything, perhaps vision calls for a more attentive response *because* it is not optical—thus standing out inexplicably from among impressions in daily life, lingering in the memory as though unreasonably and carrying a significance that mundane physical events may not exert.

Etymologically, vision (*darshana*) defines a seer (see 4.2) but vision is not defined as optical or visual only. Sivananda noted how some see, while others hear. Vasudevananda reported a long-term relationship with Hanuman through hearing. We do not know how Daivarata perceived mantras, but the internal evidence of the mantras he uttered indicate the participation of all senses. Seeing either connotes, or results in, knowing—to see past lives may also imply (as per the theory of karma) an understanding of the causes for the effects of this life and to see several yogis upside down in the inner sanctum is to know about their presence at that location. The concept that a rishi can perceive *shruti* (that which is heard), and which is a synonym for the revelatory corpus of veda (a word which means "to know") as well as tantra, suggests a conflation between seeing, hearing and knowing. Therefore, inquiry into visionary experience is also an epistemological inquiry.

Is Vision, Imagination?

After describing her visions of the Goddess, Siddheswarananda's follower Sandhya Rani asked me if I thought she had imagined it. Was this a way to express self-effacement or to strike a rapport with a researcher? I responded by asking, "How would I know either way? And how would you know?" She said, "I don't know, sometimes I have a *doubt.*" Doubt has a respectable place in the history of devotion. In 17th-century CE Vishvanatha Chakravartin's *Madhurya Kadambini* (Brzezinski 2005), the devotee is confused after the vision of Krishna:

> Recovering consciousness after some moments, the devotee, anxious to see the Lord again, opens his eyes, and not seeing the Lord, he begins crying. "Was I merely dreaming? No, no, I was not dreaming, because I have neither drowsiness, nor any contamination in my eyes from sleep. Was it some hallucination. No, for a hallucination could never give real bliss. Or was it from some defect in the mind? No, because all the symptoms of unsteady mind are absent. Was it the fulfillment of some material desire? No, no material fancy could ever approach what I have seen. Was it a momentary meeting with the Lord. No, because it is completely different from all previous visions of the Lord that I remember." In this way, the devotee remains in uncertainty. (8.10)

Discussing Chakravartin's descriptions, Travis Chilcott (2015) points out that perceptual experiences of a deity share structural and phenomenological detail with hallucinations—there is no corresponding external stimuli publicly accessible, it is perceived as real, it is not under the subject's direct and voluntary control, and occurs in a waking state (535). A hallucinator's meta-cognitive skills become disrupted after an experience and s/he may wonder if it is an inner or outer vision (548). Mantra-sadhakas would not be too perturbed by such a comparison, for imagination is *also* a part of their experience. Mantras are considered natural substances (*dravya*), just like ghee that is offered to deities in yajnas/homas.

Sometimes, the very profusion of phenomena is reason for skepticism. G. Y. N. Babu, a follower of Siddheswarananda, remarked wryly that he felt uncomfortable saying if or not he had a vision of the Goddess, it would make the Goddess seem commonplace. We laughed; in Shakta circles, visions and visitations were plentiful—if one had seen the edge of Goddess's sari, another had heard her anklets. However—and this is what differentiates the experiencing practitioner from the skeptical observer—Babu's concern is for the status of the Goddess rather than the epistemological acumen of practitioners. Babu's point was that the abundance of visions does not serve the Goddess well, she comes across as readily available and that reduces her status as well as the striving for her vision. Sandhya Rani's skepticism is about her own experience, not about the existence of the Goddess.

Practitioners *admit* anticipation and imagination as harbingers of experience. Chilcott (2015) writes that in hallucinations and deity visions, expectations create lower thresholds for perceptual experiences (546). The term "expectation" is reminiscent of conception and *sankalpa* (intention) which Shulman (2012) translates as "generative intention" in *More than Real*. Mantra-sadhana *consciously* works with sankalpa, an intention which is a kind of expectation, and thus, with a low threshold. How imagining the form of the deity helps intensify feeling (*bhava*) is similar to the technique shared by mantra-sadhakas. Mani Prasanna stressed the importance of imagining with *bhava* and always feeling connected to the deity. Siddheswarananda who spoke about deities as though they were another species emphasized the role of imagination—"you frame a body by your imagination. They (deities) will come into that frame."

If some practitioners were uncertain about some visions, they were also certain about some other visions, and when questioned, explained ways to differentiate between imagining (i.e., hallucinating, or seeing what is not there) and vision (what is there). Determining whether a vision is illusion or reality is important because the stakes are high—every step of the sadhana serves as a ratification that leads to the next. How do sadhakas arrive at a conclusion that deities and mantras exist independent of their imagination? Firstly, in the case of precognitive visions where actual events occur (i.e., where the vision is not only visual), internal image precedes external event—Lakshmi's vision of a Shivalinga surrounded by water was not understood by her at first; later that day, when she visited a temple where the Shivalinga had once been surrounded by water, she interpreted the dream vision as a call. Precognitive dream visions of several practitioners including Appaji reinforce for them that vision is not *just* imagination. Secondly, unusual vision is likely to be a vision rather than imagination. When I discussed categories of mantra with Amritananda, he told me about his vision of letters in Arabic, and called them mantras. Karunamaya also emphasized unpredictable visions, distinguishing them from memory leaks which were more predictable. Thirdly, persistence of the vision is another indication—Mahi said that what is imagined is often forgotten, but visions persist in the memory. Potturi's dream vision of mantra-initiation persisted for years until he acted upon it by doing the mantra. Fourthly, collective vision is an obvious verification—Babu was among a group of people who saw the sudden appearance of Goddess Kali (and interrogating all the living members of this group could be a project for a researcher with objectives different from mine). Finally, phenomena recur and are replicable with sadhana (e.g., chakra sounds, OṂ-sound and specific deities and effects from specific mantras) and this too is evidence.

In mantra-sadhana, visions of deities are neither isolated phenomena nor spectacles, nor only in a cause–effect format (mantra in, deity out), but they indicate milestones for the sadhaka and a budding relationship with the deity. If and when sadhakas doubt the reality of their vision, the very occurrence of the vision testifies to the intensification of their devotion. Thus, even in Chakravartin's writing, doubt is a part of the final stage of devotion called *prema*.[4] Deity visits are a sign of progress in mantra-sadhana and may be an evidence of otherwordly company. Practitioners may experience sensational visions but they are actually seeking something else—success, good health, enduring relationships with deities, self-transformation or liberation. Phenomena occur during mantra-sadhana, like in mining where a range of extracts or by-products become first available even as one digs deeper. Experienced practitioners discourage too much attention to phenomena, urging practitioners to carry on with the sadhana for greater, deeper goals.

Vision of Meanings

Mantras with words may have a meaning—Daivarata's vedic mantras with words, lines and stanzas have meaning, as do Karunamaya's mantras with words and a syntax. According to practitioners, understanding the meaning helps them stay focused on the sankalpa or the generative intention of the mantra. In the words of Swami Madhavananda, whom I met in Thogutta: "As you will be clear about the meaning and the upcoming changes, your sankalpa can be even more clear. And also can be prepared and come out of the obstacles that can disturb your sankalpa." It may also take a visionary experience to connect with the "hidden meaning" of a mantra, as in the case of Karunamaya.

This is not only the case with tantric practitioners, as I heard several anecdotes from vedic practitioners about understanding an alternative meaning, and I will illustrate this point with the case of Maunish Vyas, who learned to chant vedic mantras at Puttaparthi.[5] When Maunish was perusing a dictionary for the meaning of a word in a mantra, he encountered the first word of another mantra, and instantly had a vision of its meaning.

> MAUNISH: I was trying to translate "*Kātyāyanāya Vidmahe*" [a mantra that begins with those words]. So, *ka+ ati+ayani; kāti+ayani; kātyā+ayani*

Maunish is referring to the various ways in which the first word may have been compounded.

> And I kept on thinking, and then I kept on opening dictionaries.
>
> [....] I was looking at the dictionary at this kā+*ati, kāti, ayani*. And there was an entry: "*Kāṇḍa*", and next to it there was a mantra, "*kāṇḍāt kāṇḍāt prarohantī paruṣaḥ paruṣaḥ pari.*"
>
> And then I see in the middle of air, I see a .. a brain .. with the.. spinal cord hanging down from it. No bone structure, nothing. Just the brain and then a… bolt of electricity shooting up from below going to the brain. Which is clearly kundalini. So then, I get the inner message: kāndāt kāṇḍāt prarohantī paruṣaḥ paruṣaḥ parī.

Entries in some Sanskrit dictionaries include a textual reference in which that word is found. Maunish had thus chanced upon *a single line* from the Durva-suktam and had an immediate visionary experience of what he took to be the meaning of that mantra. Translations of this mantra tend to explain "durva" as grass—but Maunish's vision had given him a different meaning. Maunish spoke about this meaning, which he called inner meaning:

> MAUNISH: Of course it [durva] is a grass. But that is the "sthūla," y'know, gross meaning. The inner meaning is Kundalini. And then I translated the whole hymn as per the Kundalini meaning.

Maunish's understanding of the vedic mantra is not according to rituals (*yajnika*), etymology (*nairukta*), or history (*aitihasika*) (Gopal 1983). His interpretation cues in yoga or tantra, with their focus on Kundalini energy. In yoga and tantra, the *prana* (life force) of a person is mapped along the spinal cord along seven chakras or energy centers.

We can consider both Karunamaya's and Maunish's meanings as a *parivrajaka* or mystical interpretations, similar to "anagogical" in Biblical hermeneutics. Discussing meaning in mantras, scholars often quote Yaska's *Nirukta* 1.16 where he refutes Kautsa's accusation that mantras are meaningless. The same Yaska also derives the etymology of "chandas" (i.e., veda) from its nature of being *hidden*—"*chandāṃsi chādanāt*" (*Nirukta* 7.2). Quoting Yaska, S. K. Ramachandra Rao (1998) explains: "The real meaning of the mantras are in fact hidden behind words. Mere involvement with words, however brilliant and meticulous, fails to provide the insight necessary for understanding the meaning" (III).

A single line triggered a vision for Maunish. Karunamaya was brushing his teeth when the meaning of the Shuklambharadharam-mantra suddenly arrived in his mind. His discoveries of new mantras were in tandem with the meanings in the Lalita-Sahasranamam. One may argue that these are interpretations, or insights rather than visions. Nevertheless, understanding a mantra by way of ordinary language does not call for vision; it is when, and because, a meaning is hidden that vision (or insight) is called for.

8.5 How Mantra Works in Sadhana

Imagination, Intention, Feeling

Contemporary mantra-sadhakas actively use imagination, intention and feeling when doing mantras. Devipuram sadhakas visualize syllables in their body, and after some time, they are able to see syllables in their body. Does this mean that if I visualize protons, I will soon be able to see protons? The missing—and the crucial—component, is mantra. As Mani Prasanna narrated, Goddess Bala told her that "if you need to go inside your body, every part of your body should be affected by the mantra." Here, the sadhaka is both subject and object—uttering the mantra with the body helps recognize the mantra that is already in the body and which therefore becomes tangible. There is a difference between sankalpa, intention and cause. In Indian aesthetics, intention was regarded irrelevant in language, since the observance of aesthetic rules would create the *rasa* (the aesthetic effect or mood). Sankalpa, on the other hand, is an active and dynamic intention that may be different from the meaning (say, of the words), and a sentence can have a sankalpa as well as a meaning. Thus, Shulman's (2012) translation of "sankalpa" as "generative intention" is apt. The difference between cause and intention is illustrated in a tale in Ariel Glucklich's (2003) *Climbing Chamundi Hill*. A snake bites a boy and when accused, passes the blame on to Death. It claims that it had no "intention" and was a mere "bit player," a "secondary cause" and not the "instigator" and gives an example: "I mean, would you blame the branches of dry trees for spreading a forest fire?" Death then appears and confesses that he had indeed sent the snake on this task (26). When we apply this format to mantras, we may call the mantra the cause—like the snake and its poison, it causes the results, but it has been instigated by the mantra-practitioner's intention. This is an explanation that also accommodates sadhana *sans* mantras.

Next, "bhava" refers to an emotional intensity as contradistinct from intellectual acumen. Calling the Lalita-sahasranama mala-mantra his *prana* (life force, breath), Karunamaya demonstrated to me how to chant—not mechanically, but with feeling. Mani Prasanna's point about seeing syllables in the body is worth repeating here:

> It can be imagined. For example, "aṃ," when you imagine "aṃ," you need to imagine the "a" and the sunna [ṃ sound] beside it. You can imagine it being written and one day, even when you don't imagine, it will appear to you. The important thing is, we need to be connected to the deity all the time. If we have to stay connected, we need to find a way. We need to first feel the deity. If you don't feel it, it can't happen. That feeling is the imagination.

"If you don't feel it, it can't happen." This may be a clue for why legends are necessary, for they help generate intense feelings. As Sivananda had said, "If you choose japa of a god you *like*, it will happen. The moment you say Krishna, all the *lila* [divine play] of Krishna is right in front of you."

Even though thought is not involved, mantra-sadhana is not a thoughtless space open to random impressions as there is a focused and *directed* intention on the mind. Indian conceptions have (not five, but) six sensory organs including the mind. Is there a role for intuition? Even though most of the practitioners often spoke in English and used words such as "imagination" and "feeling," nobody used the term "intuition" which is also common parlance in spoken English in India. (The equivalents to "intuition" in Sanskrit and Telugu dictionaries are *sahajagna* which means "natural knowledge," *antarjna* which means inner knowledge and even "*pramananirapeksha*" which means not dependent on authoritative sources.)

Levels of Sound, Levels of Experience

Mantra-japa can be *vachaka* (aloud), *upamshu* (muttering) or *manasika* (mental) which is considered the most effective. Sadhakas speak about inaudible mantra in terms similar to sound vibrations, and about doing japa without the *interference* of other thoughts, and *using* japa to stop the flow of thoughts—this is regarded a necessary prerequisite to hold steadily on to any deeply felt intention. Appaji called vedic mantras "sonic" and tantric mantras, "supersonic and subsonic." When Sivananda spoke about finding the "pitch" and "frequency," she was referring to inaudible japa. Sadhakas help us reimagine sound as vibration. Vibration is known to have an effect on material which vibrates at a specific rate—soldiers break stride on a bridge because matching the frequency of the bridge can result in breaking the bridge.

20th CE scholar and practitioner Swami Pragyatmanada Saraswati ([1961] 1971) in *Japasutram*[6] explains the idea of shabda using the terms "stress," "causal stress" and "impulse":

> When the Śruti [veda] talks of śabdabrahma, what is actually meant is not that particular sound made by God has brought into being a particular type of thing. The word Śabdabrahma indicates the urge of the original

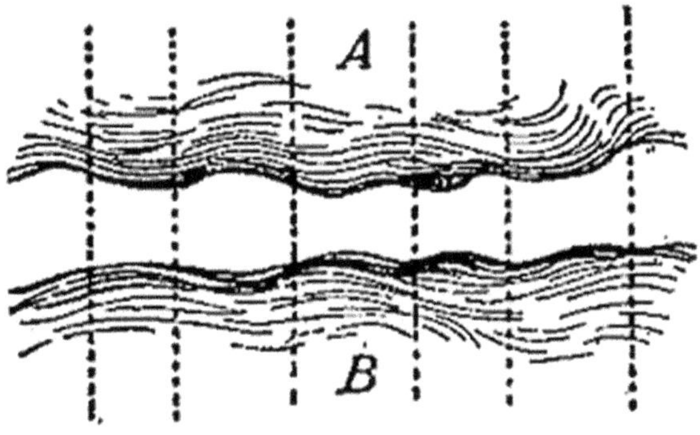

Fig. 8.1 Ferdinand Saussure's diagram

> cause (ādi karaṇa) to express itself in different forms. The urge is a kind of stress which tends to express itself in many forms (bahuśyām). … original stress and sound are inseparably associated and sound is the most conspicuous result of stress vibrations. (104)

"Urge," "impulse" and "causal stress" are useful terms by which to think about how mantra can be an intention beyond discursive thought, as well as linked to material results.

A diagrammatic illustration of the planes of thought, phonic substance (and by extrapolation, the material world) is to be found in the lecture notes from the classes of the linguist Fredinand de Saussure [1916] 2001) (Fig. 8.1).

Here, the letter A designates "the indefinite plane of jumbled ideas" and the letter B, "the equally vague plane of sounds" and the waves "resemble the union of thought with phonic substance" (967).

> Visualize the air in contact with a sheet of water; if the atmospheric pressure changes, the surface of the water will be broken up into a series of divisions, waves; the waves resemble the union or coupling of thought with phonic substance. (967)

The waves in this diagram represent what occurs *before* diachronic language (which is shown by the vertical markings). Vibrations and wave diagrams are speculations and analogies to explain and understand what practitioners are telling us happens when they do mantras.

8.6 Natural Form

It was because I asked Amritananda, "whose *language* are mantras," that he responded, "the language of the panchabhutas." My own tendency had been to rely on the concept of language to understand mantra. Thus, Karunamaya's state of mind when intuiting new mantras reminded me of automatic writing, I turned to Saussure to imagine how ideas and intentions could exist before the word, and I attempted to understand diksha through the analogy of aksharabhyasa (learning the alphabet). However, the idea that mantras are a "language" is figurative, like calling human beings, seashells or trees, the language of Nature, or God.

Even though early Indian thought has an extensive discussion about language, one often forgets that it is language that originates from Shabdabrahman (i.e., mantra), and not the other way around. Sounds and words can be articulated by us, but it takes a visionary experience, a guru's initiation or an authoritative source to make a syllable or combination of syllables or words, a mantra. Mantra-sadhakas in this fieldwork endorsed connections between cosmic/divine sources and syllables/letters, between cosmic/divine sources and grammar, and between syllables or letters and mantras, but not between mantras and human language, and never attributed mantras to human composition. Even though meaning—and hidden meaning—played a role in the relationship of the practitioner to the mantra, the implication was that *language* was also mantra, not that mantra was language. Mantra-sadhakas in my fieldwork maintain the ontological view of mantras held by ancient theorists that mantras are a priori, naturally occurring *forms*. This displaces such language-based frameworks as speech act theory to appraise mantras (unless the framework can accommodate such a divine speech act as "let there be light and there was light").

Mantras were inextricably bound with deities and with (the body of) the practitioners. When practitioners speak about mantras in relation to their own bodies the areas of the body mentioned are not sensory organs such as eyes or skin, but those of thought and feeling—heart and mind. Another area suggested is that of *prana* (breath, life force), and the chakras. Don's practice integrated the Chandi mantra to his breath, and Karunamaya used the metaphor that the L.S. mantra *is* his prana. During japa, one automatically adjusts to one's own breath; conversely, one brings the breath in line with the rhythm of the mantra. When uttered mentally, there are no restrictions imposed by breathing; but—and as the reader will be able to experience this even with a brief trial—the rhythms of breathing and the rhythms of utterance (including silent utterance) play off each other.

How does one appraise natural form? A 1865 entry in the journals of Gerald Manley Hopkins ([1953] 1988) is a dialog where a Professor of Aesthetics, and a scholar, discusses the formal values of a chestnut fan. As they proceed to examine a leaf, or the shape of a tree, they discover that beauty is "a relation"—e.g., it is "not the likeness of the leaves but their likeness as thrown up by their difference in size" (101). The principles that lead us to admire things that exist in nature are not the same as that by which we evaluate human compositions. In his early writings on poetics, Hopkins coined a term for intrinsic form and for the relationships between its parts—"inscape." Further, he coined the term "instress" to denote our perception of inscape. In an essay on seashells, Paul Valéry ([1937] 1988) reflects on their slow and continuous formation in the "making" of nature, and aspects of form we may admire, as we might, music.

> ...invincible and one might say flawless progression of form, which involves and develops its whole setting according to the continuous fatality of its convolutions and seems to create its own time, we admire the combination of rhythm, marked by the regular spots or spines, and of indivisible movement. It is like seeing music .... (16, 17)

Holding and turning the shell between his fingers, he observes the themes of "the helix and the spiral" and other aspects of form involve him "in a degree of astonishment and concentration that leads where it may: to superficial remarks and observations, naïve questions, "poetic" comparisons, beginnings of reckless "theories" (24). In both cases, the seashell and the tree are complete and perfect in themselves, without comparison to anything outside themselves, and any relationships are those of parts relative to each other. Moreover, the response is that of self-mockery at one's own habit of aesthetic criticism. Valéry writes about the seashell as if it were a moment frozen in time. Hopkins' leaves are perfect, regardless of symmetry. When scholars Frits Staal, Jayant Burde and Wade Wheelock point out the patterns of mantras, and when I appreciate a mantra for its poetic structure, it is both exciting and problematic, like a well-patterned leaf; a symmetrical leaf is not "better" than an asymmetrical leaf. To summarize, mantras have defined forms, but they are regarded natural forms—while it is possible to discuss their aesthetics and think of them as language, and one may also refer to the "poet" that authored them, such an approach would be dissonant and distant from the perspectives of mantra-sadhakas. From the practitioner's perspective, uttering a mantra is really a remembrance or imitation with a view to *real*-izing it. Articulating a mantra that already exists (within nature, and within oneself) creates a resonance with that mantra, which makes it possible to harness its power. As Ananda K. Coomaraswamy (1997) expands in his essay titled "Imitation, Expression, Participation," imitation also serves as expression and participation. To this extent, then, the sadhaka is a participating-author in a mantra.

8.7 OṂ

After some fieldwork, I inferred that when practitioners do the OṂ-mantra, it is the natural OṂ they are imitating, or with which they are resonating. I met other sadhakas who had heard the Pranava and some who pointed to the region of their heart-chakra. An experienced practitioner with whom I discussed the Pranava was Swami Madhavananda Saraswati at Thogutta. Thogutta is a two-hour drive from Hyderabad; I had gone there in August 2014 to attend a Chaturmasya yajna and to chit-chat with vedic ritualists. Madhavananda did not attend the yajna, and I waited for his visitors to leave before we could talk. When I explained my topic of research, he said that he did not do *Mantropasana* (mantra-sadhana), as "all that" was for ritualists; he was a sanyasi and did not care for karmas (rituals). I asked if he did not even do the Pranava (OṂ)? Yes, of course, he said, then told me that there were many ways to do OṂ, and shared insights from his practice and experience of the Pranava.

> MADHAVANANDA: In some traditions *(sampradayas)*, they practice only A-kara, some Ma-kara, some U-kara. And there are divisions in it. 'A,' 'U,' and 'Ma' are the main divisions. And then there is nadam [Mmm-kara] in it. There are people who meditate on the end-part of this sound. And so it is so deep in the Pranavopasana [sadhana of OṂ-mantra]. So some do individual sections, some do all three sounds of OṂ. And then the last section of the sound... so deep!

I had never heard of so many divisions nor come across anyone who focused on these fragments in their sadhana.

> MANI: So they pronounce the complete Pranava, but meditate on only one particular part of it?
>
> MADHAVANANDA: Right, if they don't pronounce the complete Pranava, then the sound will not be heard or produced. So they do pronounce 'OṂ' but meditate on a particular part. So if you consider OṂ as the total universe, there will be ones who do the dhvani [vibration], the ardha matra [Mmm-kara]. The last section in the ardha-matra is also meditated upon. Again in ardha-matra, there will be twelve different sections and there is a method to practice that. So this is a task involving high experience.

I asked if there are shastras (doctrinal source) about this, for I had read about divisions of the OṂ mantra, but never heard about twelve divisions within just the *ardha-matra* of OṂ and never could have imagined focusing on these divisions.

> MADHAVANANDA: There are many shastras on Pranava. In every Upanishad, there is the same thing. And that Pranavopasana should be there. Among them, people who can explain it in detail, on each part, that is, only direct from the mouth of a Guru (guru-mukhatah). It remained in shruti, the detailed part. It was never written anywhere.

"*Guru-mukhatah*" literally means "from the mouth of the Guru," or oral, personal teaching. Madhavananda continued to explain in much more detail about the various parts of OṂ that become objects of meditation. According to Madhavananda, this information has not been inscribed or written down, continues to remain within the oral tradition, and guidance for the practice of OṂ in this manner cannot be found in written sources anywhere. As the sadhaka proceeds, further guidance comes from *within* the practice:

> MADHAVANANDA: It is all based on personal experiences. Because, when you are at a stage where you are keenly observing the universe, it [OṂ] takes you to the path of eternal wisdom. And that wisdom itself automatically takes you to that stage of practice. During that journey, depending on the progress, the Pranavopasana method also changes.

Madhavananda's description of Pranavopasana is also a general description of sadhana. It begins with a Guru, followed by sadhana and then experience leads to an understanding that in turn acts upon the sadhana, fine-tuning it and leading to another understanding.

> MADHAVANANDA: It has to come through a Guru. And upasana method keeps changing. As you progress, the power of the upasana grows and improves. It reveals itself gradually. That is why, the meaning shouldn't come from outside sources, it is better if it is progressing from within.

We discussed the results of doing sadhana on OṂ. Madhavananda said that by adding OṂ before any mantra, "the vowel power that is at the final note of the Pranava, that power affects the mantra. So it brings fruit [results] to the mantra." The second manner was to focus on OṂ per se, and it would take the sadhaka toward ***advaita*** (non-duality and non-differentiation) and "tattva-jnana" (knowledge of truth).

> MADHAVANANDA: And where is that? It is you. ONLY YOU! Then it can be called the Advaita stage [non-dualism]. Until then it is not Advaita stage. Until then, even if you see the shabda [word/sound/mantra] it is not Advaita. Even when you are seeing all the vishayahara [objects]. "That shabda is I, the sparsha is I, that rasa is I, the rupa is I." That is one kind of Advaita.
>
> When someone says, God appeared, that means that did not happen. It is true when he says, that is me, I am God… he is in me. If you see other, it is not Advaita state then. Advaita cannot be obtained until that state where you cannot see the other form besides yourself. Not through words either. Advaita is a practical siddhanta [philosophy]. Not theory-based. One has to experience it personally.

When I told Madhavananda about my OṂ experience; he was blasé:

> MADHAVANANDA: Whether we hear or not, the Anahata shabda comes out of us. The vast form of that Anahata shabda is Pranava. And also the core form of the Anahata shabda. Both are Pranava.
>
> This is how it is. *Sadhanat sadhyate sarvam.* [Everything is accomplished through sadhana]. That is through sadhana, the universal form, the Chaitanya Svarupa [divine itself] can be seen / experienced. The Sadhana is all… like taking one step at a time. These are all stages. When you meditate on OṂ, it is in fact a symbol, the A-kara, U-kara and Ma-kara, when

> written, it is in the form of a varna [letter]. When heard, it is in the form of shabda [sound-form] when understood it is in artha-krama [meaning-stage], when experienced it is in the jnana-krama [wisdom-stage] and when it occurs, you do not know what it is. It is in ananda [bliss]. Inexpressable.

Potturi (see Chapter 6) practiced the OṂ-mantra but had not heard it; I had heard the OṂ-mantra and integrated it into my sadhana, but had not realized its parts or plumbed the depths indicated by Madhavananda. This conversation made me much more informed about the practice and potential of OṂ than reading a number of sources. Madhavananda's point about how OṂ results in a detachment had also been made by Potturi. Madhavananda's statement about how the methodology of the OṂ-sadhana had been passed on through the oral tradition vindicated my methodology.

8.8 Summary

Mantra-sadhakas consider mantras ontological—mantras are natural forms that exist in nature, both within and outside us, and can be perceived in revelatory experiences. Mantra-sadhana is hard work, but has results and can be gratifying to the extent that practitioners get attached to mantra-sadhana and continue to develop a lifelong practice, and may even consider themselves as researchers. Mantras must not be confused with audible sound, for they are also uttered and thought silently, and they become the directed intention and creative will of the practitioner. Mantras charged with earnest effort, imagination and intention are effective. Mantras help change the status quo and transform the practitioner. People do mantras to seek the favor of deities, overcome obstacles, gain or maintain health and prosperity and even to achieve ultimate knowledge and bliss. According to scholars, mantras are unverifiable and unfalsifiable—and advanced sadhakas or seers and gurus advice that phenomena must be ignored—but sadhakas rely on phenomena to ratify progress and success. Phenomena are effects, or side effects, of progress in mantra-sadhana, and among visionary experiences, visions of deities are desired and cherished. Mantras are inseparable from deities; they help contact, communicate with and build relationships with deities. Imagination is a methodology in mantra-sadhana; at the same time, sadhakas discriminate between what is imagined and what actually occurred. Mantra is a link between the human and divine, between guru and disciple, desire and action, intention and manifestation, imagination and reality, and even between sound and silence. Mantras received from deities, seen and heard mantras, hidden mantras, lost mantras, dormant mantras, mantras with hidden meanings, mantras given silently and even mantras done unconsciously—there is an entire taxonomy of mantras when considered from mantra-practice and experience.

Notes

1. Devipuram official website, under "5 Saraswati 1981," http://www.devipuram.com/gurujis-experiences-part12/, accessed 1 April 2015, italics mine. See Chapter 5, Note 5.
2. Such a case is in the legend of the deity Rama signing and fulfilling a promissory note to the Golconda king Tanishah, to secure the release of his devotee Ramdas from prison.
3. A narrative about the nature of the gods is in the Brihadaranyaka Upanishad 5.1. A cryptic message from Prajapati (a creator) is communicated through thunder, and the message is, simply, "*da*." This utterance is interpreted differently by gods, titans (*asuras*) and humans, based on their nature. Human beings get the message of "*datta*" (be charitable), the titans interpret it as "*dayādhvam*" (be compassionate) and the gods understand it as "*dāmyata*" (control yourself). A popular explanation for the gods' interpretation is that they live lives of supreme bliss and pleasure. (Olivelle 1998, 133).
4. The last verse in *Madhurya Kadambini* lists the stages of devotion: shradda (faith), sadhu sangha (association with devotees), bhajana kriya (devotional activities), anartha nivritti (clearing of obstacles), nishta (steadiness), ruchi (taste), asakti (attachment), bhava (feeling) and then prema (pure love).
5. This was the case not only in Andhra, but even among vedic pundits in Maharashtra. In Satara, Maharashtra, Vivek Shastri Godbole told me that when he was a young boy, he asked his father for the meaning of the Mrityunjaya mantra. His father told him "*padte jao, padte jao*" (keep studying) and the meaning would suddenly be revealed to him—it did, but only decades later.
6. Originally in six volumes, in Sanskrit and Bengali, *Japasutram* includes thousands of sutras (aphorisms), and commentary by Pragyatmananda based on his scholarship as well as sadhana. An abbreviated book of the same title published in 1961 presents a summary of his treatise in English.

References

Brzezinski, Jan K., ed., and trans. 2005. *Madhurya Kadambini* of Vishvanatha Chakravartin. Mathura: Sri Krishna Chaitanya Shastra Mandir.

Buhnemann, Güdrun. 2003. *Maṇḍalas and Yantras in the Hindu Traditions.* Leiden: Brill.

Chilcott, Travis. 2015. "Directly Perceiving Kṛṣṇa: Accounting for Perceptual Experiences of Deities within the Framework of Naturalism." *Religion* 45 (4): 532–552.

Coomaraswamy, Ananda K. 1997. "Imitation, Expression, and Participation" In *The Door in the Sky: Coomaraswamy on Myth and Meaning.* Princeton, NJ: Princeton University Press.

de Saussure, Ferdinand. [1916] 2001. *Course in General Linguistics.* Edited by Charles Bally and Albert Sechehaye, translated by Wade Baskin. In *The Norton Anthology of Theory and Criticism*, edited by Vincent B. Leitch, et al., 960–977. New York and London: W.W. Norton.

Glucklich, Ariel. 2003. *Climbing Chamundi Hill: 1001 Steps with a Storyteller and a Reluctant Pilgrim.* New York: HarperSanFrancisco.

Gopal, Ram. 1983. *History and Principles of Vedic Interpretation.* New Delhi: Concept.

Gupta, Sanjukta. 1989. "Pancharatra Attitude to Mantra." In *Understanding Mantras.* Edited by Harvey P. Alper, 224–248. Albany, NY: State University of New York Press.

Hopkins, G. M. [1953] 1988. "From 'On the Origin of Beauty: A Platonic Dialgoue' (1865)." In *Poems and Prose.* Edited by W. H. Gardner, 92–104. New York: Penguin.

Jung, C. G. 1971. *The Portable Jung.* Edited and translated by R. F. C. Hull. New York: Viking.

Morgan, David. 2012. *The Embodied Eye: Religious Visual Culture and the Social Life of Feeling.* Berkeley: University of California Press.

Olivelle, Patrick. 1998. *Early Upaniṣads—Annotated Text and Translation.* New York: Oxford University Press.

Pragyatmananda Saraswati, Swami. [1961] 1971. *Japasutram; the Science of Creative Sound.* Madras: Ganesh.

Rao, Ramachandra S. K. 1998. *Ṛgveda Darśana*, vol. I, p. III. Bangalore: Kalpatharu Research Academy.

Shulman, David D. 2012. *More Than Real: A History of the Imagination in South India.* Cambridge, MA: Harvard University Press.

Smith, Frederick M. 2006. *Self Possessed—Deity and Spirit Possession in South Asian Literature and Civilization.* New York: Columbia University Press.

Valéry, Paul. [1937] 1998. *Sea Shells.* Translated by Ralph Manheim. Boston: Beacon Press.

Glossary

Ashram (*Āśram*)	Spiritual community.
Bhava (*Bhāva*)	Feeling, emotion.
Brahman (*Brahman*)	Formless, nameless non-object in Indian thought arguably equivalent to "God."
Brahmin (*Brāhmin*)	A person of a lineage (*varṇa*/"caste") entitled to perform vedic rituals and mantras, a ritual priest.
Chakra (*Cakra*)	Energy-center in the human body.
Darshana (*Darśana*)	Mutual seeing between devotee and deity.
Devi (*Devi*)	A goddess.
Devata (*Devatā*)	A god or goddess.
Diksha (*Dīkṣā*)	Initiation.
Guru (*Guru*)	Spiritual teacher.
Homa (*Homa*)	A small-scale yajna.
Ishvara (*Īśvara*)	A personifiable God.
Japa (*Japa*)	Repetition of mantra.
Japamala (*Japamālā*)	Rosary.
Kavya (*Kāvya*)	Poetic composition.
Mandala (*Maṇḍala*)	Mystical drawing, group, chapter.
Mantra (*Mantra*)	Invariant combinations of "sounds" which may include words, used for a range of results from the therapeutic to soteriological; revelations.

M. Rao, *Living Mantra*, Contemporary Anthropology of Religion,
https://doi.org/10.1007/978-3-319-96391-4

Mudra (*Mudra*)	Codified hand-gestures.
Prana (*Prāṇa*)	Breath, life, that which animates breath.
Puja (*Pujā*)	Ritual honoring of deities.
Sadhaka (*Sādhaka*)	Spiritual practitioner.
Sadhana (*Sādhanā*)	Spiritual practice.
Sadhu (*Sādhu*)	Ascetic.
Samadhi (*Samādhi*)	Deep meditation.
Samadhi (*Samādhi*)	Sacred tomb.
Sankalpa (*Sankalpa*)	Intention, generative imagination.
Sanyasa (*Sanyāsa*)	Ascetic orders.
Sanyasi (*Sanyāsi*)	Celibate sscetic.
Shabda (*Śabda*)	An authoritative source or revelation such as a veda or tantra.
Siddhi (*Siddhi*)	Extraordinary powers.
Tantra (*Tantra*)	Sources considered revelations, ritual and philosophical content.
Vak (*Vāk*)	Speech, Goddess of Speech, or authoritative revelation of veda or tantra.
Varna (*Varṇa*)	Social grouping based on birth and tendencies, "caste."
Veda (*Veda*)	Sources considered revelations, ritual and philosophical content.
Yajna (*Yajña*)	Ritual with offerings of substances and mantras to the deity of Fire, Agni.
Yajnashala (*yajñaśālā*)	A space where yajna is conducted.
Yantra (*Yantra*)	Device, instrument, drawing, mystical diagram.

Index

A
Abhinavagupta, 16
Agni, 3, 53, 76, 156, 157, 171
Akasha, 5, 59, 119
Alper, Harvey P., 10, 17, 23
Amritanandanatha Saraswati, 10, 35, 39, 69–73, 76, 78, 79, 81, 83, 84, 92, 93, 98, 100–108
Anandavardhana, 18
Andhra-Telangana, 5–8
Appaji, 86, 114, 116, 122–127, 139, 198
Apparao, D.V. *See* Appaji
Arabic mantra, 101
Asiddhi, 105
Atharvaveda, 3, 55
Atman, 34, 173
Avesha, 158

B
Baba, Sathya Sai, 3, 4, 32, 176, 186
Babu, G.Y.N., 114
Bala, 57, 58, 61, 70, 76, 79, 100, 101, 190, 197
Bave, Vinoba, 60
Bhakti, 20, 126, 127, 151, 158
Bharati, Agehananda, 21, 173
Bharati, Swami Siddheswarananda, 10, 33, 35, 39, 114, 116, 135, 141, 144, 191
Bhartrihari, 16, 22, 185
Bhava, 158, 161, 162, 193, 197
Bhavana, 44, 81, 138, 144
Brahman, 14, 43, 60, 61, 122, 173
Burchett, Patton E., 19

C
Chakra, 68, 75, 82, 85, 132, 151, 165, 178, 194, 202
  definition, 5
Chandas, 14, 36
Chandi, 78, 83, 84, 88
Chandodarshana. *See* Daivarata, Maharshi
Chandraghanta, 156
Chilcott, Travis, 192, 193

D
Daivarata, Maharshi, 39, 51, 54–57, 61, 95, 191

M. Rao, *Living Mantra*, Contemporary Anthropology of Religion,
https://doi.org/10.1007/978-3-319-96391-4

Dasha-Mahavidyas, 113, 126
Dattatreya, 101, 163
Deities, 187–190
Devipuram, 67
Diksha, 33, 90, 100, 134, 173–174, 176
Doubt, 192

E
Eliade, Mircea, 40, 71

G
Ganapati, 73, 97, 98, 131, 132
Ganapatimuni, Vasishtha, 54, 55, 98
Ganesha. *See* Ganapati
Geertz, Clifford, 8, 28, 29
Ghantakarna, 130, 132
Guntur, 10, 57, 86, 113, 116
Guru, 185–186

H
Hanuman, 69, 100, 127, 130, 132, 187–189, 191
Hladini, 70
Hufford, David, 31

I
Intention, 107, 121, 127, 138, 139, 167, 170, 193, 196–199
  Panchakshari, 7, 123
Itihasa-purana, 35, 36

J
Jackson, Michael, 44, 45
Jaimini, 14, 22, 185. *See also* Mimamsa
Japa, 4, 120, 123, 131, 161–163, 175
  ajapa, 59, 178
  japamala, 4, 151
  kinds of japa, 198
Jillelamudi, 116, 120

K
Kala-Bhairava, 131, 134–138, 143, 187, 191
Kalavahana, 72–76, 80, 82, 108
Kali, 6, 88, 89, 92, 113, 114, 116, 131, 136, 151, 171, 190
Kalpana, 44, 81, 143
Kamakhya, 71
Kapre, Narendra, 39, 51, 54–56
Karma, 125, 131, 133, 192
Karna, 125
Karunamaya, 30, 93–100, 108
Khadgamala, 68, 108
Knipe, David, 20
Kodgal, 149
Kosha, 44, 165–166, 188, 189
Kundalini, 79, 151, 177, 195
Kunti, 127

L
Lalita, 30, 38, 67, 70, 73, 76, 93, 100, 188
Language, 200–202
Latour, Bruno, 31

M
Madhavananda Saraswati, Swami, 195, 202, 203
Mahabharata, 56, 125, 127, 152
Maheswari, 170–173
Mandala, 10, 184
Mantra
  Aksharamala, 17, 73
  Anahata, 175, 177, 204

Ashtakshari, 154
Bala, 57, 79, 108
Bhramari, 175
Bija, 17, 75, 119
Chandi, 85, 87, 88, 200
Durga, 161, 190
Durva-suktam, 195
Ganapati, 104, 132
Gayatri, 4, 7, 53, 56, 59
Guru, 175
Hanuman, 129, 130, 132, 134
Hanuman-Chalisa, 128, 129
Kalabhairava, 134
Kala-Bhairava Ashtakam, 137, 191
Kali, 134–136, 155, 161
Khadgamala, 68, 100
Kilakam, 119
Lalita-sahasranama, 81, 118, 197
Maha-Shodashi, 84, 87
Maha Vyadhi Vinashi, 103
Mantra-vetta, 115
Mantra-vihina, 144, 197
Mrityunjaya, 96
Naga-mantra, 124, 127–129
Nagastra-mantra, 124, 125, 128
Narayana-suktam, 71
Navadurga Stotram, 156
"No"-mantra, 166
Panchakshari, 174
Permutations, 123
Pranava, 5, 119, 120, 202–204
Pranayama-mantra, 175
Purusha-suktam, 71
Radha, 134
Radha-Krishna, 134
Rama, 129
Rudram, 4
Saundarya-Lahari, 89–91
Shirdi Sai Baba, 174
Shodashi, 7, 59, 84, 92
Svapna-mantra, 114
Ucchishtha-Ganapati, 116
Vijay-Ganapati, 131
Mantramahodadhi, 160
Marriot, McKim, 43
Matangi, 126
McCarthy Brown, Karen, 32
McKenna, Donald, 83–88
Meaning, 15
Mimamsa, 42, 173
Mimamsa-Sutras, 14, 22
Moore Gerety, F.M., 18
Mudra, 123, 151, 154, 156–161

N
Nachiketa, 178
Nachiketa Chaitanya Kriya, 158, 175
Nachiketananda Puri, Swami, 10, 34, 39, 137, 149, 150, 158, 166
Nachiketa Tapovan, 149
Nadi-Ganapati, 132
Names, 162–163
Narayan, Kirin, 28, 29, 33
Navaratri, 155

O
OṂ, 4, 17, 18, 60, 61, 119, 120, 122, 175, 194, 202–205
Orsi, Robert, 31, 32, 44

P
Padoux, André, 14, 17, 20, 159, 160
Panchabhuta, 59, 104
Panchakshari Kalpa, 39, 123
Paramahamsa, 41
Parashurama Kalpasutra, 39
Pashyanti, 15, 16
Patanjali Mahabhasya, 37
Patanjali Yogasutras, 17, 41
Patton, Laurie L., 53

Phenomena, 4, 41–43, 92, 123, 134, 170, 179, 184, 191, 193, 194
Phenomenology, 39–44
Piette, Albert, 44, 45
Pollock, Sheldon, 36, 37
Potturi, Venkateswara Rao, 119–122, 191
Pramana, 13, 36
Prana, 178, 196, 197, 200
Prasad, Leela, 28, 36
Prasadarao Kulapati. *See* Bharati, Swami Siddheswarananda
Prasanna, Mani, 76–83
Pratyangiras, 126, 139
Purana, 7, 16, 22, 72, 114, 118, 142, 144
Purusha, 68
Puttaparthi, 3–5, 32, 43, 177

R
Radha-Devi, 117
Radha-Krishna, 134
Rama, 129, 130
Ramakrishna Paramahamsa, 139, 151, 168
Ramana Maharshi, 39, 54, 56, 61, 98
Ramdas, 129
Rani, Siva Sankar Sarma, 57
Reddy, Prema, 73–76
Reddy, Vasundhara, 152
Rigveda, 3, 14, 53, 55, 60, 184
Rishi, 8, 9, 14, 37, 51–53, 55, 81, 118–120, 122, 123, 192
  -etymology, 52
  sapta-rishis, 52
Rudraksha
  ekamukhi, 91, 137

S
Sadhaka, definition, 4
Sadhana, 3, 4, 30, 33, 34, 56, 81, 82, 95, 117–120, 125, 129, 131, 133, 135–137, 139, 140, 144–146, 154, 161, 165, 166, 169, 170, 173, 174, 177, 179, 189, 193, 194, 198, 202–204
Sahasrakshi, 67–71, 83, 91, 108
Samadhi, 41, 54, 58, 69, 117, 118, 153, 160
Samaveda, 3
Samhita, 4, 53
Sankalpa, 44, 127, 170, 175, 193, 196–198
Saraswati, 70, 187
Saraswati, Pragyatmananda, 13
Sastry, Chandole, 57–61
Sati, 72
Saussure, Ferdinand de, 199
Sayana, 14, 15, 22, 185
Shabarabhashya, 14
Shabda, 13, 16, 198, 204, 205
Shabdabrahman, 16, 200
Shakta, 6, 69
Shakti, 6, 16, 67, 79, 116, 119, 155
  -pitha, 6, 59, 72, 114
Shankara, 41, 42, 185
Sheela, 87–93
Shiva, 6, 16, 67, 76, 91, 97, 124, 125, 133, 134, 137, 163, 174, 190
Shivalinga, 6, 67, 124, 129, 133
Shruti, 6, 14, 36, 52, 53, 192, 203
Shulman, David D., 44, 82, 193, 197
Shyama, 73
Siddhi, 4, 42, 105, 118, 123, 174
  ashta-siddhi, 41
Silence, 167, 175

Sivananda Puri, Swami, 10, 35, 38, 39, 152, 153, 173, 174, 187, 191, 198
Smith, Frederick M., 20, 157, 188
Sound-spectrum, 199
Srichakra. *See* Sriyantra
Srividya, 6, 38, 59, 69, 73, 77, 82, 93, 95, 118
Sriyantra, 10, 67, 69, 80, 83, 85, 95, 150
Staal, Frits, 13, 18, 53, 201
Svadhyaya, 14, 17
Svayam Siddha Kali Pitham, 10, 113, 114

T
Tadepalle, Raghava Narayana Sastry. *See* Sastry, Chandole
Tanmatra, 104
Tantra, 17, 58, 76, 107, 116, 157, 160
Telugu, 6, 7, 42, 57, 88, 117
Tirtha, 184
Transcendental Meditation, 185
Tulsidas, 128

U
Upanishad, 40, 154, 203
  Ishavasya, 69
  Katha, 178
  Mundaka, 34
  Shvetashvatara, 60
  Taittiriya, 14, 165, 189
  Tripuratapini, 39
Uttara-mimamsa, 173

V
Vadlamudi, Venkateswara Rao, 39, 43, 117–119, 191
Vak, 15, 16, 53, 54, 56, 57
Varahi, 73, 190
Vasudevananda, Swami, 100, 127–130, 191
Veda, 3, 14, 36, 58, 62, 97, 192
Venkatalakshmi, Akella, 130–135
Vishvanatha Chakravartin, 192
Visionary experience, 185–194
Vision of meaning, 14–15
Vivekananda, Swami, 151
Vyas, Maunish, 195
Vyasa, 52, 149

Y
Yajna, 3, 14, 41, 58, 59, 70, 71, 88, 171, 191, 193
Yajurveda, 3, 14
Yama, 178
Yaska, 14, 52
Yoga, 17, 56, 58, 70, 80, 117, 151, 165, 175
Yogini, Ramya, 135–140, 191
Yoni, 71, 75
  yoni-pitha, 72

Milton Keynes UK
Ingram Content Group UK Ltd.
UKHW021506210624
444565UK00028B/355

9 783030 071844